WATER AND POWER IN WEST MAUI

WATER AND POWER
IN
WEST MAUI

JONATHAN L. SCHEUER AND BIANCA K. ISAKI

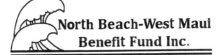

North Beach-West Maui
Benefit Fund Inc.

Lahaina, Maui, Hawai'i

First printing, 2021
Second printing, 2024

ISBN 978-0-8248-8452-9 (pbk : alk. paper)

Published by the North Beach-West Maui Benefit Fund, Inc.
P O Box 11329
Lahaina, Hawaiʻi 96761

Distributed by University of Hawaiʻi Press
2840 Kolowalu Street
Honolulu, HI 96822-1888

Every effort has been made to trace copyright holders
and to obtain their permission for the use of copyright material.
The publisher apologizes for any errors or omissions and
would be grateful if notified of any corrections that
should be incorporated in future reprints or editions of this book.

This book is printed on acid-free paper and
meets the guidelines for permanence and durability
of the Council on Library Resources.

Print-ready files provided by North Beach-West Maui Benefit Fund, Inc.

*For all who love and seek to protect
the people and places of West Maui.*

I ʻauheʻe o Kaʻuiki i ka wai ʻole.
Kaʻuiki was defeated for lack of water.
—ʻŌlelo noʻeau no. 1151

Contents

FOREWORD

Like land, water is a necessary element to the sustaining of life.

This project was originally envisioned as a history of the use and diversion of the waters of West Maui as well as its description in modern times. However, intervening events transformed the scope and aim of this project to what it is now.

Starting in 2017, the Commission on Water Resource Management began the process of adopting inflow stream standards for Ukumehame, Olowalu, Launiupoko and Kauaʻula Hydrologic Units. On March 20, 2018, the Commission did approve new instream flow standards. The Commission then adopted instream flow standards for the Kahoma Hydrologic Unit that includes Kahoma and Kanahā Streams on November 20, 2018. In September 2019, the Commission took up the Honokōwai, Honolua, and Honokōhau Streams with public fact gathering. The Commission deferred action at its December 2019 meeting held at Waiola Church in Lahaina intending to take up the matter earlier this year. That has been put on hold due to the novel corona virus pandemic emergency declaration. In short, a portion of the original intent of the project is now available in the form of publicly available staff reports.

Instead of duplicating that work, the project was modified to be more useful to West Maui communities by focusing on how public trust resource advocacy can occur.

This volume is the latest in a series of projects to help expand the base of knowledge and understanding of West Mauiʻs history, to help support planning for the possibilities of the present and the future.

Lance D. Collins
Hāʻenanui, Honokōwai

Acknowledgments

We assembled this book from many kinds of knowledge from more people than we can name here. Mahalo nui to Darryl Aiwohi, Hannah Bernard, Dr. Lance D. Collins, Dr. Paula Cutillo, Dr. Mark Deakos, Kapule Eubank, Sy Feliciano, Dr. Scott Fisher, Geoffrey Fricker, Archie Kalepa, Karyn Kanekoa, Maka Kanekoa, Kalani Kapu, Keʻeaumoku Kapu, Uʻilani Kapu, Kai Keahi, Kapali Keahi, Keith Keahi, Cami Kloster, Tiare Lawrence, Ed Lindsey, Kaleo Manuel, Jen Mather, Elizabeth Pa Martin, Jen Mather, Isaac Moriwake, Kai Nishiki, Linda Nye, Victoria Palafox-Kaluna, Aimoku Pali, Tamara Paltin, Hokuʻao Pelligrino, Kanani Puou, Saul Scheuer, Kapua Sproat, Kanoe Steward, Dr. Ayron Straunch, Kainoa Wilson, Nicole Wood, Wili Wood, and Jonathan Yim.

Chapter 1

HORNER V. KUMULIʻILIʻI

> *The Plantation has persecuted these Hawaiians by having them*
> *arrested and by forcibly taking their water and because one or two*
> *have been instrumental in trying to get their rights, it has deter-*
> *mined to crush the whole settlement in the Kauaula Valley.*
>
> —J. A. Magoon, 1895[1]

> *Commanding the pristine North Kāʻanapali Beach, The Westin Kāʻanapali*
> *Ocean Resort Villas offers six outdoor pools, with two dedicated to chil-*
> *dren's pools and one for adult serenity. Located in garden-style settings with*
> *panoramic ocean views, the pools offer splashing fun to guests of all ages.*
> *Children will be especially delighted with the pirate ship pool that is ideally*
> *situated near the Westin Family Kid's Club and keiki playground area.*
>
> —Westin Kāʻanapali website, 2017[2]

Behind the town of Lahaina and the beaches and resorts of Kāʻanapali to the north, Mauna Kahālāwai (one name for the West Maui Mountains) rises in increasingly steep slopes. Above the easily cultivated hills, narrow and deep valleys like Kauaʻula are small folds in the cliffs. The peak rises to nearly 6,000 feet and is frequently shrouded in clouds. The rainfall gradient on this volcano is tremendous: at the summit, mean annual rainfall is over 312 inches a year; at Lahaina it is a scant 13.5 inches.[3] In a direct line, it is only seven miles from the summit (Puʻu Kukui) to the resorts at Kāʻanapali, just north of Lahaina.

Even as the cloud-shrouded summits and the hot and dry coastal lands of West Maui are distinct, there is far greater dissonance between the indigenous approaches to living in this landscape and the sometimes violent transformations enacted here by the developers of plantations and resorts. As will come up throughout this book, the challenges and opportunities presented by the natural distribution of water have been managed in significantly different and conflicting ways. Kānaka Maoli[4] have diverted streams emerging from the mountains multiple times for the flow-through cultivation of kalo and other crops, and water was returned from these flooded fields into the streams of origin. Cultivated wetlands managed as fields and fishponds gathered these waters near the coast. In the midst of one of these ponds lay Mokuʻula, an island on an island that was the seat of the kings of Maui, and later of the whole Kingdom of Hawaiʻi.

However, during the rise of sugar cultivation in this area beginning in the 1860s, streams were increasingly diverted out of watersheds for the consumptive uses of growing and milling sugar cane. Since the rise of mass tourism in the 1960s and the demise of the plantations in the late 1990s, stream diversions and groundwater wells have taken water from wetter inland areas to deliver them to coastal developments. At the same time, partially treated sewage has been pumped into near-coastal injection wells, while just offshore algal blooms have impacted near-shore reefs. The landscape of Mokuʻula and its surrounding freshwater pond, Mokuhina, once the capital of the nation of Hawaiʻi, now lay hidden beneath a baseball field and parking lot. Water from Kauaʻula and other valleys, and the groundwater that fed coastal springs, flows to municipal systems, resort complexes and luxury homes rented to visitors or occupied by residents a few months of the year.

For both sugar and tourism, the proximity of relatively abundant water near dry areas where sugar can grow and tourists can sunbathe has been a tremendous asset. Its development required, however, the forceful displacement of existing land-holders and water users. The transformation and dispossession in water management has been neither uncontested nor complete, despite its invisibility to those enjoying a resort pool with faux pirate ship amenities.

A mere few miles from the Westin Kāʻanapali and other resorts, kalo cultivation continues in Kauaʻula and other West Maui valleys today. For over a century and a half, Kānaka Maoli and others who live in this area have wielded lawmaking, litigation, and other tools to contest this partial takeover. Their efforts have been significantly focused on trying to manage water in a way that allows for the preservation of traditional and customary practices, as well as the maintenance of a healthy environment that these practices rely on and promote.

In its simplest form, this book seeks to be a faithful (if necessarily incomplete) account of those struggles, in both their complexity and their uncertainty, in an attempt to counteract the many ways the struggles and the people struggling are made invisible. But this book also seeks to shed light on an underexamined area of political contest in the islands.

From Land and Power to Water and Power

Our title deliberately echoes the seminal 1995 book *Land and Power in Hawaiʻi* by George Cooper and Gavan Daws. That work concluded that in Hawaiʻi, "There never has been a ruling class or governing group that has not drawn its strength and sought its continuing advantage from land."[5] While that is true in West Maui and across Hawaiʻi, the control of water has also been key to the creation and transformation of political and economic power and advantage. Unfortunately, the academic and popular focus on land as compared to water has been one factor that has allowed the efforts of foreign capital and settler decisionmakers to control water to be less contested and less recognized.

This historic focus on land also misses the ways fights over water are in many ways even more complex and significant than struggles over land ownership and jurisdiction. This is because unlike land, Hawaiian Kingdom law and State Constitutional provisions define water as a trust resource that cannot be bought and sold as private property. Water is also, due to escalating demand and declining supply, an increasingly scarce resource. Across Maui, if the land already entitled for development were built out to what is legally allowed, demand would exceed the supply that the state calculates is available from groundwater and streams.[6] Thus we also seek in this book to shed light for Hawaiʻi-interested audiences on the fact that a sometimes single-minded focus on the politics of land ignores one of the most significant areas of struggle in the islands, historically and currently.

The purposes of this book, *Water and Power in West Maui*, are however not solely historical nor academic. In equal importance, this book seeks to serve in the following ways:

- To be a resource for residents and others who care about West Maui to gain a historically grounded understanding of the current regime of water resources management;
- To be an example of the larger story of how settler agriculture has impacted but not totally transformed native agriculture and resource management;

• To illustrate how flaws in state management of water play out in this area and indicate the implications for other places of Hawai'i; and

• To highlight the ongoing tensions pervading current state efforts to "balance" native rights to and foreign desires for water.

ORGANIZATION OF THE BOOK

Following this introductory chapter, chapter 2 grounds the rest of the book by describing the current legal regime of water management in West Maui. This description consists of an introduction to the State of Hawai'i water resource management framework, the Maui County interface with that state framework (and respective water management responsibilities), and various private water systems in West Maui. It will also describe, on a broad level, hydrologic characteristics of the area. Standing alone, this chapter serves as an overview for those who simply want to understand the management framework of water in West Maui.

Chapter 3 describes the historic and existing physical infrastructure that moves water across the landscape of West Maui. It emphasizes a discussion of West Maui agricultural ditch systems. These ditch systems use both surface and ground water sources. At the beginning of the twentieth century, Honolua Ranch and Pioneer Mill Company constructed the Honokōhau Ditch, Honolua (Honokōhau) Ditch, Honokowai Ditch, Kahoma Ditch, Kanaha Ditch, Kaua'ula Ditch, Launiupoko Ditch, Olowalu Ditch, and Ukumehame Ditch. This chapter will inventory these ditch systems, their associated water system developments, such as hydroelectric pumps, and water tanks, and their present use. The development of the Kaua'ula water system, including the well-documented construction of the Kaua'ula tunnel, will be discussed in finer detail. Rather than merely examining this physical infrastructure acontextually, however, we simultaneously look at how these systems displaced native agriculture. We also note how narratives celebrating plantation ditch systems persist in struggles over water today in West Maui.

Chapter 4 revisits some of the legal review of chapter 2, but places these state and county policies in a historic context. It begins with an examination of the development of legal understandings of water from the 1850s through the present, and moves on to a review of current judicial guidance on the management of water, the record of failure by the CWRM before Hawai'i appellate courts, and a description of anti-Hawaiian bias in CWRM decisionmaking.

By examining these concrete decisions by the Commission we can see how the narratives celebrating plantation ditch systems help to shape water management actions today.

In chapter 5, we review how the state is supposed to protect Public Trust uses of surface water, including instream uses, by the setting of Interim and permanent Instream Flow Standards (IIFS and IFS, respectively). However, the process of IIFS determination has been very slow, and has been hampered by poor implementation during CWRM's early attempts to "certify" surface and ground water uses in existence when the state Water Code was passed. The slow nature and other aspects of the state's IIFS-setting approach, like other management schemes, privileges diverters over Kanaka Maoli rights holders and is deferential to developer needs. Disrepair in the IIFS determination process can also be tracked to a lack of capacity in CWRM, demonstrating a system that is destined—and perhaps designed—to fail. Certification failures at onset of implementation of the water code should have signaled these issues. This chapter describes these challenges and will also review potential remedies.

In chapter 6, we examine the state's process of managing groundwater in West Maui and elsewhere, which is supposed to accomplish the same ends as its management of surface water—protection of the resource and Public Trust uses. However, if sustainable management of groundwater is understood to protect and sustain these public trust uses—water left in its natural state supporting ecological functions, water used for the traditional and customary practices of Hawaiians, the domestic needs of the general public, and water for homesteading under the Hawaiian Homes Commission Act—then management by sustainable yield (SY) is not sustainable.

In chapter 7, we address barriers for aloha ʻāina[7] who want to farm loʻi kalo or access kuleana lands for traditional purposes. Barriers include CWRM's failure to recognize some appurtenant rights holders, and kuleana lands that have been adversely possessed or subject to quiet title actions by Pioneer Mill, Maui Land and Pine, and their successors. New developments and landowners often cut off physical or water access to kuleana lands. Several instances of specific dewatering of lands by large-scale diversions are also reviewed.

Chapter 8 concludes the book by looking critically at the different ways in which the Public Trust doctrine is used and interpreted, especially in light of a decolonization framework. It is an attempt to situate the large efforts of managing West Maui waters within the much larger political context of Hawaiʻi in history.

Over a Century of Water Struggles

We begin, however, in this introductory chapter by laying a foundation in a particular legal contest: *Horner v. Kumuliʻiliʻi*, 10 Haw. 174 (1895). In this Hawaiʻi Supreme Court case, agents for the largest sugar plantation in the area, Pioneer Mill, sued sixty West Maui Kānaka Maoli who held, were believed to hold, or thought to have claimed water rights. This included men, women, and even a child. Pioneer Mill sued specifically regarding control of water from Kauaʻula Valley.[8]

Looking at *Kumuliʻiliʻi* is a means of introducing the main concerns that gave rise to this book and acknowledging the assumptions on which it is based. In particular, beyond honoring one of the earliest well recorded struggles over water between Kānaka Maoli and foreigners, it particularly illustrates the challenges faced by Kānaka Maoli to continue practices such as kalo cultivation, the legal tactics used by foreign interests (including the appropriation of Hawaiian traditions), and the complicated and incomplete role of the courts in protecting Kanaka Maoli interests.

The Political Economic Context of *Kumuliʻiliʻi*: Struggles Over Land, Water, and Food

The disputes that led to the *Horner v. Kumuliʻiliʻi* case in 1895 originated and were enmeshed in the changes that occurred in the Lahaina area soon after the Māhele (1848–1852) and the subsequent rise of sugar cultivation for export. The privatization of land that occurred at the time of the Māhele explicitly did not include a privatization of water. The land awards to the King and Aliʻi were subject to the rights of kuleana holders to enter into privately held lands for subsistence purposes. Similarly, while the Māhele allowed for the distribution of parcels of land to individual Hawaiians, the waters that were associated with that land were never directly deeded to them as private property. Rather, it was assumed in the legislation that traditional water rights would be guaranteed. As noted in Section 7 of the Kuleana Act of 1850 (emphasis added) and discussed later in the book in detail:

> Where the landlords have obtained, or may hereafter obtain, allodial titles to their lands, the people on each of their lands shall not be deprived of the right to take firewood, house timber, aho cord, thatch, or ki leaf, from the land on which they live, for their own private use, but they shall not have

the right to take such articles for profit. *The people shall also have a right to drinking water, and running water, and the right of way. The springs of water, running water, and roads shall be free to all*, on all lands granted in fee simple; provided that this shall not be applicable to wells and water courses, which individuals have made for their own use.

This clause recognized that kamaʻāina depended on access to a variety of resources that would not be available immediately on their own small lots. All land and water in the kingdom, as a result, was subject to the rights of the kuleana holders and other native tenants. This was supposed to be a bedrock legal principle that secured the rights of native tenants during this massive change to private property ownership.

In practice, the securing of land and water by both sugar planters and Kānaka Maoli was complex and highly contested. Individuals and firms began to acquire, by fee and lease, ahupuaʻa exclusive of kuleana awarded therein— including lands that had traditionally not been cultivated but were suited to sugarcane.

Because the area was so heavily settled and so many land claims were awarded, along with other challenges, the expansion of sugar in Lahaina occurred in fits and starts. The firm of Pioneer Mill that came to dominate the area and initiated the Horner litigation were not the first planters. Kepā Maly has described a series of investors: "... The first proprietor of Lahaina Mill Co. sacrificed over $25,000 before he got out of the business; Walker & Allen (Honolulu agency that later failed) lost $30,000; before Campbell & Turton bought the mill their debt to Walker & Allen was $50,000 and it was entirely lost to Walker & Allen's creditors."[9] What would later become Pioneer Mill was established by James Campbell through the acquisition of smaller interests, and later came to be held by Horner and Isenberg, the named plaintiffs in *Kumuliʻiliʻi*.

Even as nascent sugar industrialists lost money, Kānaka Maoli sometimes lost much more. Maly also documents that famine became so great in the formerly heavily cultivated and abundant area that a committee was appointed to investigate matters in 1867, a mere fifteen years after the Māhele laid the basis for successful capitalist agriculture. D. Kahaulelio, S. W. Nailiili, M. Ihihi, and D. Baldwin were appointed to investigate the matter and make a report; D. Kahaulelio and M. Ihihi would later become defendants in *Kumuliʻiliʻi*. In the Hawaiian language newspaper *Nupepa Kuokoa* on April 12, 1867, Kahaulelio presented the nine conclusions of the committee for the causes of the famine (translated by Maly):

1. The many sugar mills in Hawaii nei, there are 33. They do not farm, but instead, they burn up the food of the kalo lands. Such as Honokōhau, Halawa, Waipio, &c.

2. In Lahaina, there were many loi and dryland sweet potato fields before, but in these days, they have been turned over to planting cane.

3. There was plenty of water gotten by the people who farmed before, but in this time, the water has all gone to the sugar cane; and the foreigners are now making great efforts in places formerly cultivated by the people who planted taro, sweet potatoes, bananas, gourds, and such.

4. The high price gotten for sugar cane, cause those who cultivate taro, sweet potatoes, and gourds to consider it a waste, because they want more money, but there is not ample food, and that is the mistake.

5. There are 250 men who work the sugar mill in Lahaina. They work strongly in this work, but not in farming, and these words apply as well to the lands cultivated in sugar cane throughout all Hawaii; there is burden and hardship.

6. There are also many idle young people who dwell in Hawaii, thus the farming is left to the elderly people.

7. On Hawaii and Maui, many of the strong people have gone off to the work of gathering pulu (tree fern down), pepeiao (forest mushrooms), and such, to earn money, not food.

8. There are many people to eat the food in this time, as in the time of Kamehameha III, but, beware, the number of people cultivating the food is decreasing.

9. God is not the reason for this lack, nor is it because there is a lack of rain—instead it is the lack of thought by men. Those of Lahaina are quick to judge, they think that in putting their land to sugar planting, that they shall have paiai (thick slabs of taro mash, into which water is added to make poi). So this is what the committee finds is the problem of famine in the district of Lahaina.

Narratives of Hawaiian "Idleness" as a Prelude to Privatization Laws

These things were not supposed to happen as the result of the Māhele, at least in the eyes of some. Westerners had advocated for the privatization of land specifically to improve the lives of Kānaka Maoli. One Westerner in the islands expressed this clearly in the lead up to the Māhele, in 1838:

The character of this people, their ordinary means of subsistence, the absence of inducements to labor, and the systematic policy of the government, are considerations of peculiar interest.... The very natural effect of these circumstances, is, to depopulate the islands... [for] the very facility with which the kalo can be cultivated, has doubtless contributed to arrest the progress of improvement in these islands... Necessity awakens industry, and this calls forth the intellectual powers of men. When these are developed, man does not sit in his cabin, gathering his little patch of kalo, asking no greater luxuries, and proposing no higher ends in life, than to eat or sleep. The idleness of the Indian keeps him where he has been for ages, while the industry of the European, surrounds him with the blessings of society, with its comforts, its affections, its virtues....[10]

Soon after the passage of the acts of the Māhele, however, disputes arose over land and water. Because of the increasing number of fights over access and water use in the new context of private land holdings, dispute management entered into the Kingdom's nascent justice system. In 1860, the Kingdom's legislature created the Commission on Private Ways and Water Rights in order to settle these controversies. In one form or another, this commission existed through the so-called Provisional and Republic governments to the early days of the Territory, when the duties of the commissioners were assumed by the circuit courts of the islands.

Horner v. Kumuliʻiliʻi

Kumuliʻiliʻi came to the Hawaiʻi Supreme Court as an appeal of a case brought before H. Dickenson, Special Commissioner for Private Ways and Water Rights for Maui. In 1894, when the case first came before Dickenson, the 1893 overthrow of the Kingdom was so fresh that a subpoena he issued on a form had to have "Provisional Government" written beside a crossed out "Kamehameha V."

By 1894, Pioneer Mill owned nearly all of the land in the area—except for the many kuleana that people continued to own in Kauaʻula and other small valleys tucked into the steep slopes of the mountains. According to the case, Pioneer was growing cane in the lower, more gently sloped areas and taking water that had formerly gone to loʻi kalo for that irrigation. The case first arose before the Water Commissioner, by the argument of the Plaintiffs, because some of the Defendants had begun to irrigate their kalo in Kauaʻula in defiance of how the Plantation wanted water managed.

Plaintiff allys that the water from the said stream of Kauaula to which the lands mentioned above by the Plaintiffs are entitled by use and custom from Ancient times and to which they have a right, are taken by Kumuliilii, Kalua Kanawaliwali and others of the Defendants, and this taking and changes of said water the Plaintiffs say are contrary to the laws and the rights of the Plaintiff and causes them damages.[11]

The Ancient system of managing these waters to which the Plantiffs referenced was highly complex and reflected a very sophisticated manner of managing a limited resource. The Hawaiʻi Supreme Court in their opinion described the system in detail:[12]

Generally the ahupuaas or ilis of land of a certain name situated on the level land below or "makai" has land, mainly kalo patches, in the valley above or "mauka" bearing the same name. One or two lands makai have no counterpart mauka, and at least one land mauka has no counterpart makai. These mauka kalo patches are similar to the "leles" or outlying portions of an ahupuaa, well known on other islands of this group as "leles" though as a rule they seem not to be so called in Lahaina.

In order to irrigate these lands small ditches or auwais were dug in very ancient times, through which the water was led from the main stream on to the lands. On the Kaanapali or western side there are three main auwais, the first one nearest to the head of the valley is "Piilani," then below it is "Waimana," then "Puuhuliliole." On the Olowalu or eastern side are, first, "Puupapai," then "Muliwaikane." There are numbers of other auwais of much lesser length which start from the stream, irrigate a few patches and then turn into the stream. The ahupuaas and ilis in this part of Lahaina were divided into two principal divisions each containing eleven lands. In order to make the division even, a few lesser ahupuaas were bracketed in pairs and treated as one land, and have one "water day."

Division one, for example, had the water during the day, and Division two during the night, the day being from 5 o'clock a.m. to 5 o'clock p.m., and the night being the remainder of the twenty-four hours. While during eleven consecutive days the lands in Division one were having the water in rotation according to an arranged schedule during the day, the lands in Division two were having it at night. Then, when the last land in each division had been watered, a shift was made, beginning the list again, and Division two received the water in the day time and Division one took it at night, and so on in endless rotation.

While the defendants agreed that such a system existed, they also argued that the ancient system for managing water in Kauaʻula was both more complex and flexible than the plaintiffs alleged. They believed that the most mauka lands were entitled to water when necessary for the success of their kalo crop, and that the ancient system of managing water was to be flexible when needed to support kalo cultivation.

In a very unusual outcome for the time, the court ruled against most of the complaints of the plaintiffs, the sugar planters. While the plaintiffs couched their argument in the supposed immovability of the ancient system and the supposed violations of it by the defendants, the court ruled that "the testimony shows that during a good portion of the twenty years last past the plantation had not insisted that the 'eleven day' system of supplying the water should be strictly executed, but, about three years ago efforts were made to confine the natives cultivating the kalo land mauka to the old system."

While the court ruled that the attorneys' fees be split between the parties, they did not hand to the plantation the complete victory that had been sought. Thus the courts at least on paper upheld a native rights victory. However, the necessity to absorb the costs of litigation, even of itself, made the victory mixed—presaging a century of future water court decisions, discussed later in this book. Nonetheless, it was a notable example of Kanaka Maoli water rights and practices being upheld against the increasing power of plantation interests.

A SMALL FOUNDATION

One possible translation of the name of the lead defendant in *Horner*, Kumuliʻiliʻi, is "small foundation." As will be more fully discussed in the chapters that follow, the *Kumuliʻiliʻi* case is foundational in that it illustrates matters that have become recurring patterns in the struggles over water in West Maui and across Hawaiʻi.

First, as with *Kumuliʻiliʻi*, the courts of Hawaiʻi have acted to protect water and public trust interests in water more than any other venue. As has been seen in the modern water victories in Waiāhole, Oʻahu and Nā Wai ʻEhā (on the other side of Mauna Kahālāwai from Lahaina), the courts (particularly the Hawaiʻi Supreme Court) have been the one venue that Kānaka Maoli and communities that care for water have been able to reliably turn to for a defense of water rights.

Second, it points to the complexity and sophistication of more ancient methods for managing water. During contemporary discourse around plantation water systems, it is nearly inevitable that someone will invoke language praising the engineering of sugar ditches; it is rare that anyone states the same about ancient kalo cultivation systems. This bias both obscures the earlier achievements and can preclude productive, community-driven thinking about the management of water resources and what modes and models are possible.

Third, and perhaps most significantly, *Kumuli'ili'i* shows how residents of West Maui and their supporters have, against towering powers, fought to retain their water rights and practices in the past with some success. Building on these efforts in a small way, we offer this book as a hopefully useful tool in collectively implementing a more equitable and sustainable water future for this area. In that effort, our next chapter gives an overview of the current state of water regulation in West Maui and Hawai'i as a whole.

CHAPTER 2

REGULATORY OVERVIEW

INTRODUCTION

On March 17, 2016, the Maui Department of Water Supply (DWS) held the second of four public meetings on the Maui Island Water Use and Development Plan (Maui WUDP) with approximately fifteen people in West Maui.[1] Though only a small fraction of the community, engaged attendees raised questions about watershed protection, overdevelopment, continued plantation diversion of streamwater, the cost of water from the Kapalua Water Company, and a plethora of other concerns.[2] These questions indicate the breadth of issues surrounding the management of water in and for West Maui communities. This chapter describes the overall system of water management within the state, as well as West Maui's place within that system.

The island of Maui was built by two volcanoes: Haleakalā and Kahālāwai, the west Maui mountains.[3] Kahālāwai has been translated various ways, including to mean "House of Water." Kahālāwai is a deeply dissected volcano 5,788 feet high. The flat isthmus connecting these two volcanoes was created by lava from East Maui banking against Kahālāwai. Other than at the active volcano of Kilauea, the only "thermal water" in Hawai'i exists in West Maui.[4] These unique water resources are governed under the State Water Code, Hawaii Revised Statutes (HRS) Chapter 174C, as well as through implementation of regulations and various county laws concerning the transmission and development of water resources.

The state's legal regime for water management entangles these geologies with multiple objects of law—resources, rights, policies, and institutions—to govern water rights and make certain uses and deprivations "lawful."[5]

The state manages West Maui much as it manages every other region in the island chain. First, we describe this uniform regulatory system, then address ground water management in West Maui separately, and finally surface water management. This chapter leads into the historical discussion of West Maui ditches in chapter 3 by here tracking the interplay between West Maui communities, commercial water users, and government actors over the best set of ways to use West Maui water.

Regulatory Overview

As discussed in chapter 1, tradition and Hawaiian Kingdom laws imposed complex systems of water resource management. One of the first mentions of the Territory's attempts towards a concerted management of water resources, however, was not until 1915. G.K. Larrison, superintendent of hydrography to the Board of Agriculture and Forestry, used a report noting that the governor of Hawai'i had "on several occasions called on this office for data and advice relative to water resources of the Territory. Special reports relative to water resources in the vicinity of Honolulu and Kapaa, Kauai have been furnished."[6] Larrison described progress in other areas, including a reconnaissance of the upper valleys of Honokōwai, Olowalu, and Ukumehame, with locations selected for new continuous stream measurement stations on Olowalu and Ukumehame streams.[7]

Currently, West Maui's fresh water resources are governed through a complex legal regime of authorities shared between the state and county. Ground water provides approximately 99 percent of the water used for domestic uses across the state, and approximately 50 percent of all freshwater uses.[8]

Water Commission Regulation Overview

The state Water Code, HRS Chapter 174C, provides the overarching framework, with reference to other laws governing water quality, Hawaiian traditional and customary rights, and Hawaiian Home Lands. Hawai'i's Water Code was enacted in 1987 and the first administrative rules implementing the Water Code were adopted in May 1988. In December 1988, the Commission on Water Resource Management (CWRM) selected consultants to prepare the first few component plans that with others comprise the Hawai'i Water Plan: (1) Water Resources Protection Plan, (2) Water Quality Plan, (3) State Water Projects Plan, (4) Kaua'i Water Plan, (5) Hawai'i Island Water Plan, (6) O'ahu Water Plan, and (7) Maui Water Plan. Later, the Agricultural

Water Use and Development Plan was developed and adopted as part of the Hawai'i Water Plan.

The overarching principle of Hawai'i's state management regime is that the state, which includes its agencies and counties, must manage water resources as public trustees who have fiduciary duties. CWRM is the state agency tasked with administering the State Water Code. CWRM's mission is to protect and enhance the water resources of the state.

The CWRM consists of seven members. All are appointed by the governor and confirmed by the State Senate. One is the chairperson of the State Board of Land and Natural Resources, who by that role serves as chairperson of the Water Commission, and another is the Director of the State Department of Health. Five others are at-large members required to have "substantial experience in the area of water resource management; provided that at least one member shall have substantial experience or expertise in traditional Hawaiian water resource management techniques and in traditional Hawaiian riparian usage such as those preserved by section 174C-101"[9]

In practice, as will be described in this book, the management of West Maui's water resources has turned on the directives of large landowners.[10] This is accomplished by county operations as well as by private water corporations, like the Kā'anapali Water Company, which operate systems that generally intersect with and run parallel to those of the counties' departments of water supply.

CWRM manages Hawai'i's water under a bifurcated system of water management areas (WMAs) and non-WMAs. The authors of the Water Code anticipated all areas of the state would eventually be designated WMAs. That this has not come to pass may be attributed to a lack of resources at CWRM and opposition to state management over water. The latter has come from land use developers, counties, and misunderstandings about the nature of WMA designation. The 'Īao Aquifer System is the sole groundwater WMA on the island, and Nā Wai 'Ehā is currently the state's only surface water WMA. The West Maui area of this study, however, contains no WMAs.

The primary distinction between WMAs and non-WMAs is a water use permitting system that operates in WMAs. All water users are required to apply for permits in WMAs, but "water user" has a specific meaning that excludes, for practical purposes, the everyday domestic user. "Water users" include county municipal water supply purveyors, well drillers, and other, generally larger scale, water system developers.

The WMA system prioritizes the needs of existing water users by considering their permit applications in the first year after the designation of a WMA.

New proposed water uses may apply for water use permits after this period. To obtain a permit, however, new water users must establish that their proposed water use: (1) can be accommodated with the available water source; (2) is a reasonable-beneficial use, which means "the use of water in such a quantity as is necessary for economic and efficient utilization, for a purpose, and in a manner which is both reasonable and consistent with the state and county land use plans and the public interest"; (3) will not interfere with any existing legal use of water; (4) is consistent with the public interest; (5) is consistent with state and county general plans and land use designations; (6) is consistent with county land use plans and policies; and (7) will not interfere with the rights of the department of Hawaiian home lands as provided in section 221 of the Hawaiian Homes Commission Act (HHCA), which prioritizes the foreseeable water needs of DHHL. HRS §174C-49. These criteria are consistent with the legal status of water as a public trust resource.

Most water users, particularly those seeking to use water for commercial uses such as private golf courses and hotel resort developments, have faced this litany of permitting criteria with trepidation. Amongst other reasons, when CWRM considers a water use permit application, it holds a public hearing and solicits input from a variety of other agencies and groups. CWRM, other agencies, or certain members of the public may call for a contested case on the water use permit application. The contested case hearing is primarily a fact finding proceeding oriented towards the overarching question of whether the proposed water use meets the seven criteria under which CWRM could grant the permit. Yet the process is quasi-judicial, certainly less expeditious and more costly than a simple administrative law proceeding, and subject to court appeal.

As has been done elsewhere on Maui and described above, CWRM may designate either groundwater or surface water WMAs. In designating a surface water WMA, CWRM is required to consider:

1. Whether regulation is necessary to preserve the diminishing surface water supply for future needs, as evidenced by excessively declining surface water levels, not related to rainfall variations, or increasing or proposed diversions of surface waters to levels which may detrimentally affect existing instream uses or prior existing off stream uses;
2. Whether the diversions of stream waters are reducing the capacity of the stream to assimilate pollutants to an extent that adversely affects public health or existing instream uses; or
3. Whether serious disputes respecting the use of surface water resources are occurring.[11]

CWRM has not designated any surface or ground water areas as WMAs in West Maui. In determining whether to designate a ground water WMA, CWRM is required to consider the following:

1. Whether an increase in water use or authorized planned use may cause the maximum rate of withdrawal from the groundwater source to reach 90 percent of the sustainable yield of the proposed groundwater management area;
2. Whether there is actual or threatened water quality degradation as determined by the Department of Health;
3. Whether regulation is necessary to preserve the diminishing groundwater supply for future needs, as evidenced by excessively declining groundwater levels;
4. Whether the rates, times, spatial patterns, or depths of existing withdrawals of ground water are endangering the stability or optimum development of the ground water body due to upconing or encroachment of salt water;
5. Whether the chloride contents of existing wells are increasing to levels that materially reduce the value of their existing uses;
6. Whether excessive preventable waste of ground water is occurring;
7. Whether serious disputes respecting the use of ground water resources are occurring; or
8. Whether water development projects that have received any federal, state, or county approval may result, in the opinion of the commission, in one of the above conditions.[12]

Further, where ground water withdrawals in the proposed designated areas reach 80 percent, CWRM "may invite the participation of water users in the affected area to an informational hearing for the purposes of assessing the ground water situation and devising mitigative measures."[13] However, even where none of the criteria are triggered, CWRM may (and is supposed to) designate an area as a WMA if the water resources in an area may be threatened.

CWRM Actions in Non-WMA-Designated Areas

CWRM has oversight over some aspects of West Maui fresh water resources, even though none of its aquifers or surface water areas have been designated as a WMA. Those seeking to construct wells or install pumps for those wells are required to apply for a CWRM permit and report their water usage on a monthly basis. CWRM may impose reasonable conditions on well construction or pump installation permits, but generally lacks authority to deny them when the water resources are available. CWRM has no oversight over the location of wells installed on private lands, in which case those wells may compete with other wells for the same "pockets" of aquifer waters. No public hearing is held on the permit application; however, CWRM publishes a monthly *Water Resource Bulletin* that announces its receipt of a well construction or pump installation permit application. Their process allows for a public comment period, but neither the applicant nor the Commission is required to respond to any comments.

CWRM is also involved in water governance outside WMAs because it inventories and issues water plans for the protection and development of water resources. The Hawai'i Water Plan consists of five separate plans: (1) a Water Resource Protection Plan (WRPP), which is prepared by CWRM, (2) a Water Quality Plan, which is prepared by the State Department of Health (DOH), (3) a State Water Projects Plan, which is prepared by DLNR's Engineering Division with the input of other state agencies, (4) an Agricultural Water Use and Development Plan, which is prepared by the State Department of Agriculture (DOA), and (5) Water Use and Development Plans, which are prepared by the boards of water supply in each county (Maui, Kaua'i, the City and County of Honolulu O'ahu, and Hawai'i).

To prepare the WRPP and water quality plan, CWRM is required to study, review, and inventory all of the state's water resources and means of conserving water resources; state and county land use plans and policies; the impact of those plans and policies on the environment, fish, wildlife, and water quality; quantify the existing and contemplated water needs for irrigation, power development geothermal, and municipal uses; identify rivers or streams that "may be placed within a wild and scenic rivers system, to be preserved and protected as part of the public trust"; and drainage, reclamation, flood hazards, floodplain zoning, dam safety, and selection of reservoir sites as they relate to the protection, conservation, quantity, and quality of water (HRS §174C-31(c)). These studies, reviews, and inventories of state water resources are important public sources of information about West Maui's waters.

Many of West Maui's agricultural ditches are described in the *State Agricultural Water Use Development Plan* (AWUDP) (2004). The state legislature required the AWUDP to ensure that plantation irrigation systems, even after plantation closures, would be rehabilitated and maintained for agricultural use. In 1998, the legislature enacted Act 101, which authorized the AWUDP as a part of the Hawai'i Water Plan under HRS Chapter 174C, putting it on par with county water use and development plans.[14] Act 101 authorized the State Department of Agriculture (HDOA) to: (1) inventory the irrigation water systems of the State, (2) identify the extent of rehabilitation needed for each system, (3) subsidize the cost of repair and maintenance of the government systems, (4) establish criteria to prioritize the rehabilitation of the systems, (5) develop a five-year program to repair the systems, and (6) set up a long-range plan to manage the systems. HDOA put together this information in its report, *Agricultural Water Use and Development Plan* (AWUDP), *December 2003*. Act 101 also required CWRM to incorporate the AWUDP into the Hawai'i Water Plan. Unfortunately the plan is out of date, and does not suggest any prioritization scheme for management and repair of these ditch systems (nor abandonment and restoration for those with little value to agriculture).

West Maui Water Resource Management

West Maui's highest peak is Mauna Kahālāwai, which, as its name indicates, is the "meeting" of many water sources.[15] Orographic ascent of trade winds up the windward slopes produces persistent rainfall at West Maui's Pu'u Kukui.[16] The Honokōwai and Kahoma streams receive the most rainfall (over 320 inches of rain), followed by Kaua'ula and Wahikuli streams (240 inches), then Honolua, Kahana, and Olowalu streams (180–200 inches), and then Honokahua and Launiupoko streams and Ukumehame gulch (140 inches).[17]

Although the Water Commission's management chooses to address Lahaina aquifers as separate sections and the Lahaina aquifer as separate from Waihe'e and 'Īao aquifers, many have critiqued the administrative separations between these areas because they may draw from a single source in the West Maui Mountains. As discussed more in chapter 6, the hydrological realities of West Maui likely lie somewhere between CWRM's neat pie-slice-like aquifer boundaries and a wholly communicating single water source underlying all of West Maui. The Lahaina aquifer area identified by CWRM is composed in traditional Kanaka Maoli resource management schemes into three districts, or moku, and more than a dozen ahupua'a.

CWRM draws administrative boundaries around aquifer section areas and aquifer system areas, although the systems are hydrologically connected. The Lahaina aquifer section area is composed of six aquifer system areas (ASAs): Honokōhau, Honolua, Honokōwai, Launiupoko, Olowalu, and Ukumehame.

As discussed much more extensively in chapter 6, aquifers are assigned a "sustainable yield," which predicts the amount of water that can potentially, theoretically be withdrawn without harming future consumptive withdrawal.

Table 2.1. The Lahaina aquifer area resource management scheme

MOKU	AHUPUA'A	
Kā'anapali	Honokōhau	Mailipali
	Honolua	Kahana
	Honokahua	Mahinahina
	Napili	Honokōwai
	Honokeane	Makaiwa
	Alaeloa	
Lahaina*	Hanakao'o	Polanui
	Ilikahi	Puaaiki
	Wahikuli	Puaa Nui
	Molalii	Paunau
	Waiamahole	Puunau
	Kaua'ula	Puunau Iki
	Kuia	Launiupoko
	Makila	Koonepolaielaie
	Pāhoa	Awahia
Kealaloloa	Olowalu	Kumaalaea
	Ukumehamehame	Pokahea
	Papalaua	

* Lahaina, particularly in the Makila and Kaua'ula ahupua'a, is characterized by a unique land division system. See Chap. 2, n. 19.

Sustainable yield may be met where wells and other points of withdrawal are perfectly spaced in relation to underground water storage areas. However, as a practical matter, well drillers lack the information and resources to space their wells this way. In 1990, CWRM first established sustainable yields for the Lahaina aquifer systems, and updated them in 2008. As discussed further in chapter 6, the sustainable yield figures for West Maui ASAs are too crude a tool to provide meaningful protections for actual water resources. Instead, an approach based on actual information of West Maui's hydrological connections, and just as importantly, priorities for protected water uses, should be implemented. Despite their shortcomings, sustainable yield figures are embedded in state and county planning and are therefore useful for understanding some assumptions associated with those plans.

The total state-calculated sustainable yield for the Lahaina aquifer is 34 million gallons per day (mgd). Current groundwater withdrawals from the

Lahaina aquifer sector are predicted to rise from 5.8 mgd to 11.2 mgd by 2030.[18] Most of that demand is due to private water systems. By contrast, demand for municipal groundwater from the Maui DWS is estimated to increase from 2.1 mgd to 3.5. mgd by 2030. "Recharge" describes the rate at which fresh groundwater is replenished within the aquifer. Recharge is calculated by considering the following factors: rainfall, fog drip, irrigation, direct surface runoff, change in soil-moisture storage, and evapotranspiration. Under average climate conditions, the recharge for Lahaina aquifer is 164 mgd, and drops to 126 mgd under drought climate conditions.

CWRM also recognizes specific ground and surface water hydrologic units. West Maui's groundwater hydrologic units are: Honokōhau, Honolua, Honokahua, Kahana, Honokōwai, Wahikuli, Kahoma, Kauaʻula, Launiupoko, Olowalu, and Ukumehame. Surface water hydrologic units are:

> Wahikuli (Honokōhau Ditch, Honokōwai Ditch, Wahikuli Pump Ditch, Wahikuli Reservoir)
> Kuia (Lahaina Pump Ditch, Lahaina Pump Ditch 2, Lahainaluna Ditch, Paupau Ditch, Piʻilani Ditch)
> Kauaʻula (Kauaʻula Tunnel)
> Launiupoko (Launiupoko Ditch, Makila Reservoir Ditch)
> Olowalu (Olowalu Ditch)

As explained by Kepā and Onaona Maly, Lahaina, particularly in the Makila and Kauaʻula section, is characterized by a unique land division system. Instead of two distinct ahupuaʻa, some twenty-five traditional land divisions were found in the section of Lahaina that extends from Launiupoko to Wahikuli. Rather than a mauka-to-makai configuration, the "ahupuaʻa" were not contiguous and rather appeared as "lele," or detached parcels with portions of other lands between them.[19] This accounts, in part, for the distinct configuration of water resources in West Maui.

As noted, the Lahaina aquifer sector has a total sustainable yield of 34 mgd. Within the Lahaina aquifer sector are component aquifer system areas (ASAs) with sustainable yields.

Sustainable yield is a problematic administrative tool, but it is also a critical trigger for potential designation as a WMA. As discussed above, when actual uses or "authorized planned uses" of groundwater reach ninety percent for an aquifer sector or aquifer system area, CWRM is called to designate the area as a groundwater WMA.[20]

Table 2.2. Lahaina aquifer sector component aquifer system areas

AQUIFER SECTOR AREA	AQUIFER CODE	SUSTAINABLE YIELD (MGD)
Ukumehame	60206	2
Olowalu	60205	2
Launiupoko	60204	7
Honokōwai	60203	6
Honolua	60202	8
Honokōhau	60201	9
Total	602	34

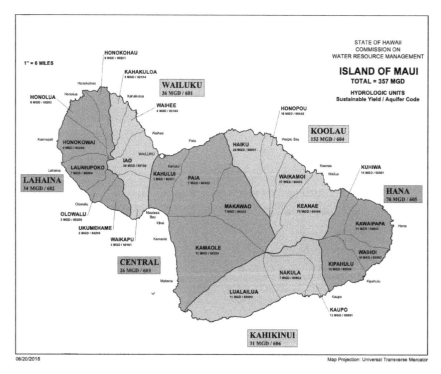

Maui aquifers and section numbers. Figure from CWRM, *Water Resources Protection Plan*, Section 3 (2008).

Maui County Roles in Water Management

The Maui WUDP is a twenty-year plan that, like the WUDPs for other counties in the state, is a component of the State Water Plan.[21] Within the Maui WUDP, tracking the state WRPP, Maui is broken up into aquifer sectors: Lahaina, Central, Kahikinui, Koʻolau, Hāna, and Wailuku. Within aquifer sectors there are existing regional groundwater transfers, such as from Honolua to Honokōwai and Launiupoko to Honokōwai. For Honokōwai, the sustainable yield of its aquifers is significantly less than the projected 2035 population (not agricultural-based) demand for water.[22]

The following describes 2013 Public Water Systems (PWS) within Lahaina aquifer as reported in the draft Maui WUDP.[23] These systems used a total of 8.937 mgd in 2013.

In 2014, the total reported pump capacity for Lahaina aquifer was 53.181 mgd, although the average 2014 groundwater pumpage was 6.207 mgd. This is only 18 percent of the 34 mgd sustainable yield.[24] The population served in Lahaina in 2014 was 31,051 persons, which included resident and visitor populations. Maui DWS, however, uses resident population projections only as the basis for calculating future water demand.[25] Visitors constituted between 25–30 percent of the total population in Maui County.[26]

Lahaina customers rely on a mix of surface and ground water. County water treatment facilities for West Maui are located above Lahainaluna School and near the Kapalua Airport. There are also many other communities in West Maui, such as Honokahau, Kahakuloa, Launiupoko, Olowalu and Ukumehame, that have local or independent water systems not reliant on the DWS systems. All of these rely on a water supply that originates from within the West Maui Watershed.

Public Utility Commission Regulatory Controls on Water in West Maui

In addition to the overarching role that the CWRM has as a trustee of water, and the county's Public Trust obligations as an administrative subdivision of the state as well as the County DWS's role as a water provider, the state Public Utilities Commission (PUC) plays a role in West Maui water management. This is because the provision of water to paying customers by private entities is regulated by the PUC. As new landowners have been adapting plantation irrigation systems to deliver potable and irrigation water to new large-lot agricultural/luxury home customers, they have fallen under PUC regulation, even when CWRM management was nascent or absent. Two examples of this regulation follow.

Table 2.3. 2013 Public Water Systems (PWS) within Lahaina aquifer

PWS NO.	ASA	OWNER	POPULATION SERVED	NUMBER OF CONNECTIONS	AVERAGE DAILY MGD	SOURCE
204	Kapalua	Kapalua Water Co., Ltd.	4,200	555	0.45	Ground
205	Kāʻanapali	Hawaiʻi Water Service Co.	8,000	700	2.8	Ground
209	Olowalu	Olowalu Elua	100	38	0.052	Ground
214	Lahaina	MDWS	18,122	3,236	5.522	54% surface/ 46% ground
218	Honokōhau	MDWS	42	15	0.013	Purchased PWS 204 ground
251	Mahānalua nui subdivision	Launiupoko Water Co., Inc.	587	275	0.1	Ground

OLOWALU WATER DEVELOPMENT

In its 2008 application for licensing from the Public Utilities Commission, the Olowalu Water Company described its potable public water system for the Olowalu area. The Olowalu water system is supplied from Well No. 4937-02 and is identified as Public Water System (PWS) Number 209. The West Maui Land Company conducts the daily operations and fiscal administration for the Olowalu water system. The well water is pumped into a 50,000-gallon tank, where it is chlorinated and stored. From this area, the water is pumped to a 500,000-gallon reservoir tank through a six-inch pipe. From the larger reservoir tank, the water is distributed to new agricultural lots. From the new subdivision, the Olowalu system connects to the older Pioneer Mill system to transport water approximately a mile to Olowalu makai lots and existing homes on those lands.[27]

LAUNIUPOKO WATER COMPANY

In 2002, the Makila Land Company, which is itself a subsidiary of the West Maui Land Company, created both the Launiupoko Water Company and the Launiupoko Irrigation Company (LIC). LIC operates Kauaʻula stream diversions and intake structures as part of their irrigation system, which provides water service to agricultural subdivision estates as well as kuleana users. Makila Land Company refers to their water development in Kauaʻula and Launiupoko as the Makila water system. This system is serviced by two stream diversions, with intakes at Kauaʻula and Launiupoko streams. From the diversions, water is collected in reservoirs and then distributed to agricultural lands below.[28]

The highest element of the current water diversion system in Launiupoko is a tunnel above the Launiupoko intake system at an elevation of 1,425 feet on the north side of the valley. Tunnel No. 15 is 1,320 feet long, cut through 20 dikes, and is reported to withdraw about 100,000 gallons per day, or 17 percent of the median flow diverted from Kauaʻula stream. The intake is located in the back of Kauaʻula Valley at an elevation of approximately 1,280 feet. The intake diverts water from a 742-acre watershed into a cut stone ditch with an eight-inch PVC pipe approximately one mile long to a three- MG reservoir below. From the reservoir, the surface water is sent to a filter station and then to transmission lines servicing the Mahanalua Nui subdivision to the south and to Makila Plantation subdivision to the North. Between 1956 and 1975, the Launiupoko Plantation intake diverted an average of 0.78 mgd with a maximum diversion of 4.75 mgd.[29]

Kauaʻula stream diversion, June 20, 2017.

Kauaʻula stream above the diversion, June 20, 2017. Lance D. Collins and Keʻeaumoku Kapu pictured.

The Kaua'ula diversion system begins as a water flow from a tunnel at approximately 1,530 feet into a forebay and then a penstock that runs the Kaua'ula hydroelectric plant. From the hydro plant the water enters a ditch, then a siphon, and back to a ditch, which flows to a 4 MG reservoir at 725 feet. From the reservoir, the water is sent to a filter station located at approximately 640 feet. Then the transmission lines split, allowing the water to service the Makila Plantation subdivision to the south and the Pu'unoa subdivision to the west. Between 1956 and 1975, the Kaua'ula intake system diverted an average of 5.22 mgd and a maximum of 25.5 mgd.[30]

DESIGNATED WATER MANAGEMENT AREAS

The stickiest concept in the eight considerations for groundwater WMA designation by CWRM has been "Authorized planned use (APU)," which means "the use or projected use of water by a development that has received the proper state land use designation and county development plan/community plan approvals."[31] APU amounts are added to the amount of existing water usage to determine whether 90 percent of the sustainable yield (SY) has been reached. If West Maui communities or CWRM itself sought to designate any West Maui aquifer as a groundwater WMA, it would likely have to establish that APU would reach 90 percent of the applicable sustainable yield.

In its other considerations of groundwater WMA designation petitions, CWRM has applied varied definitions in calculating APU. An APU need not have a water commitment or development agreement with DWS, nor all permits required to proceed with development.[32] CWRM has issued findings that rely on proposed new developments that had not obtained proper state land use designations (the Mānele Bay project in the 1990 Lāna'i WMA petition and in its 1992 Moloka'i designation: "The results of these authorizations [for planned use] are summarized by the County Community Plans, which are expected to be *generally consistent* with State land use designations" [emphasis added]);[33] or county zoning or building permits (1992 Windward O'ahu WMA: APU "includes all existing and projected developments with the proper land use classification and county development plan/community plan approvals even if they do not yet have the zoning or building permits").[34] The following recounts the ways CWRM has earlier calculated APU in determining whether or not to designate a groundwater WMA, included here insofar as it will inform how any community efforts to seek designation may need to engage with calculation of APU.

Lāna'i WMA Considerations

In its 1990 consideration of a petition to designate Lāna'i as a WMA, CWRM used "maximum demands stated from all development related reports" based on residential and visitor population growth projections and standard Maui water use measures to determine the total water demand for APUs.[35] CWRM determined 4.95 mgd as the total APU requirement, and recommended, "To be further conservative, the Commission should consider a future demand from the high-level aquifer of 5 mgd."[36] Projected domestic water demands for Lāna'i development through 1991 totaled 1.72 mgd for nonpotable uses and 4.63 mgd for potable uses, with 0.32 mgd of potable waters being used to make up for a shortage of nonpotable water for a total demand of 4.95 mgd.[37] These projections were based on Maui County standards of 600 gpd per single-family residential unit and 175 gpd per visitor.[38] Golf course water uses were projected based on a standard of 1,000 gpd/acre. CWRM concluded, "Future planned development on Lanai will increase total annual average withdrawals from the high-level aquifer to no more than 5 mgd."[39] The sustainable yield of the Lāna'i high-level aquifer was six mgd and the total projected future demand was five mgd, or 83 percent of the high-level water source.[40] CWRM determined none of the eight criteria for WMA were met, and did not designate Lāna'i as a WMA.[41] CWRM's Lāna'i APU calculation included proposed developments that had not received state land use district amendments.[42] CWRM relied on the Lanai Resort Partners' Water Resources Development Plan for the Island of Lanai (March 1989).[43] Consequent to this reliance, CWRM used estimates for Lanai Resort Partners' proposed Manele Bay golf course and residential developments to calculate APU in 1990, even though petitions to redistrict lands required for those projects were not approved by the State Land Use Commission (LUC) until 1991 and 1994.[44]

O'ahu WMA Designation

In 1990, CWRM determined withdrawals from individual aquifer systems comprising the Windward O'ahu WMA would, at most, meet 85 percent of the sustainable yield in the case of the Kahana aquifer system.[45] In 1992, however, CWRM staff determined "future water demand" for all of O'ahu through 2010, based on 105 percent of the upper limit of population projections, would be a 40 mgd increase—and because APUs were calculated on the basis of *all* areas affected by Windward O'ahu water, this amount accounted for 86 percent of the islandwide sustainable yield through 2010.[46]

They did this because O'ahu had the infrastructural capacity to transport

Windward water to Honolulu and Central Oʻahu, and so APUs "in all geographic areas affected by Windward water must be included in the determination under HRS 174C-44(1) whether the ninety percent sustainable yield figure for the ground water area in question could be exceeded."[47] After subtracting groundwater from areas where there was a direct interaction between ground and surface water, CWRM staff stated APUs would account for 96 percent of the developable yield islandwide.[48]

CWRM relied on the 1992 staff submittal in determining the designations of Oʻahu WMAs.[49] CWRM staff cited the 40 mgd future water demand from the 1990 Oʻahu WUDP, which projected 40 mgd as the maximum increased water demand by 2010 on the basis of their two biggest water users: sugar plantations and the City and County of Honolulu BWS.[50] The Oʻahu WUDP calculation of future water demand supports: (1) the use of historical water consumption as recited in the Oʻahu WUDP as a basis for calculating per capita water demand; and (2) summing future water demands of municipal, military, and private developments, irrespective of whether proposed developments had already obtained approvals for appropriate state land use designations, SMA permits, approvals, zoning amendments, or environmental review documentation; (3) use of proposed water demands from private developments noted in county plans; and, alternatively, (4) an estimate based on 105 percent of the upper limit of population growth multiplied by DWS's historical consumption per capita coefficient.[51]

Molokaʻi WMA Designation

CWRM found APUs for domestic and municipal water on Molokaʻi to account for 4.35 mgd, based on a target resident population (10,600 persons with 3,800 residential dwelling units, 1,800 dwelling units for non-residents, and supporting commercial and industrial facilities).[52] CWRM also found APUs for irrigation/ agricultural water to be greater than 21.6 mgd.[53] Molokaʻi APUs were based on an economic forecast by Hastings, Martin, Chew & Associates, Ltd. (Jul. 1981),[54] which took the form of projected demands for housing and visitor accommodation units and commercial and industrial space through the year 2000.[55]

CWRM relied on the then-current 1984 Molokai Community Plan (MCP 1984) and background information and technical data for the MCP 1984, which was published in the "Molokai Community Plan Technical Report" (1981) (MCP Technical Report 1981).[56] CWRM summarized MCP Technical Report 1981 land development data and Maui DWS municipal water demand data from

1985. The Hastings, Martin, Chew & Associates, Ltd. economic forecast and its underlying methodology was not available at the time of this writing. The MCP Technical Report 1981 specified that the economic forecast produced a population projection upon which water demands were calculated under water system standard usages.[57] CWRM designated the island of Molokaʻi as a WMA on May 13, 1992.

ʻĪao and Waiheʻe Ground Water WMA Designations

In its November 14, 2002 findings of fact regarding ʻĪao and Waiheʻe WMAs, CWRM "assumed" Maui BWS's projection of 7.147 mgd of additional withdrawal "[met] the definition of authorized planned use."[58] CWRM, however, described APUs as "[l]ong-range authorized planned future demands from community plans and specified in the Maui County Water Use and Development Plan[.]"[59]

CWRM compared population-based water demand projections in a community plan that called for concurrency with Maui BWS projections based on pending/approved building permits, contractual obligations, and water commitments and determined the former were irreconcilable with the much higher amount calculated under the projection-based method.[60] CWRM found, "[t]he [Kīhei-Mākena community plan (1998)] plan states that water supply increases will be concurrent with planned growth, and supports the projected development of the Central and East Maui water systems. However, using county water demand standards of 600 gal/day per single-family unit, and assuming four residents per unit, this population growth would translate to an increase of 1.25 mgd. This number cannot be reconciled with Table 11[.]"[61] Table 11 of CWRM's 2002 findings are reproduced in Table 2.4.

CWRM findings of APUs in 1996 and 2002 discussions about ʻĪao aquifer designation depended on estimates of future water demand provided by Maui BWS and as described in the Maui WUDP (1990). In 1996, CWRM found criterion 1 for WMA designation was met for ʻĪao aquifer on the basis of existing use, which alone exceeded SY.[62] CWRM's 1996 APU calculation was based on Maui BWS's existing water commitments (8.116 mgd to 8.366 mgd) and its projections of increased future demand of 2 to 2.5 mgd by 1998.[63] No method for Maui BWS' projections of 2 to 2.5 mgd to 1998 was provided.

In 2002, CWRM again found criterion 1 was met for ʻĪao aquifer designation on the basis of its "discussions" with Maui BWS and "update[s]" to four categories of "estimate[d] new development" reflected in its 1996 findings.[64] The 1996 findings were based on Maui BWS water commitments under an unspecified time-

Table 2.4. Water Use

DESCRIPTION OF AUTHORIZED PLANNED USE	1990	1996 FOF MGD	2002 MGD
1. Existing water commitments (Water System Development Fee Rule)		0.410	0.411
2. Approved building permits w/o commitments		0.480	NA
3. Pending and approved building permits		0.476	6.736
4. Central Maui Joint Venture (contractual obligation)		6.750 to 7	NA
Additional demand total		8.116 to 8.366	7.147
12-MAV pumpage for CMSA for calendar year	15.4	20.35	22.040
Total projected use	31.1	28.5 to 28.7	29.2

frame, whereas the 2002 findings included approved building permits without commitments and omitted Central Maui Joint Venture projected demand because those projects "have such a long timeframe (some have been on hold since the 1980s); any additional amount following a resolution of the [Joint Venture] commitment are commensurate with the total buildout by 2020."[65]

CWRM explained the 2002 figure for pending projects "simplifie[d]" the "projects without commitments" category to include projects with approved permits, and those with approval still pending, which included many of the Central Maui Joint Venture projects, and omitted "20 to 30 very small projects totaling less than 0.25 mgd."[66] CWRM noted 2010 projected water production requirements for the Central Maui system area were 31.1 mgd according to the 1990 Maui County Water Use and Development Plan (Maui WUDP), but found "current ultimate demand, based on current plans, is 29.19 mgd" apparently due to its 2002 simplifications of the four categories.[67] CWRM calculated water demands as a function of population growth by using Maui County water demand standards of 600 gal/day per single-family unit, and assumed four residents per unit.[68] At its November 20, 2002 meeting, CWRM carried a motion "find[ing] that meeting criteria [*sic*] §174C 44(1) constitutes a current reasonable threat to the Iao Aquifer system" and designated Iao as a WMA.[69]

In Maui, administrative models do not predict water scarcity based on an absence of resources. Rather, as observed by former Maui DWS Director, David Craddick, "Water controversies... [are] in my estimate currently more along the lines of who will pay for developing water and not so much that we have run out."[70] Craddick's observation, taken in tandem with CWRM's tendency to base its WMA designation determinations on whether 90 percent of groundwater resources will be foreseeably used, may tend to lead to the conclusion that WMA designation is unwarranted.

However, administrative predictions of sufficient amounts of West Maui groundwater resources are predicated on "sustainable yield," which is meant to describe the amount of water that can be withdrawn without harming the aquifer system. As discussed *supra*, many have criticized "sustainable yield" as an impractical concept that does not describe on-the-ground realities and impacts to communities and natural resources. Further, for many decades, West Maui residents have observed that expanding water development would not reduce water needs. This is primarily due to increasing resort and residential development.

In the 1970s, Nāpili residents complained of contaminated water that was not chlorinated, and with coliform bacteria content so high that it did not meet U.S. Public Health Service standards.[71] At that time, Nāpili residents obtained approximately 0.5 mgd of water from Honokōhau Stream, which carried surface water to the area's homes. Despite announcements of a new one-mgd storage tank and new well, William Iaconetti of Nāpili observed that nothing will change overall, because new housing developments would be taking the new well's water. As an example, he cited the proposed Maui Land & Pineapple Company's large residential and tourist development project planned in the Honolua area.[72]

West Maui (Lahaina) Aquifer Surface and Groundwater Uses

As discussed above, CWRM has recently emphasized the criterion under which actual pumping or authorized planned use has reached 90 percent of the sustainable yield of the aquifer WMAs may be designated ground water management areas. How this would be approached in Lahaina will be informed by some of the following considerations.

The Lahaina Aquifer Sector Area (ASA) has a total of 82 wells, with 72 of those wells drilled for irrigation and municipal use. In 2014, those wells pumped approximately 6.208 mgd, with 96 percent of that pumpage devoted to municipal uses. Surface water usage amounts to 20.3 mgd, with 17 percent of that use coming from irrigation and agricultural uses. Further, none of the aquifers comprising the Lahaina ASA have come close to reaching their sustainable yields. The following chart of surface water uses is based on Maui DWS's latest update to their Water Use and Development Plan for Lahaina.

Table 2.5. Surface Water Uses

STREAM	LOW FLOW Q50	# DIVERSIONS	REPORTED WATER USE
Papalaua	0 (mgd)	0	0
Ukumehame	3.23	1	0
Olowalu	3.94	2	1.622
Launiupoko	0.304	1	0.405
Kauaʻula	6.137	1	2.610
Kahoma	3.747	7	0.416
Kanaha	3.165	0	1.622
Wahikuli	(dry 50% of the time)	0	0
Honokōwai	3.488	2	0
Kahana	(dry 50% of the time)	0	0
Honokahua	(dry 50% of the time)	0	0
Honolua	2.455	4	0
Honokōhau	13.566	8	13.54
Anakaluahine	0	0	0
Total	40.03	27	20.21

DESIGNATION OF A GROUNDWATER MANAGEMENT AREA IN LAHAINA?

In 2008, the sustainable yield for the Lahaina aquifer sector was set at 34 mgd. This figure went under review as part of the update of the State Water Resources Protection Plan,[73] but did not change.[74] As noted, one factor CWRM is required to consider in determining whether to designate an aquifer as a WMA is:

> Whether an increase in water use or authorized planned use may cause the maximum rate of withdrawal from the ground water source to reach ninety percent of the sustainable yield of the proposed ground water management area[.]

HRS §174C-44(1).[75] According to the Maui WUDP, water use of Lahaina aquifer system areas as of 2014 is not yet at 90 percent of sustainable yield, however, calculations of authorized planned use may yield a different assessment.

Although none of the aquifer system have a reported usage approaching ninety percent of sustainable yield, there are often discrepancies between

Table 2.6. Lahaina aquifer system use in mgd

AQUIFER SYSTEM	SUSTAINABLE YIELD	2014 REPORTED USAGE[a]	2017 12-MO. MOVING AVG.[b]
Honokōhau	9	0	0
Honolua	8	2.601	2.561
Honokōwai	6	3.052	3.568
Launiupoko	7	0.479	0.864
Olowalu	2	0.069	0.104
Ukumehame	2	0.007	0.043
Total	934	6.208	7.14

[a] Maui WUDP Update at 22.
[b] CWRM Submittal for Regular Meeting Item B-2, at 11 (Table 7) (Nov. 20, 2018).

Table 2.7. Aquifer system usage

(AQUIFER NUMBER) AQUIFER SYSTEM	SUSTAINABLE YIELD (MGD)	EXISTING WATER USE (MGD)	SY MINUS PUMPAGE (MGD)	WATER USE AS % OF SY
(60101) Waikapū	3	0.19	2.81	6.3
(60102) ʻIao	20	14.19	2.84	71.0
(60103) Waiheʻe	8	4.67	3.33	58.4
(60104) Kahakuloa	5	NRU	NRU	NRU
(60201) Honokōhau	9	NRU	NRU	NRU
(60202) Honolua	8	2.56	5.44	32.0
(60203) Honokōwai	6	4.020	1.98	67.0
(60204) Launiupoko	7	0.40	6.61	5.7
(60205) Olowalu	2	0.12	1.88	6.0
(60206) Ukumehame	2	0.04	1.96	2.0

Source: WRPP Draft 2018, Appx. H at 23.

reported water usage and actual usage. Approximately 5.956 mgd of ground water usage (96 percent) is from public water systems, most of which is used by the Lahaina DWS system. Further, new wells have been permitted since 2014. CWRM's current draft of the Water Resources Protection Plan also reports a relatively low usage of Lahaina aquifers as of December 2016.

According to the update to the Maui WUDP, several new wells are planned for development across Lahaina.[76]

Table 2.8. Wells permitted in Lahaina Aquifer 2014–2018

ASA	TMK	APPLICANT	PROPOSED USE (MGD)	DATE APPROVED
Launiupoko	(2) 4-7-012:004	Strombeck	0.072	09/22/2018
	(2) 4-7-009:016	Duvall	0.036	10/08/2018
	(2) 4-7-001:049	Moyer	0.005	06/23/2018
	(2) 4-7-003:005	McDonald	0.2	08/06/2018
	(2) 4-7-003:004	LIC 1	0.700	10/06/2016
	(2) 4-6-032:001	Puamana Assn	?	09/18/2015
Honokōwai	(2) 4-4-004:002	DHHL/DWS	0.680	10/21/2018
	(2) 4-4-014:005	Starwood	3.4	05/24/2015
	(2) 4-4-004:018	Hawai'i Water	0.72	03/31/2008
Honolua	(2) 4-3-001:017	DWS	?	10/22/2014

The proposed uses (not the capacity of pumpage) of these new wells added to the existing water use increases in percentage of sustainable yield used, arguably is an authorized, planned use.

More recently, two new subdivision developments in Kaua'ula and Launiupoko have sought approvals from the Maui County Council: Makila Rural-East and Polanui Gardens. A new well in Launiupoko has been proposed to service these developments. Polanui Gardens, a project proposed by Kipa Centennial, LLC, is proposed to include 50 single-family lots with allowances for 50 'ohana units. Adjacent to Polanui Gardens is a proposed Makila Rural-East housing project consisting of 46 lots with allowances for 46 'ohana units.[77] A third development, Makila Kai, was proposed a few years back but met with a complaint against its noncompliance with land use procedures and environmental review requirements.[78]

Based on 2017 existing water uses and new proposed development of water sources since 2014, the Honokōwai aquifer may be the closest to approaching a threshold of 90 percent use of sustainable yield. Maui County observed: "Projected development in the Honokowai aquifer system could exceed sustainable yield if withdrawals from that aquifer were exclusively used to meet projected demand."[79] However, developers have also planned to meet demand by using surface water diverted from northern streams, including Honokōhau Stream.

Sustainable yields for these aquifers, however, are undergoing revision as part of CWRM's Water Resources Protection Plan in 2019. Chapter 6 includes an in-depth unpacking of the concept of sustainable yield.

South Lahaina – Ukumehame Development Projects, Long Range Planning Division, Maui Planning Department, dated May 1, 2016.

Kapalua – North Lahaina Development Projects, Long Range Planning Division, Maui Planning Department, dated May 1, 2016.

CWRM's 2018 Draft Water Resources Protection Plan describes a situation that further illustrates some shortcomings of the sustainable yield concept. Since August 2001, CWRM has been able to monitor the transition zone of the Honokōwai aquifer through the installation of the Māhinahina Deep Monitoring Well, located at an elevation of 665 feet above median sea level, just upslope of the Kapalua Airport.[80] Conductivity, temperature, and depth (CTD) profiles "indicate a thinning of the fresh water zone"—specifically that the top of the transition zone between fresh and sea water has risen by 50 feet, the midpoint of the transition zone by 13 feet, and the seawater level by 11 feet.[81] The cause of this aquifer lens thinning is attributed to changes in land use. Whereas the plantation irrigated sugarcane, contributing to recharge, "the rise in construction and water demand in the Kāʻanapali and Honokōwai areas near the beach have imposed additional demands on the thin basal lens from wells installed upslope from the Māhinahina well, resulting in the upward trend of the top of the transition zone (TTZ), denoted the dramatic thinning of the fresh water lens in recent years."[82] The upconing of aquifer lenses is one criterion that CWRM considers in determining whether to designate a water management area.[83] As of the time of this writing, CWRM staff have independently discussed whether to designate Honokōwai as a ground and surface WMA, as well as other areas in West Maui.

Surface Water Regulation and Issues

The legal terms for the management practice to protect stream water uses are the determination of Interim Instream Flow Standard (IIFS) or the more permanent Instream Flow Standard (IFS). The state defines IIFS as "a temporary instream flow standard of immediate applicability, adopted by the commission without the necessity of a public hearing, and terminating upon the establishment of an instream flow standard."[84] The IFS is defined as "a quantity or flow of water or depth of water which is required to be present at a specific location in a stream system at certain specified times of the year to protect fishery, wildlife, recreational, aesthetic, scenic, and other beneficial instream uses."[85] The current IIFS for West Maui is set forth in HAR §13-169-48, and became effective on December 10, 1988:

> *Interim instream flow standard for West Maui.* The Interim Instream Flow Standard for all streams on West Maui, as adopted by the commission on water resource management on October 19, 1988, shall be that amount of water flowing in each stream on the effective date of this standard, from year to year without further amounts of water being diverted offstream through

new or expanded diversions, and under the stream conditions existing on the effective date of the standards.

In other words, as was the case for similar administrative rules for other areas across Hawai'i, the West Maui IIFSs were set at whatever happened to be in the stream at that time. Since most plantation diversions were still capturing 100 percent of base flow, whether or not those plantations were still operating in 1988, it cemented a state in which dry streams were considered to legally meet the state's IIFSs.

In the last few years, a single CWRM staff member was tasked with assembling proposed revised IIFSs for West Maui. These standards describe not just a number, but as described in the definition of an IFS, a number that encapsulates a balance of protections for the "fishery, wildlife, recreational, aesthetic, scenic, and other beneficial instream uses." An "instream use" is further defined by the Water Code to mean beneficial uses of stream water for significant purposes that are located in the stream and which are achieved by leaving the water in the stream. Instream uses include, but are not limited to:

1. Maintenance of fish and wildlife habitats;
2. Outdoor recreational activities;
3. Maintenance of ecosystems such as estuaries, wetlands, and stream vegetation;
4. Aesthetic values such as waterfalls and scenic waterways;
5. Navigation;
6. Instream hydropower generation;
7. Maintenance of water quality;
8. The conveyance of irrigation and domestic water supplies to downstream points of diversion; and
9. The protection of traditional and customary Hawaiian rights.[86]

Given this breadth of beneficial uses, setting the IIFS involves an inexact but wide-ranging consideration of interests. CWRM reports for three of West Maui's southernmost streams are due to be released to the public presently.

Lahaina has eleven perennial streams and 27 declared stream diversions (see table 2.9).

In Lahaina, agricultural diversions consume approximately 20.214 mgd.[87] Ground and surface waters interact under varied conditions, such as when high-level water seeps into stream channels to provide streamflow; basal water

Table 2.9. Lahaina streams and diversions

AQUIFER	STREAM	# DIVERSIONS	BASE STREAM LOW FLOWS[a]
Papalua	Ukumehame	0	8 mgd
Ukumehame	Ukumehame	1	0 mgd at Olowalu
Launiupoko	Launiupoko	1	1.5 mgd
Kauaʻula	Launiupoko	1	9.5 cfs
Kahoma	Launiupoko	7	5.7 cfs near Lahaina
Kanaha stream	Launiupoko	0	4.9 cfs
Wahikuli	Honokowai	0	
Wahikuli gulch	Honokowai	0	Dry under low flows
Hahakea gulch	Honokowai	0	Dry under low flows
Honokowai	Honokowai	2	1.1 cfs near Lahaina
Kahana	Honokowai/Honolua	1	Dry under low flows
Honokahua	Honolua	0	Dry under low flows
Mokupeʻa gulch	Honolua	0	Dry under low flows
Honolua	Honolua	4	4.6 cfs
Papua gulch	Honolua	0	Dry under low flows
Honokōhau	Honokōhau	8	14 mgd above diversions
Anakaluahine	Honokōhau	0	

[a] Draft Maui Island Water Use & Development Plan, Public Workshop Draft, Lahaina, at 6 (Nov. 28, 2016) available at: http://www.mauicounty.gov/DocumentCenter/View/106353.

flows into stream channels; stream water infiltrates into groundwater; and basal water discharges through basal or caprock springs, providing water to wetlands and ponds. This interconnection is recognized in CWRM's definition of a "hydrologic unit" as a "surface drainage area or a ground water basin or a combination of the two."

In August 2006, Maui Land and Pineapple Company (MLP) petitioned CWRM to establish amended instream flow standards for Honokōhau and Honolua Streams. In November 2008, CWRM determined that MLP's petitions would be delayed pending determination of issues in the contested case concerning Nā Wai ʻEhā.

On June 21, 2011, CWRM entered into a $648,000 joint funding agreement with USGS to conduct a low-flow study of the main streams within ten watersheds in the Lahaina District. The ten streams studied included Honolua, Honokahua, Kahana, Honokōwai, Wahikuli, Kahoma, Kauaʻula, Launiupoko, Olowalu, and Ukumehame. CWRM expanded its study area "due to development pressures and changes in land use in West Maui."[88] In 2014, USGS published its low-flow stream study for West Maui streams.[89] CWRM has been preparing instream flow assessments since 2016, including assessments for West Maui. CWRM also worked with the United States Army Corps of Engineers (USACE) to undertake a watershed assessment management plan in West Maui.[90] As discussed further in chapter 3, CWRM is currently updating its interim instream flow standards (IIFSs) for West Maui surface waters. These updated IIFSs are expected to govern and shape many disputes over surface water.

West Maui Watershed Partnerships

In 1998, Maui DWS, Kamehameha Schools/Bishop Estate, C. Brewer, Amfac, MLP, the Nature Conservancy, and DLNR agreed to protect the 50,000-acre West Maui Mountain watershed, which fed the ʻĪao, Waiheʻe, and Lahaina aquifers. Their agreement was modeled on the successes of the East Maui Watershed Partnership. Common to both were agreements that native flora and fauna should be conserved and that wild pigs, whose rooting caused erosion, should be eradicated.[91] Kamehameha Schools also later became part of the Partnership.[92]

The West Maui Mountain Watershed Partnership office is located at 820 Olowalu Village Road in several neat trailer offices. While lean, WMMWP has been able to remain a vital part of conservation efforts across West Maui. The Partnership operates in a niche where no conflicts arise in large part because forest conservation has benefits that are not seen as controversial.[93] Partnership staff have found themselves in the position of being an informal bridge between community groups and landowners tied to the vestiges of Lahaina's plantations. The Memorandum of Agreement between Partnership partners essentially agrees to manage the mountain as a cohesive unit and try to share resources to further their mission of protecting the forest's ecological integrity, with emphasis on native biota. Partners provide labor, materials, sometimes funds, and shared resources.

In July 2008, the US Army Corps of Engineers (USACE) initiated the development of a West Maui Watershed Plan to be completed in collaboration with the State Department of Land and Natural Resources (DLNR), Department of Health, and various other federal agencies. In September 2012, USACE and DLNR entered into a $3 million cost-share agreement to develop a watershed plan in support of the West Maui "Ridge to Reef" Initiative. In 2013, the West Maui Mountains Watershed Management Plan was made public and described the operations, goals, and rationale behind the Partnership's actions.

Fencing, which has been a hugely controversial issue between watershed managers and hunters, has been less of a problem in West Maui mostly due to the consolidation of lands by the plantations.[94] Plantations were self-serving—they would only allow employees to have hunting privileges; the rest of their lands were ranched. During West Maui's plantation era, there were plantations 360 degrees around the mountains, so access was severely controlled and limited. Ranchers and sometimes ranch employees were also given access to hunt. Because general public hunters and Kānaka Maoli were historically cut off from access to mountain hunting grounds, there has been less of a hunting community to protest against Partnership fencing as compared with other watershed areas. Further, West Maui did not have pigs until the 1950s. Pigs were introduced by the plantations for game.[95] Today, MLP has a hunter program for its lowland fallow lands. The Nature Conservancy used to have a similar program, but does not currently.

Watershed management efforts have meant collaborations between the large landowners and environmental protection groups, largely under the West Maui Mountains Watershed Partnership. MLP owns approximately 22,000 acres on Maui, with nearly half of it dedicated to conservation management, including 141 acres within the project watersheds.[96] Of these, 1,588 acres are in the Honokōwai Watershed. MLP ceased cultivation of pineapple in 2008 and continues to operate resort communities in Kapalua. Kaanapali Land Management Corporation is also a partner with WMMWP, although its lands are in the agricultural district. KLMC's subsidiary is Kā'anapali Coffee Farms, which offers four- to seven-acre farm lots in a "plantation-style" arrangement covering 300 acres in which workers grow coffee on lands owned by homeowners. Kamehameha Schools owns approximately 1,000 acres within WMMWP areas and is also a partner.

Development-associated pressures, such as the influx of new populations that need to be educated on watershed and conservation issues, complicate Partnership work. Liability issues for hikers and dirtbikers on mountain trails have also become problematic. The enlarging population of West Maui also means that more people live in proximity to the watershed due to mauka development. Enlarged populations are also a risk factor for wildfires, which also threaten the watershed.

Private Landowners and Water Companies

West Maui's water systems, as with those across the Islands, demonstrate tight continuities between plantation water usage to resort tourism water usage.

West Maui Land Co. manages three water companies: Launiupoko Irriga-

Table 2.10. List of Potable water systems

POTABLE WATER SYSTEM NAME[a]	OWNER	SOURCE	2014 DAILY AVG. (GPD)
Honokōhau	County DWS	Groundwater purchased from Kapalua Water Co.	13,000
Kapalua	Kapalua Water Co.	Groundwater	450,000
Kaʻanapali	Hawaii Water Service	Groundwater	2,800,000
Lahaina	County DWS	54% Surface, 46% Groundwater	5,522,000
Olowalu	Olowalu Elua Associates	Groundwater	52,000
Mahanalua Nui Subdivision	Launiupoko Water Co.	Groundwater	100,000

[a] Maui DWS, WUDP Draft at 9. Available at: http://www.co.maui.hi.us/DocumentCenter/View/104326.

Table 2.11. Wells

REPORTER	WELLS[a]
Maui DWS	Honokahua, Napili, Kanaha, Wai Puka
Hawaiʻi Water Service Co., Inc.	P-1 to P-6, Hahakea, Honokowa
Maui Land & Pineapple Co., Inc.	Kapalua
Launiupoko Water Co., Inc.	Mahanalua Nui
Puamana Community Assoc.	Puamana
Olowalul Water Co., Inc.	Olowalu Elua

[a] U.S. Geological Survey, Pacific Islands Water Science Center, "Recent hydrologic conditions, Lahaina District, Maui, Hawaii. Pumpage in aquifer systems" (Jan. 15, 2013) available at: https://hi.water.usgs.gov/recent/lahaina/pumpage.html.

tion, Launiupoko Water, and the Olowalu Water Company. In 2014, the Olowalu Water System was operated by the Olowalu Water Co., Inc., with water supplied by the Olowalu Well. The Olowalu Well is a groundwater source, drawing from the underground Olowalu aquifer.[97] In its disclosure of Olowalu Water Company water service rates, West Maui Land Co. described the following:

$1.35   per 1,000 gallons up to 10,000 gallons

$1.82   per 1,000 gallons from 10,001 up to 25,000 gallons

$2.14   per 1,000 gallons over 25,000 gallons
$0.72   per 1,000 gallons over 150,000 gallons

In 2014, the Mahanalua Nui Water System operated by the Launiupoko Water Co., Inc. was supplied by the Mahanalua Nui Wells nos. 1, 2, & 3. The Mahanalua Nui Wells are groundwater sources, drawing from the underground Launiupoko aquifer.[98] Launiupoko Water Company, Inc. has disclosed the following rates:

$1.43 per 1,000 gallons up to 10,000 gallons
$1.93per 1,000 gallons between 10,00 and 25,000 gallons
$2.31per 1,000 gallons over 25,000 gallons[99]

Launiupoko Irrigation Company, also a West Maui Land company, charges $0.76 per thousand gallons and $0.38 (for a period of a one-year term, with the possibility of extensions to the term) Bulk users (over 1 million gallons per month or owner/lessee of at least 50 acres in Applicant's service area).[100] By contrast, the Maui DWS disclosed that it charged the following rates in 2014:

$2.00 per thousand gallons for 0–5,000 gallons
$3.80 per thousand gallons for 5,001–15,000 gallons
$5.70 per thousand gallons for over 15,000 gallons

On November 27, 1978, the Kāʻanapali Water Corporation (KWC) was incorporated as a wholly owned subsidiary of Amfac, Inc. KWC took over Amfac's water service provider functions for Kāʻanapali, an area of West Maui dominated by hotel resorts. In the late 1950s, Amfac began installing its water supply systems as part of its Kāʻanapali resort complex, which began operation in 1962. From that time until 1978, Amfac's subdivision, Amfac Communities Maui, operated the water systems. Pioneer Mill Company, which was another wholly owned subsidiary of Amfac, provided water to north Lahaina. Now KWC has become "Hawaiʻi Water Service Company" (HWSC), a wholly owned subsidiary of California Water Service Group.[101]

In 2016, headlines read, "Kāʻanapali hotels, condos face steep water bills, compared with county customer costs" and "Resort customers challenge private water company to 'do better.'"[102] HWSC proposed a 33 percent increase of their water bill for that year, which the State Public Utilities Commission

(PUC) granted. HWSC distributes approximately three MGD to 47 businesses and nearly 600 homes. In seeking higher water rates, the company said that, since its last hike in 2012, it had installed two tanks, pumping equipment, electrical connections and an upgraded system; replaced or repaired inaccurate meters; purchased new vehicles; and completed a water supply and facility master plan.[103]

HWSC's increase spiked monthly rates to $1,136.86 (for four-inch water meters), $4,360.20 (six-inch water meters) and $6,393.19 (eight-inch water meters), which averaged 400 percent more than the county, which were $380 (four-inch), $700 (six-inch) and $1,100 (eight-inch).[104] Kāʻanapali resort managers, however, argued that their high water rates were necessary to offset about $3 million in capital improvement projects, and that rates would gradually decrease after the first year.[105] However, as Tony Bruno, General Manager of the Westin Maui Resort & Spa in Kāʻanapali, pointed out, "When I hear that $3 million in capital improvements require $1.7 million in revenue on an annual basis, that doesn't pencil up."[106] HWSC's increase meant that some hotels now pay nearly five times as much as what Maui County charges similar customers. In its 2015 application, HWSC projected that its revenues from hotel water service would be $3.8 million in 2016.

In September 2016, the State Public Utilities Commission approved HWSC's proposal, but limited an increase of water rates to about 20 percent over present rates for Kāʻanapali hotels and condominium owners. The new rates would increase revenue from $5,317,466 to $6,378,817 in a year.[107] The PUC determined the company's rate of return of 7.75 percent was "fair." The 20 percent increase was less than the 32.8 percent increase, which would have brought in $1.7 million more in net revenues, that HWSC had initially sought.

Maui DWS and *Ka Paʻakai* Analysis

We have highlighted the Kaanapali Water Corporation water rate increase for several reasons. It raises questions about the scope of revenues that may be realized from the (albeit regulated) sale of water resources in the context of West Maui's present economy. All of Hawaiʻi's water resources are public trust resources. Had a government agency proposed to treat and deliver these water resources to Kāʻanapali, that agency, and its public beneficiaries, may have been able to utilize the revenues for public interest purposes. The Department of Hawaiian Home Lands (DHHL) is, for instance, specifically entitled to receive thirty percent of proceeds from leases or licenses for the use of water into a special Native Hawaiian Rehabilitation Fund. Just as importantly, the Kāʻanapali water rate case is notable for what it did not discuss in regard to the ongoing history of how water control has shaped settler colonialism in West Maui.

Water resources are cultural resources. Waters removed from the ground aquifer or surface waters deprive nearshore fisheries in coastal ecosystems and streams of needed flows for native fauna, flora, and loʻi kalo. Had these been considered in the PUC decision, other provisions may have been made with a longer-term vision of Hawaiʻi in view. This would not only have been a good idea, but a process that is required by law. In the groundbreaking Hawaiʻi Supreme Court case *Ka Paʻakai o Ka ʻĀina v. Land Use Commission* (94 Hawaiʻi 31, 7 P.3d 1068 [2000]), the court addressed the public trust responsibility of all government agencies relative to the protection and preservation of native Hawaiian traditional and customary practices. In *Ka Paʻakai*, the State Land Use Commission (LUC) was required to make findings as to:

1. The identity and scope of "valued cultural, historical, or natural resources" in the petition area, including the extent to which traditional and customary native Hawaiian rights are exercised in the petition area;
2. The extent to which those resources—including traditional and customary native Hawaiian rights—will be affected or impaired by the proposed action; and
3. The feasible action, if any, to be taken by the LUC to reasonably protect native Hawaiian rights if they are found to exist.[108]

The court held that the LUC had not entered sufficient findings to demonstrate that it had discharged its non-delegable duty to protect those rights and had improperly delegated its public trust duties to the developer.[109] The LUC had tasked the developer with developing and coordinating resource management plans that would ensure protections for native Hawaiian traditional and customary rights. Under *Ka Paʻakai*, requisite findings should be completed independently by the approving agencies; and the development proponent was required to provide relevant information, which the agency was to subsequently verify, analyze, and use to develop and prescribe conditions necessary to protect traditional and customary native Hawaiian rights. Requiring development proponents, including water purveyors, to adhere to a *Ka Paʻakai* analysis is entirely consistent with the Water Code case law that governs CWRM's duties and practices. In re Use Permit Applications, 94 Hawai'i 97, 9 P.3d 409 (2000) (Waiāhole I), the Hawai'i Supreme Court noted:

> Thus, insofar as the public trust, by nature and definition, establishes use consistent with trust purposes as the norm or "default" condition, we affirm the Commission's conclusion that it effectively prescribes a "higher level of scrutiny" for private commercial uses such as those proposed in this case. *In practical terms, this means that the burden ultimately lies with those seeking or approving such uses to justify them in light of the purposes protected by the trust.*[110]

Similarly, in its extensive analysis of the ways in which state and county agencies can make decisions that affect water resources and how those agencies should meet their decisionmaking responsibilities (*Kaua'i Springs, Inc. v. Kaua'i Planning Commission*, 133 Hawai'i 141, 324 P.3d 951 (2014)), the court directed: "Applicants have the burden to justify the proposed water use in light of the trust purposes."[111]

Early in 2017, the Maui DWS solicited comments on its *Ka Pa'akai* process, which it integrated into the updated Maui Water Use and Development Plan (Maui WUDP). The Maui DWS *Ka Pa'akai* analysis includes a Generalized Assessment of Impacts of Preliminary Measures and Strategies on Traditional and Customary Practices of Native Hawaiians, which with the exception of Item no. 17: Ha'ikū well development, describes preliminary measures that are generally beneficial to both ecosystems and cultural practices. By focusing on beneficial actions, however, it may not usefully inform practitioners about ways of cooperating with Maui DWS in mitigation of the latter's actions in caring for freshwater resources.

The *Ka Pa'akai* consultation might best be utilized as a process of gaining input into ways of better caretaking for the cultural resources. In developing its *Ka Pa'akai* framework, Maui DWS sent out an evaluation form, which in parts asked practitioners to understand themselves as water consumers, as opposed to stewards of the resources that sustain their cultural practices. For some practitioners, this may be culturally inappropriate or alienating to the ways they perpetuate their practices. For example, practitioners at Ka'ena Point, O'ahu produced a stewardship document titled, "Mālama i ke kai, a mālama ke kai ia 'oe," which expressed their sense of kuleana to the place, including its cultural resources and ecosystems. Cultural practitioners' positions on the ways agency decisions impact freshwater resources are often also informed by this relation of kuleana.

In light of the abundance of its water resources, those such as Kāʻanapali hoteliers and other commercial users, who can and must pay for them, and the innovative framework of the new Maui Use and Development Plan, West Maui may be poised to institute a water resource allocation system that properly protects public trust resources.

CHAPTER 3

DITCH SYSTEM HISTORY

INTRODUCTION

In 1738, the warrior Alapaʻi prepared for war with Maui by drying up the streams of Kauaʻula, Kanahā, and Kahoma so there would be no food for the forces of Ka-uhi or for the country people. Alapaʻiʻs men also kept close watch over the brooks of Olowalu, Ukumehame, Wailuku, and Honokōwai.[1] The monopolization of water resources as a war tactic has a history in West Maui.

From 1861 to 1999, sugar plantation operations drastically changed the shape of West Maui. The consolidation of thousands of acres of West Maui lands for thirsty sugar plantation crops also meant a drastic shift in the ways water reached those lands. The Pioneer Mill Company, West Mauiʻs most influential plantation, would devote over 10,000 acres of land for sugar production by 1935. The attempt to monopolize water resources as a tactic of control was no less deliberate than what Alapaʻi employed.

This chapter recounts the ways settler agribusiness transformed West Maui through diversion of West Mauiʻs streams. The story does not consist only of a description of plantation ditch development. Carol Wilcoxʻs *Sugar Water: Hawaiiʻs Plantation Ditches* (University of Hawaiʻi Press, 1996) devotes a lengthy chapter to the development of West Mauiʻs plantation ditches. Rather, we attend to the interplay of the exploitation of West Mauiʻs water resources for plantation agribusiness, the displacement of traditional Kanaka Maoli agricultural practices, new labor communities, and the environs of West Maui itself.

Frequently accounts of the plantation ditch developments celebrate them as evidence of the "indomitable," intrepid, and entrepreneurial spirit of individual pioneer men. In 1903, the *Maui News* announced two new ditches would be completed in Maui in the next year:

> Maui has been the pioneer in building ditches for irrigating cane fields, bringing the waters from the mountain streams to the fertile valley lands. The big Island Hawaii has to depend on natural rainfall, and Oahu on pumps but Maui alone in less than another year will be able to dispense with the cost of pumping machinery as its natural supply will be developed the fullest limit.
>
> Through the indomitable energy and business foresight of the Hon. H. P. Baldwin three new ditches will be finished on Maui in 1904; namely the Honokōhau ditch from West Maui mountains to supply Pioneer Plantation with water and the big Koolau and Hamakua ditches from Nahiku region to furnish additional water to central Maui.[2]

For the *Maui News,* the identity of each island was coextensive with sugar planters' exploitation of water resources. English-language news sources generally failed to note the concomitant loss of water for kuleana, streams, and the Hawaiian cultural practices and economies that depend on those waters.

Rather than re-narrate the theft of West Maui surface waters as testament to the ingenuity of Henry P. Baldwin and James Campbell, for example, we here seek to examine the systems that enabled a wholesale transformation of West Maui's society, economy, and landscape in the interests of a small minority of newcomers by also taking aim at the ways that these settler colonial exploitations of West Maui waters have been narrated. One particularly troubling example of early planter control over Maui's physical, social, and political landscape exists in the English-language news media opposition to the candidacy of Robert Wilcox for Territorial delegate to the U.S. Congress.

Plantation Labor and Racial Electoral Politics

During the turn of the twentieth century, the *Maui News*, the *Hawaiian Gazette*, and other newspapers were littered with denunciations of Wilcox as a "blatherite" and "anti-haole." The news media was specifically unable to tolerate Wilcox as a Hawaiian political leader, and made special efforts to undermine his support from Hawaiian communities. For instance, one op-ed noted: "Tom Clark accompanied the Board of Registration and Bob Wilcox to Hana for the double purpose of seeing that the Hawaiians register and that Bob don't fool 'em any more."[3] When Wilcox's election seemed assured, the *Maui News* editors proposed importing "colored laborers" from the U.S. South who would be forced to vote Republican.

> Bob Wilcox's plurality over Samuel Parker on Maui is 180. The plantations on Maui need at least 300 colored laborers from the southern States, who would undoubtedly vote the republican ticket. On Hawaii, Wilcox's majority was 230. Hawaii needs at least five hundred colored men for her cane fields, all of whom would vote the republican ticket. The latest returns from Kauai give Wilcox 160 plurality. At least 300 colored laborers from the cane fields of the South are needed on Kauai, all of whom will vote republican. *Quod erat demonstrandum.*[4]

Hawaii's Asian settler plantation laborers were not afforded suffrage until later in the twentieth century. Even when they obtained the vote, the plantation was notorious as a place in which sociopolitical liberties were tightly curtailed by supervisors and plantation managers. The "colored" laborers would undoubtedly vote Republican because they would be coerced into doing so. These political machinations contextualize a curious article, also published by the *Maui News*, that asserted the "intelligence" of Hawaiians in Lahaina lay with their will to conform to plantation regimes.

> It is a serious mistake to think that the native Hawaiians of Maui, the class generally indicated by the term "ignorant Hawaiians," will not think and act for themselves at the approaching election. Were there a rational hope for the restoration of the queen, there is no doubt that the majority of them would work and vote to that end. But the Hawaiians of Maui have abandoned all such hope, and are new thinking their way into one or other of the two leading political parties. This was well illustrated at one of Bob Wilcox's meetings in Lahaina, the other day. Bob was waxing eloquent at the loss of the taro patches, and suggested that the time would come when the cane have to go, and taro would take its place as of old. No sooner did his native audience grasp his meaning than they revolted at his proposed step backward toward their former condition, and they absolutely hooted him off the rostrum.[5]

In 1900, the Kūʻē petitions protesting U.S. annexation had only been signed and delivered a few years prior. The *Kumuliilii* case had been decided in 1895. These and other factors render the *Maui News'* opinion that "Hawaiians of Lahaina" would revolt against kalo farming highly questionable.

In the following discussion of historical water diversions in West Maui, we look at the ways this dynamic of inequality persisted from the tenure of Pioneer Mill and into the operations of West Maui Land Company (amongst other large landowners) through today. Our story of West Maui's ditch systems includes late twentieth-century community struggles to reclaim water from plantation-era diversions. We pay particular attention to the renewed efforts of Honokōhau kalo farmers, who catalyzed movement amongst government agencies and larger water diverters towards gaining a better understanding of West Maui surface water use.

PLANTATION MONOPOLIES OF WATER RESOURCES

Today, West Maui has eleven perennial streams and three that flow continuously. On average and between the years 1913 to 2005, these streams brought about 35 million gallons per day (mgd) through lower-lying areas. West Maui's thirsty plantations diverted millions of gallons of surface water from prior uses that sustained a markedly different community than that which previously existed. The "ingenuity of engineering and cultivation" of West Maui's native Hawaiian communities was documented as early as 1793 by foreigners traveling with Captain George Vancouver. They observed:

> Even the shelving cliffs of rocks were planted with esculent roots, banked in and watered by aqueducts from the rivulet with as much art as if their level had been taken by the most ingenious engineer. We could not indeed but admire the laudable ingenuity of these people in cultivating their soil with so much economy. The indefatigable labor in making these little fields in so rugged a situation, the care and industry with which they were transplanted, watered and kept in order, surpassed anything of the kind we had ever seen before.[6]

West Maui's water resources were increasingly exploited in the later 1800s as Pioneer Mill sought to capture and divert more water for its plantation uses. The traditional prescribed system of water use, touched on in chapter 1, allowed vast tracts of land to be cultivated with kalo, 'uala, 'ulu, niu, and other native plants.[7] Several important 'auwai were also constructed in Lahaina as part of its complex water management system. In the fourteenth century, an 'auwai called 'Auwaiawao was constructed and named for the sister of an earlier Maui ruler, Kaululā'au.[8] The sister was named Wao, who owned lands adjoining a water head in Lahainaluna and who had the 'auwai constructed. The 'Auwai o Pi'ilani is attributed to the reign of Pi'ilani and is believed to have been constructed during that time.[9] Pi'ilani referred to the 'auwai in texts and maps made during the Māhele.

The history of irrigation ditches in West Maui are more closely tracked to the development of sugar agribusiness and colonialism. In 1861, the Lahaina Sugar Company was founded by H. Dickenson.[10] A year later, James Campbell and Henry Turton established the Pioneer sugar mill. It was not, however, until August 1, 1865 that Campbell and Turton purchased their first parcel of land from Makekau, a native Hawaiian resident of Lahaina.[11] "Makekau" names a genealogy of Native Hawaiian lineal descendants of Lahaina: Abel Keli'ionuuanu Makekau and his wife, Mele Kahiwa Swinton (Mele Kahiwa or Mary Swinton).[12] Mele Kahiwa's mother was Kaumeaha'ulewaliekahakawai of Lahaina and Kona.[13] Kaumeaha'ulewaliekahakawai married an Englishman, Harry Swinton, and gave birth to Mele Kahiwa on June 24, 1823 in Kalae, Moloka'i. Today, the Makekau estate borders the site of the historic Pioneer Mill smoke stack in Lahaina.[14] The Makekau 'ohana house was "the tallest, biggest building—you could see it for miles around, once the sugar cane fields were cut or burned and the view up mauka was unimpeded."[15] In a few generations, Abel Wahawela Makekau would become an infamous fixture of Lahaina's tourist-focused town.[16]

Plantation and Water System Development in West Maui

The plantation era in West Maui spanned the life of Lahaina Sugar and then Pioneer Mill (1862–1999). Pioneer Mill's upper fields were each irrigated by six ditch systems within each watershed.[17] These upper field irrigation systems were named Kahoma, Kanahā, Kaua'ula, Launiupoko, Olowalu, and Ukumehame, corresponding to the streams they diverted. The Kaua'ula ditch powered a hydroelectric plant (as it still does); Olowalu ditch supplied domestic water to Olowalu village; and the Kanahā ditch supplied the Lahainaluna Ditch, Maui County, and the Pioneer Mill factory.[18] M. O'Shaughnessy, who engineered plantation ditches across Hawai'i, explained that Pioneer Mill developed its irrigation by pumping ground or artesian wells near the coast and through gravity tunnels and diversions.[19]

Like many other large agribusinesses in Hawai'i, Maui Land & Pineapple (MLP) is a legacy of the tight and overlapping relationships among white settler landowning businessmen. Dwight Baldwin, who settled in Hawai'i in 1836, is the founder of MLP. By 1853, Baldwin had acquired 2,675 acres of Mahinahina and Kahana ahupua'a for farming and pasture. By 1902, Baldwin merged with other lands to create Honolua Ranch, which held 24,000 acres.

Dwight Baldwin's son, Henry Perrine Baldwin (August 29, 1842–July 8, 1911), the catalyst for half of the Alexander and Baldwin plantation legacy, worked with David Thomas Fleming, a horticulturist, to develop coffee, aloe, and mango crops in West Maui. D. T. Fleming was also responsible for planting pine trees along Kapalua roads. Later, in 1912, Harry Baldwin, Henry Baldwin's son, planted the first twenty acres of pineapple fields in the area. By 1932, MLP was headed by Harry Baldwin's son-in law, J. Walter Cameron. Cameron's son, Colin Cameron, later developed Kapalua Resort.

By 1850, it was claimed to be well known that Lahaina had the finest sugar in Hawai'i.[20] By 1861 the Lahaina Sugar Company was established, and a year later, Pioneer Sugar Mill.[21] In 1883, the McCandless brothers drilled the first well on Maui for Pioneer Mill Company. Pioneer Mill's fields extended 14 miles long and 1½ miles wide at altitudes between 10 and 700 feet, drawing all of the water resources it needed for irrigation and to support its workforce from artesian wells and the West Maui Mountains.[22] In 1901, Pioneer Mill constructed eight reservoirs to store waters drawn from the artesian wells: three at Lahaina, four at Kā'anapali, and one at Wahikuli.[23] The reservoirs, connected by 25 miles of ditches, meant that Pioneer Mill no longer needed to irrigate fields at night and further provided water for another 600 acres of land.[24]

Water was long recognized as a decisive factor in the economic value of the plantations. In 1877, Pioneer Mill was considered overvalued at $1 million, but by 1899, it was valued at $7 million.[25] "The advance is due mainly to the recent discovery that unlimited water supply for pumping could be obtained from surface wells near the shore. By this means cane is now being grown along a belt of ten miles in length, extending each side of Lahaina, giving a present crop of 12,000 tons and a prospective one of 20,000."[26] Pioneer Mill's water infrastructure in Lahaina areas appropriated the structure and technologies of earlier water resource development.

In 1883, Pioneer Mill constructed its Lahaina Pump Ditch 1.[27] However, the ditch's construction owed to earlier development by Lahainaluna Seminary, who was credited with creating the Lahainaluna Ditch in 1842–1846. In 1842, the Sandwich Island Mission Station held a general meeting at which they decided to develop the Lahainaluna Ditch to draw water from Kaua'ula Stream and bring it to Lahainaluna.[28] "While general records of the missionaries and teachers indicate that the ditch was then a "new" undertaking, native accounts as those cited above provide us with a traditional name, 'Auwai o 'Awaiawao, and implications that portions of the 'auwai date back to the 1300s."[29] Pioneer Mill later modified the alignment of the Lahainaluna Ditch, resulting in Lahaina

Pump Ditch 1. Just below the ditch was Pioneer Mill's Pump B reservoir, which stored water pumped by Pump B from a water tunnel.[30]

Pioneer Mill's Lahaina Pump camp (aka Waineʻe Camp) was named for the pumps the plantation used to pump water to its lands above Lahaina-luna. When its diversions ran dry, Pioneer Mill would use its Lahaina pump machinery to pump groundwater.[31] "So they used to have pumps all over the place. Just for backup."[32] The pump house, powerhouse, and the ditch are in Kauaʻula Valley. Lahaina Pump had regular worker housing, but: "In the beginning, when you went into the camp, there was a huge house, the entrance was just like the camp boss. And my [former Pioneer Mill employee Anthony Vierra's] uncle Joe was living in that house. So just like he was the—if any problem arises in the camp like that, they run to him, and he in turn gets in touch with everybody else."[33] The importance of Joe Vierra's work in facilitating water flow to the fields was reflected in his receipt of housing on par with other bosses' homes.

When it was first constructed at the end of the nineteenth century, Lahaina Pump Ditch 1 was unlined. By 1920–1921, Pioneer Mill had been facing water shortages and therefore decided to add a four-inch-thick concrete liner to reduce water loss.[34] In 1922, Lahaina faced a drought. Pioneer Mill then-president Allen W. T. Bottomley wrote in the company's annual stockholder report:

> The crop varies in almost exact proportion as the water per acre increases or decreases; and likewise, that the water per acre increases or decreases according to rainfall. Considerable criticism has come from time to time because of the short crops and poor showing made by your Company, and the reason for these short crops is a lack of water.[35]

By 1935, over $3,000,000 had been spent on water development, including gravity systems and underground supplies. Pioneer Mill was also increasingly mechanizing its sugar production. In 1948, Pioneer Mill initiated a three-year rock removal program to rehabilitate 3,153 acres of land for mechanized planting, cultivating, and harvesting. In 1953, the company was using new feeder tables that were conveying cane directly from cane trucks into the factory.[36] While these innovations maintained sugarcane as a profitable enterprise, they did nothing to augment the water demand of sugar cane.

By 1970, Pioneer Mill was classified as a "distressed plantation" by sugar industry analysis.[37] By 1980, Amfac management was running Pioneer Mill at a loss, subsidized by the Kāʻanapali resorts.[38]

PLANTATION-ERA DIVERSIONS

Today, West Maui's dominant irrigation system is the Maui Land and Pineapple Company/Pioneer Mill Irrigation System (MLP/PMIS), which comprises a conglomeration of three older ditches used by the plantation: the Honolua-Honokōhau Ditch, the Lahainaluna Ditch, and the Wahikuli Ditch.[39] Honolua Ranch and Pioneer Mill Co. historically operated ditches with the following average flow and capacity flow:

Ditch name	Average/capacity flow (mgd)[40]
Honolua-Honokōhau Ditch (1904)	20 mgd/35 mgd
" … " (rebuilt 1913)	18–30 mgd/50–70 mgd
Honokōwai Ditch (1918)	6 mgd/50 mgd
Kahoma Ditch (1911–1917)	3.04 mgd (upper)
Kahoma Ditch (1988–1999)	7.9 mgd (upper)
Kanahā Ditch (1916–1932)	4.98 mgd (upper)
Kanahā Ditch (1911–1916)	3.68 mgd (lower)
Kanahā Ditch (1988–1999)	1.55 mgd (overall)
Kauaʻula Ditch (1912–1917)	6.08 mgd/25.5 mgd
Launiupoko Ditch (1996)	0.76 mgd
Olowalu Ditch (1911–1967)	4.85 mgd (upper)/11 mgd
Olowalu Ditch (1988–1999)	3.55 mgd (upper)
Ukumehame Ditch (1988–1999)	3.88 mgd/15.5 mgd

In the late 1800s, Pioneer Mill initiated the first plantation-level diversion in West Maui. By 1931, Pioneer Mill used approximately 50 to 60 million gallons per day of surface water through eight separate diversion systems. The Honolua-Honokōhau Ditch, maintained by MLP, diverted water from Honokōhau, Kaluanui, and Honolua streams to the northwest; Honokowai, Amalu, Kapaloa, and Kahoma streams from the west; and other sources to irrigate cane fields on the northwestern slopes of West Maui between Lahaina and Kapalua. The Honolua-Honokōhau Ditch diversions of water from Honokowai, Amalu, Kapāloa, and Kahoma Streams on the western slopes of the West Maui Mountains have been abandoned.

Pioneer Mill operated a second diversion system through the Honokōwai ditch, which drained the Amalu and Kapāloa streams.[41] These diversions took between 5.494 mgd and 5.688 mgd between 1912 and 1989.[42] The remaining six smaller diversion systems are Kahoma, Kanahā, Kauaʻula, Launiupoko, Olowalu, and Ukumehame.

The Lahainaluna Ditch conveyed water from Wahikuli Reservoir to sugarcane fields south of Lahaina. It extended 4.4 miles to Launiupoko on the southwestern slopes of the West Maui Mountains. Surface water from sources south of Lahaina, including Kanahā, Kauaula, Launiupoko, Olowalu, and Ukumehame streams, were diverted into the Lahainaluna Ditch, as well as waters from part of the Honolua-Honokōhau Ditch. "The Honolua-Honokōhau and Lahainaluna Ditches were complex irrigation systems comprised of stream intakes, transmission and development tunnels, ditches, flumes, inverted siphons across gulches, hydropower plants, and large-capacity sources of ground water from coastal infiltration galleries, called Maui-type shafts."[43] The Wahikuli Ditch also conveyed water from the Wahikuli Reservoir, but served cane fields at a lower elevation along a 2.6-mile stretch towards the north, where it ended at the Puʻukoliʻi Reservoir. Former Pioneer Mill worker Frederick Higuchi commented, "We had a good water system up there, so we had real good [water]—as far as Lahaina is concerned, I think Puʻukoliʻi had the best water cause direct from the mountain."[44] Mountain water would refresh the reservoir, water from which was then piped to the camp house.

Beginning of the PMIS

Initiated in 1878 by H. P. Baldwin and S. T. Alexander, the Honokōhau ditch, with a 30 mgd capacity, was completed in 1904.[45] At completion, it was 13.5 miles long and cost $185,000. At the time, the Honokōhau ditch was hailed as smartly preserving the use of otherwise "waste" streams by diverting them towards plantation uses. As reported by the *The Pacific Commercial Advertiser*, "The Honokōhau ditch is another enterprise brought to completion during the year, whereby waste streams of Honokōhau valley are brought out on to the Kaanapali lands, and in to Lahaina for extending cane fields of the Pioneer plantation."[46] English-language media focused on the intrepid settler men who initiated the diversion project. "Through the indomitable energy and business foresight of the Hon. H. P. Baldwin, three new ditches will be finished on Maui in 1904; namely the Honokohau ditch from West Maui mountain to supply Pioneer Plantation with water and the big Koolau and Hamakua ditches from the Nāhiku region to furnish additional water to central Maui."[47] Portions of the ditch required importing lumber. On Saturday, December 13, 1903, the *S.S. Hawaii Bennett* touched at Kahului harbor with 35,000 feet of flume lumber for Pioneer Mill's Honokōwai Ditch.[48]

A year later, in 1904, the Honokōhau Ditch was completed to great appro-
bation for its engineers, managers, and investors. "The conception of this work
is due to the enterprise of Mr. H. P. Baldwin, foremost of ditch builders, and
its successful completion to the energy and resourcefulness of Mr. L. Barkhau-
sen, manager of the Pioneer Mill Co."[49] Others recognized for their part in the
Honokohau Ditch were J. S. Molony, J. Dow, H. Doden, J. Andrade, H. Hal-
vorsen, and H. Reinicke, who were the engineers and project managers. *The
Hawaiian Gazette* mentioned, "There were three deaths and some minor acci-
dents due to unavoidable causes." The people injured and killed in the effort
remained unnamed.

The *Pacific Commercial Advertiser* crowed "Big Ditch Completed" (1904).
The ditch was "the private property of Hon. H. P. Baldwin," leased by Baldwin
to the Lahaina plantation.[50] Water infrastructure development blurred the lines
between public good and private investments, with reports concluding, "The
Lahaina people are fortunate in obtaining such an abundant supply of fresh
water. It will prove a good investment."

Not all held the view that Pioneer Mill's water infrastructure development was a public good. By 1904, the relationship between Pioneer Mill and
Lahainaluna School, for example, had grown tense over their competing use
of water resources. At that time, John Richardson, an attorney employed by
Pioneer Mill, was reportedly "fight[ing] the government in its endeavor to give
the Lahainaluna school a share of the water of Kauaʻula, and that means that
Richardson is working against the interest of the people and therefore not in
favor of helping Lahainaluna, the institution where the poor Hawaiians can
expect their children to receive an education."[51]

At the time of its construction, the Honokōhau ditch carried an estimated
daily average flow of about ten million gallons and cost approximately $150,000
to construct.[52] A few years later, in 1909, the *Evening Bulletin* reported that the
Honokōhau ditch had a yield of 30 mgd.[53] In 1911, Pioneer Mill sought to increase
the elevation of the ditch across 150 acres and at a cost of $16,000.[54] Three years
later in 1915, Manager D. T. Fleming stated that a blast of dynamite let off in
the tunnel construction would increase the amount of water yielded from the
Honokōhau ditch by three mgd. This water would go to Pioneer Mill.[55]

Ecological Impacts of Plantation Operations

The plantations not only monopolized water resources, but often used them in
ways that were ecologically unsound. Another side of water resource exploitation is wastewater disposition.

Kazukiyo "Jiggs" Kuboyama, a former resident of Pioneer Mill's Kelawea Camp, offered a view on the ways Pioneer Mill used water for domestic and agricultural purposes. Prior to the 1946 great sugar strike, raw sewage from the plantation toilets emptied into irrigation ditches, so all the waste was then used as fertilizer on the field.[56] It was not until after the 1946 territory-wide sugar strike that Pioneer Mill installed something "close to the regular plumbing set up." Yet, Kuboyama was careful to note that it was not necessarily labor's demands that led to the changes. Rather, each home began to have their own shower or bath after Pioneer Mill started to sell the homes.

The plantation's irrigation ditches provided a place for the resident children to swim.[57] Also, they would ride the sugarcane flume above Lahainaluna. "From the irrigation they let the water out into this flume, and then you wen ride down. So when they throw the cane into the flume, we used to get to a certain area and then when the cane came down, we used to jump on the bunch of cane and ride that cane all the way down. And some people were too slow getting off, so they have to put the gate down to stop, because if not, it's going right into the cart where they load the cane."[58]

Some of Pioneer Mill's ditches, however, were thick with algae, which slowed the flow of the water.[59] According to former Pioneer Mill worker Minoru Hinahara, the plantation imported tilapia to eat the algae.[60]

Transitions to Tourism Development

In the 1960s, Pioneer Mill took 2,000 acres of cane production land to develop Kā'anapali lands into a tourist resort destination. By 1986, it had reduced its active agricultural acreage to 4,000 acres, down from the 14,000 acres it had cultivated at the height of its sugar operations. The economic development and transition from an agricultural to a resort development focus also intensified uses of land, and brought in more visitors and non-agricultural workers. A new social component of West Maui included different citizen and resident groups who mobilized around quality-of-life issues differently than plantation workers. Whereas company workers organized through unions and against Pioneer Mill, new residents took to public processes.

By the 1970s, more citizen groups were criticizing Pioneer Mill operations. In September 1971, a group of Maui environmentalists were reportedly opposing Pioneer Mill's request for designation of ocean discharge areas for power plant wastewater, and in case of floods, the company also asked permission to release the heated water from Kahoma Stream, Kaua'ula Stream, and the Launiupoko outfall.[61] John Siemer, Pioneer Mill's manager at the time, said he did not believe discharge from any of the seven areas would cause ecological harm—but the company's environmental record did not support his belief.

As was also documented in 1971, the Maui chapter of the community action group Life of the Land called out Pioneer Mill for its practice of dumping wastewater into the ocean at Launiupoko, and of holding wastewater in settling ponds, which create strong unpleasant odors.[62]

> If you've driven from Lahaina to Wailuku lately, you've probably noticed the rotten-egg stench encountered some three miles outside of town at Launiupoko Point. This odorific assault is produced by the six million gallons of brackish water released daily into the ocean by Pioneer Mill. According to Mike Nelson, Pioneer Mill factory superintendent, the plant uses some 11 million gallons of water each day for washing sugar cane delivered from the fields, and for cooling purposes. Nelson said this water, which contains decomposing sugar residue and a variety of complex compounds, first passes through one of the two primary settling ponds situated near the plant. It is then pumped through a ditch, which tapers from Pioneer Mill toward the ocean at Launiupoko. Just before being released, the water collects in a secondary settling basin above the road—which accounts for the smell. With most of the direct solids removed, six million gallons of the black water flows out to sea. The other five million gallons are diluted with fresh water and used for irrigation. Nelson said all of the water could not be used for irrigation because of the high salt content.[63]

Former Pioneer Mill vice president and "irrigation man" Keoki Freeland recalled that the plantation's transition to drip irrigation also remedied some wastewater issues.[64] Much of the water in the Launiupoko settling pond and the other wastewater dumped into the ocean was runoff and "mill water." Pioneer Mill had to discharge the mill water and could not get rid of it in the fields along the way, so only so much of it ran into the ocean.

These transitions in plantation water and wastewater management interplayed with the development of modern centralized wastewater treatment. The Lahaina wastewater treatment plant resulted from a petition favoring its construction in advance of the county's plans to construct the Kīhei wastewater plant in March 1971.[65] Allan Parks of Maui Community College in Kahului was listed on the petition, which noted the resident population in the Kīhei-Māʻalaea-Mākena area was 1,636, and Lahaina was nearly double that at 3,718 persons. At the time, Lahaina sewage was dumped directly into the ocean through a pipeline that extended some 1,500 feet into the ocean near the Māla Wharf. Approximately 1.5 million gallons of raw sewage was pumped through the pipeline each day.[66]

Amfac was operating the first and only sewage treatment facility in Maui County in Kāʻanapali, but it was mostly used to serve its developing resort area. At the time, Amfac was also planning a larger tourist-residential development at Honolua, several miles north of Kāʻanapali.[67] Amfac used some effluent from its wastewater treatment plant for golf course irrigation, with the rest pumped into a well. Pioneer Mill hedged against accepting effluent for sugarcane irrigation as the undiluted effluent contained a lot of nutrients that might stifle the growth of cane.[68] A second method of disposal, which was implemented to much controversy, was pumping the effluent into deep wells that would take it below the island's freshwater table and into the saltwater below.[69]

Today, the Maui Department of Water Supply operates both the Lahaina and Mahinahina surface water treatment plants, which together supply approximately 60 percent of the demand in the West Maui system. Groundwater is also pumped from eight major wells within the Honokōwai aquifer.

In the early 1970s, Pioneer Mill, along with MLP, the Wailuku Sugar Co., and the State Dept. of Transportation, held state Department of Health water discharge permits that allowed release of wastewater into the ocean.[70] One condition of Pioneer Mill's state permit was a requirement for construction of a wastewater recycling system by December 31, 1974. For many years, the West Maui Preservation Association (WMPA), along with the Earthjustice Mid-Pacific office, have sought to curb discharges of various entities into injection wells along Lahaina's coast.

As described in Ikaika Hussey's "The Modern History of Wastewater Management in West Maui" in *Social Change in West Maui*, WMPA was initially formed in response to the expansion of the Westin Kaanapali Ocean Resort Villas, a Starwood timeshare property. WMPA raised concerns about near-shore water contamination, traffic, and drainage, and succeeded in obtaining protections including nearshore water quality testing and a dunes preservation program.[71]

DITCHES V. WEST MAUI STREAMS

West Maui's plantation "ditch" system and current diversions support a vastly different range of uses and communities than those it displaced. Settler plantation water infrastructures were preceded by a complex of ʻauwai developed by

Hawaiian tenants and konohiki. The latter modified and extended the streams flowing from Kahoma, Kanahā and Kauaʻula to water extensive agricultural developments on the kula flat lands and the kula kahakai lying below. Foreign visitors reportedly first arrived in Lahaina in 1793.[72] These visitors described extensive cultivation and waterways engineered to transport water across otherwise dry lands, which instead became fertile fields.[73] Through the early 1800s, the kula kahakai nearshore lands of Lahaina were densely populated, containing fishponds, taro pond fields, and stands of trees that provided resources for Hawaiians' daily lives. Above those lands, the kula lands were planted in kalo and other foods through dry and wetland methods, as well as loko iʻa kalo (fish and kalo ponds). These were watered through the ʻauwai channels and fed thousands. In 1846, it was reported, "Irrigation clothes the most barren spots with rich vegetation in a very short time, and the trees have grown more in two years than in ten at Honolulu."[74]

Beginning in 1823, missionaries began arriving to Lahaina. Missionary letters and journals from the early 1800s described their particular interest in the irrigated fields spread across Lahaina, and the prescribed system of water usage enforced: the planters, on every fifth day, had a right to the water necessary to care for the taro pond fields.[75] While settlers thus drew an erroneous conclusion in viewing the "image of desolation" that was Lahaina in 1819 and blaming the situation on native indolence, "and failing to realize that the bounds of cultivation on this side of Maui were strictly drawn by limitation of water for irrigation."[76]

As Robbie Dukelow recounted, "A kupuna once told me, from mountain to ocean, you could not see any trees, just taro patches." As early as 1901, Lahaina was importing kalo from other islands, which was a sure sign of the decline of loʻi agriculture. In 1901, a "D. Kapawai" wrote to the Board of Health:

> We are keeping our taro for the Leper Settlement and if the Board will not take our bid we will send our taro to the other market and no taro will be sent to the settlement without those prices. There are plenty of Chinamen offering a price of $3.50 for 125 pounds of taro: a good price between the poi seller and the planter; but according to our bid, we keep our taro low. Now I want to beg of your kindness to let me know about that bid. If we lose that we will send our taro to Lahaina. Please remember in your mind all planters who are living in this valley, Wailau, and Pelekuna, are men and not boys or fools. I want to do this in a gentle manner. Very respectfully, D. KAPAWAI.[77]

By 1987, however, there were only six families remaining to raise taro in Kahakuloa.[78]

Pioneer Mill's diversions looked much different to its managers. Keoki Freeland was born and raised in Lahaina in 1939 and attended Lahainaluna School.[79] He went to Notre Dame for college, receiving a degree in mechanical engineering and industrial options. He returned and worked for the sugar industry on O'ahu until 1985, when he returned to Lahaina to become the vice president and general manager for Pioneer Mill until 1995.

Freeland had 34 years of experience in the sugar industry and worked in every department: cultivation, irrigation, and factory as well as managerial positions.[80] His original position, however, was "irrigation man." This meant he ensured that water was making it through the complex flumes, pipes, and gates that comprised the ditch system to reach the end of the flow. Irrigation occurred only during daylight hours, which required large reservoirs to ensure that sufficient water got to the fields. Later in the 1960s, plantations converted to drip irrigation, which suffused water needs over a 24-hour period. Manpower went way down—less than 10 percent of irrigation men used previously were needed. In the early days of the plantation, everything was done by hand. Pioneer Mill originally had about 1,600 employees, but near the end, due to mechanization, the same amount of land could be cultivated by just 110 people.[81]

Water was taken from the ditch on an "as needed" basis. Ditches on flat grades tended to be concrete, rectangular, and open. But to flow water down ditches into the field, Pioneer Mill could not use open flumes—too much water would splash out. So instead, they used pipes.[82] If streams ran dry, water was moved from other streams. Originally, the Honokōhau Ditch used to distribute water to a large reservoir in Launiupoko. Kaua'ula stream water was used, but it was not enough. "Pioneer Mill moved water all over the place because it owned all the land."[83] Upper fields were irrigated with valley stream water while lower fields were irrigated with saltier, pumped well water.

Freeland's reference to Pioneer Mill's automation intersects with its history of labor relations. In the 1940s, Pioneer Mill required workers to ensure its fields were watered. Pioneer Mill's dependency on water resources was also an Achilles' heel that striking workers exploited during the territory-wide 1946 Sugar Strike. Forty-four days after other plantations across the territory settled with the International Longshore and Warehousemen's Union (ILWU), Pioneer Mill persisted. "Mac" Masato Yamauchi, the local unit's strike strategy committee chairman, ordered strikers to stop any attempt by Pioneer Mill management to irrigate the fields.[84]

On November 6, 1946, union members attacked Pioneer Mill's Harlow Wright, the industrial relations manager; Mike Nelson, the chief mill engineer; and James Backlund, the steam plant engineer. Striking workers, including Ichio "Hawaiian" Hirata and Hiromi "Impoc" Mishima[85] beat Wright and knocked Nelson and Backlund into irrigation ditches. "He water; he get hurt," reported one man. Nelson and Backlund were irrigating the fields. The matter was later settled by the courts, with Yamauchi receiving a $600 fine. Fines levied against the other defendants ranged from $25 to $200. The Pioneer Mill strike ended on January 2, 1947.[86]

Freeland's perspective on West Maui's water resource allocations was oriented by the practical issue of delivering water over a smooth space of disseminated consumers and users. He raised the issue of the future of West Maui's plantation ditches. Once a ditch had failed, would it be permitted to be put back? And if ditches were not maintained, who would have the money to fix them? For Freeland, "Bottom line, whoever wants the water, someone has to agree to who is going to take care of the ditch. No one will get water."[87] This practical concern continues to orient the state in its decisions (or lack thereof) on the fate of the Pioneer Mill Irrigation System.

Kaua'ula and Launiupoko

Two 'auwai were notable early in the Kaua'ula and Kahoma ahupua'a. The earlier built, 'Auwaiawao, was reportedly named for the Chiefess Wao, sister of Kaululā'au, who ruled a portion of Maui in 1390.[88] The other, 'Auwai o Pi'ilani, continues to take water from the Kaua'ula stream. The 'Auwai o Pi'ilani, or Pi'ilani 'Auwai, was named for King Pi'ilani, who ruled Maui and neighboring islands in 1450. In the early nineteenth century, the Pi'ilani 'Auwai irrigated lands along both sides of the stream with waterways extending to at least the 'ili of Pi'ilani in the ahupua'a of Paunau, below Lahainaluna.[89]

Between 1842 and 1847, the Pi'ilani 'auwai system was modified into the Lahainaluna Ditch to serve Lahainaluna School.[90] Also during this time, Lahaina molasses gained notoriety for being "the finest available in the islands."[91] Plantation sugar crops proliferated above Lahaina. By the 1860s, longtime West Maui natives reported that in areas where water once flowed, none could then be found.[92]

Through the 1930s, a few Hawaiian families continued to cultivate lo'i in Kaua'ula gulch, above Waine'e.[93] In his 1940 publication *The Hawaiian Planter*, E. S. Craighill Handy observed that Hawaiian families cultivated lo'i through Kaua'ula Gulch above Waine'e.[94] Many of those same families continue and renew loʻi cultivation today. By contrast, in Launiupoko, Maly and Maly reported that although there was a sizeable streambed and deep valley, there was no visible evidence of wet taro cultivation, "and the Hawaiian planters at Olowalu say that *loʻi* never existed in Launiupoko. It is possible that there may have been few terraces on the level land at the base of the valley, but this is wholly arid land now and covered with dense brush."[95] Maly and Maly found references to 1,765 loʻi at one time in the Kauaʻula and Launiupoko area.[96]

Lahainaluna School lands were once owned by Hawaiians who farmed kalo by Kanahā stream towards Kelawea and towards Kauaʻula. In 1835, these farmers protested when the missionaries from the school appealed to the kings and chiefs to give them these lands.[97] Ulu-maheihei acceded to the missionaries' request. When confronted by chiefs whose lands he had given away, Ulu-maheihei answered, "It is a fine thing; do not get excited about the land. Give your land to those who are seeking knowledge. This is the thing which will establish the government of your chiefs.... Knowledge is fundamental to living as a chief."[98] In 1842, construction of the Lahainaluna Ditch was undertaken to draw water from the Kauaʻula stream. It later became part of Pioneer Mill operations.[99] Although it was newly named Lahainaluna Ditch in the general records of the missionaries and teachers indicating the ditch was then a "new" undertaking, native accounts established its traditional name, *ʻAuwaio.*[100]

Ukumehame

Craighill & Elizabeth Handy, known for their *The Hawaiian Planter* (1940) publication, noted abandoned loʻi terraces covering the flatland below the entrance to Ukumehame Canyon and above reservoirs owned by Pioneer Mill. Loʻi on the upper terraces above the reservoirs had long been abandoned, while the ones closer to it were only "half used—that half unsuccessfully, because of insufficient water for flooding."[101] Handy further observed, "The terraces used to extend well down over the land below the valley, but, with the exception of one tiny taro plantation standing like an island in the midst of the cane, all vestiges of the ancient cultivation have been plowed under. This is excellent wet taro soil." The Handys noted some kalo terraces in Ukumehame in 1934, but by the time they were writing *The Hawaiian Planter* they wrote, "All this area, like that around and above Lahaina, is now sugar-cane land."[102]

Ukumehame was also the site of significant labor rebellion. The 1946 sugar strike lasted for about three months, from September to November, for plantations on the other islands. Pioneer Mill, however, refused to settle until later, in December 1946. Fed up with the plantation's obstinacy, Lahaina's Susumu

"Peanut" Sodetani and other striking Pioneer Mill workers went to the Ukume-hame lower makai reservoir, which was full with water. Sodetani and another worker released all of the water from the reservoir, flooding the fields below. Sodetani commented, "They don't want to settle and then we can't go back to work. And then, hell, if we can't go back to work, well, the hell with these guys, goddamn, we'll make trouble for them, too."[103] "And I don't know how the news got out so fast, we got caught and then they took us down to Wailuku jail house, courthouse, and I was the first one they questioned. So I said, no I don't know anything about it."[104] The detective did not believe him, and Sodetani was jailed in Wailuku until four or five in the afternoon.

Olowalu

The recent history of Olowalu's water resources tracks extreme weather, and especially flooding. In early March 1902, a large storm lasted several days, beginning with strong winds and then heavy rains.[105] Lahaina's Main Street was overflowed, with water so deep in places that people feared to leave their homes.[106] The bridge near Olowalu stream was carried away. Afterwards, the Olowalu stream was nearly impassable due to boulders that had accrued in the streambed.[107]

In May 1916, the West Maui mountains received copious rains. *The Maui News* reported:

> …On west Maui, while the precipitation on the lower levels has been light, and have not interfered in any way with harvesting or other field work, the mountains have been almost constantly saturated by heavy downpours, with the result that the Pioneer and Olowalu companies have had a great abundance of irrigation water, and have not been obliged to pump any for some time. Unless some unforeseen disaster occurs this seems destined to be Maui's record year in the sugar industry.[108]

The same beneficial rains, however, also washed out a pier in the bridge crossing Olowalu stream. A locomotive and three cane cars crashed through the bridge, badly hurting two employees of the Olowalu Sugar Company, while a number or others doubtless "had the narrowest escape or their lives." Antone F. Santos, a luna on the plantation, was riding in the engine cab and sustained severe cuts on the head and body. Evaristo Ramos, a laborer, sustained severe internal injuries.[109] In 1916, J. C. Foss, Jr. won the county contract to construct a new concrete bridge over the Olowalu stream for $3,892.[110]

By 1940, Olowalu, the largest and deepest valley on the southwest side of

Maui, no longer supported extensive kalo cultivation.[111] Pioneer Mill's cane fields had "completely obliterated" the lower ranges of loʻi terraces near cane fields. But "just where the sugar cane ends and the valley begins there is a little spot where five Hawaiian families, all of them intermarried, raise several varieties of taro in flourishing wet patches. Some of it is sold, but most is pounded by hand for family poi. There are said to be abandoned terraces far up in Olowalu."[112]

Despite the attrition of a traditional native Hawaiian planter community, the Olowalu residents remained organized. In April 1971, there was a proposal for an apartment house development in an agricultural district before the Maui Planning Commission.[113] George Kaaea of Olowalu used the opportunity to also testify to the commission about the impact of Pioneer Mill operations. Kaaea told the commissioners that homes have been flooded by runoff from nearby sugarcane fields and recommended construction of a flood diversion ditch.[114]

Honokōwai, Kahoma, Kanahā, and Honolua

D. T. Fleming wrote: "In all three valleys which you mention—Honokowai, Honokohua, and Honolua, as well as Kanaha, there was considerable taro raised in olden times; as a matter of fact, a great deal was raised in Honokowai, where there must have been 30 or 40 acres under cultivation at one time."[115] In 1912, H. Olstad, formerly assistant manager of the Nahiku Rubber Company, began surveying the Honokōhau Ditch for the Honolua Ranch.[116] Later, on August 1, 1920, the H. P. Baldwin estate would lease the Honolua Ditch and water rights for $80,000 to Pioneer Mill Co.[117]

Honokōhau

Honokōhau Valley holds a perennial stream whose perpetual waters conditioned the ability of thousands of loʻi kalo to flourish along its banks. Fleming reported that in 1931, a larger proportion of the patches were under taro cultivation in Honokōhau than anywhere else on Maui with the exception of Kahakuloa.[118] Fleming reports a Hawaiian *kamaʻāina,* David Kapaku, who continued to cultivate his own wet taro in 1934. Others operate commercial farms, with planting accomplished by employed laborers and the continued utilization of so many old terraces."

Until the early 20th century, Honokōhau Valley had thousands of loʻi kalo supporting a vibrant farming community. This was the most extensive system of loʻi along West Maui's coast.[119] In 1903, the Maui Land and Pineapple Company (MLP) constructed a diversion of Honokōhau stream at an 840-foot elevation, diverting 21.4 million gallons per day of surface water. The

MLP diversion had a maximum diversion capacity of 60 mgd. During low-flow periods, Honokōhau stream still discharged 11.5 mgd, making it one of the few perennial streams in West Maui.

At one time, the government treated Honokōhau Stream as a game resource without regard for its native species. In 1922, H. L. Kelly of the territorial fish and game commission introduced trout fry into three streams on Maui, including Honokōhau stream. Arthur Gordon and Elbert Gillin carried two cases of trout fry far up Honokōhau Valley on horseback as far as they could and then walked on two or three miles further. "Gordon and Gillen said they took the trout well above the Honokōhau intake and that there were other fish in that vicinity so they hoped all would be well."[120]

As late as 1971, approximately 0.5 mgd of untreated surface water diverted from Honokōhau Stream was used for domestic resident uses in Nāpili. Residents complained of dirty, contaminated water that was not chlorinated and with coliform bacteria content exceeding federal standards.[121] In that same year, however, West Maui communities had become critical of the area's large landowners and the tension between development for new and part-year residents and existing community needs. Much-needed water improvements promised for Nāpili were met with skepticism by William Iaconetti of Nāpili, who said nothing would change: "The new well will not meet the future needs of the area because of plans for new housing developments." As an example, he cited the proposed Maui Land & Pineapple Company project planned in the Honolua area. "The large residential and tourist development will be using water from the county supply."[122]

Lahaina resident and community advocate Kapali Keahi described some of the issues community members seeking to restore loʻi had encountered.[123] Most of them had to do with the recalcitrance of large landowners, including Maui Land and Pine (MLP), to comply with agreements to reduce their diversions. Kapali recalled the strong community organization in Honokōhau in the 1990s, when they challenged MLP's diversions of Honokōhau. "Industry is a veritable vacuum for everyone," Kapali commented. "A lot of people backed off from farming taro. This was a generational shift—the older generation was getting too old to farm, and the younger generation did not have enough water to farm anyway."

Kapali remembered that a former MLP manger, Wesley Horcajo, had organized workshops to persuade taro farmers in Honokōhau to raise dryland kalo instead of loʻi kalo.[124] Many community members understood the aim as only to facilitate MLP's theft of water resources.

Future of the Honokōhau Ditch

For Keoki Freeland, maintenance of the Honokōhau Ditch is a critical problem. Freeland pointed to Peter Martin, principal of West Maui Land Company, who acquired much of Kahoma lands and thus sought to use Honokōhau Ditch to irrigate Kahoma as well as Kauaʻula lands. To Freeland, it seemed fair for Martin to maintain the Honokōhau Ditch, and in exchange, to get some of the water. To underscore the critical import of the ditch systems, Freeland described a big landslide in 1992 when the water intake system in Kanahā Valley, and therefore a major water system for Lahainatown, was "wiped out." At that time, state and county officials needed to figure out another way to get water. The solution was found in construction of the Mahinahina water treatment facility, built on state lands later deeded to the Department of Hawaiian Home Lands near the Kapalua West Maui airport. Prior to the installation of the Mahinahina facility, the only water sources aside from a small well at Lahainaluna School were Honokōhau Ditch sources.

Despite the critical importance to certain actors, the state has not put forward a strong position or comprehensive plan for whether and how to maintain the PMIS, for which Honokōhau ditch is a metonym. Of the 6,200 acres irrigated by Pioneer Mill's ditch system, 1,600 acres were owned by the state. According to Pioneer Mill, all the waters transported in the ditch are developed or taken from the lands owned by Maui Land & Pineapple, Inc. The quantity of water delivered to Pioneer Mill at or near the north boundary of the state land of Honokōwai averages 20 million gallons per day.[125]

In 1989, DLNR solicited and ACM appraiser Ted Yamamura submitted an appraisal for the approximately 17.242 acres of state lands proposed to be leased to Pioneer Mill.[126] Yamamura appraised the lease at $2,011.00 per year. The appraisal was based on the previous five years of rental payment of sugar leases ($114.37 per acre).

On August 5, 1997, a general lease for strips of state land underlying Honokōhau Ditch and Honokōwai Tunnel issued to Pioneer Mill was executed after many years of appraising and negotiating. GL S-5262 includes paragraph 22, which provides:

> The Grantee acknowledges and agrees that the subject easements covers only a right-of-way for the Honokōhau Ditch and Honokōwai Tunnel which runs over and across portions of government land and does not in any way

grant any right or interest in any government-owned waters nor does it grant any right to take any government-owned waters.[127]

The oddity of leasing lands underlying the ditch, instead of the public trust water resources within them, triggered a host of legal questions about evasions of responsibility that would come up again after Pioneer Mill's lease expired in 2014.

At a June 25, 1999 BLNR meeting, the Land Division administrator advised that the state acquire the ditch to protect its lands in West Maui.[128] AmFac "vehemently" opposed the acquisition. Board member Colbert Matsumoto questioned whether deferral to AmFac would not be a better option, because then they could undertake the cost. Board chair Timothy Johns, however, raised concerns that the ditch infrastructure could fall into disrepair if Amfac abandoned it. The Board voted to authorize negotiations for the acquisition of the Honokōhau Ditch. On December 9, 1999, DLNR Land Division consulted with the attorney general regarding condemnation of AMFAC lands under and surrounding Honokōhau Ditch.[129] No state acquisition occurred.

For its part, Amfac Hawaiʻi, LLC, which owned Pioneer Mill Co. at that point, filed for bankruptcy in 2002.[130] DLNR also communicated with the West Maui Soil Conservation District concerning ditch repair and maintenance in light of Amfac's bankruptcy.[131]

In 2005, Kaanapali Land Management Company (KLMC) emerged from the closure of Amfac Hawaiʻi. At the time of this writing, KLMC was trying to obtain a long-term lease of an easement for state lands through which the Honokōhau Ditch and Honokōwai Tunnel pass.[132] DLNR staff prepared a recommendation to grant a thirty-year non-exclusive easement over the 16.28 acres of public lands to KLMC for the BLNR's January 12, 2018 meeting.

Persistent advocacy and cogent inquiry into the circumstances giving rise to the proposed easement from the Office of Hawaiian Affairs and the Department of Hawaiian Home Lands (DHHL) resulted in the matter being removed from BLNR's agenda indefinitely. Amongst the issues raised were whether and how the apparent avoidance of issuing a water lease for the ditch lands would allow BLNR to meet its public trust obligations.

Earlier, on April 5, 2010, the Hawaiʻi Housing and Finance Development Corporation (HHFDC) wrote to DLNR requesting denial of Pioneer Mill's extension of Easement S-5262.[133] HHFDC stated that its residential Villages of Leialiʻi development in Honokōwai could not accommodate any overflow discharge from the Honokōhau Ditch irrigation system, and also opposed the lease extension based on discharge of overflow waters to Crater Reservoir.

KLMC seeks control over the Honokōhau ditch to transport water for the irrigation of agricultural and other lands owned by KLMC, including lands mauka of Lahaina. If granted a long-term lease, KLMC intends to repair the ditches, but would not likely expend that amount if their control is subject to a month-to-month permit. KLMC reportedly has an agreement with the county and MLP to obtain some of the water from Kanahā Stream, which is currently used by the county and directed to its Mahinahina water treatment facility. Some of the water obtained by KLMC may be directed towards the controversial Kaanapali 2020 project.

As private developers such as KLMC, Kahoma Land Company, West Maui Land Company, and Olowalu Elua Associates LLC as well as public developers including the State ERS and DHHL race to obtain entitlements for new construction, the lack of developed water resources will certainly be an issue. DHHL is distinguished from the other developers because of its mission and purpose in returning native Hawaiian beneficiaries to useable lands. However, DHHL, like other public developers, is handicapped by the relatively increased number of steps it must go through to ensure that its procurements, decision making, and other aspects of its institutional administration comply with laws requiring transparency. This disadvantage may allow private developers such as KLMC, despite enjoying no special legal protections as a commercial developer, to "outrace" DHHL for entitlement to water resources.

The State's narrow focus on KLMC being permitted to succeed to the lease for state ditch lands under condition of maintaining the ditch may later prevent it from examining alternatives to large-scale stream diversions. Chapter 7 addresses ways that West Maui's Native Hawaiian communities are seeking to take back their kuleana lands and the waters appurtenant to them to revive traditional and customary cultural practices.

On April 23, 2019, Ka Malu o Kahālāwai and the West Maui Preservation Association filed a water wasting complaint with the State Commission on Water Resource Management. The complaint alleges that Maui Land and Pine (MLP), the Kapalua Water Company, and the KLMC failed to properly maintain intakes, diversions, and ditches that withdraw water from Honokōhau stream and released water elsewhere in West Maui.

As described earlier, the Honokōhau Ditch diverts stream water to areas between Lahaina and Kapalua. The intake and diversions are mostly on MLP lands. The Kapalua Water Company is a subsidiary of MLP and provides private water services, primarily in Kapalua. KLMC holds revocable permits for state lands underlying the Honokōhau Ditch, including in areas where wasting was observed. For many decades, the groups observed warm Honokōhau Ditch water flowing out to the ocean. In late 2018, however, several large events occurred, including an early December dumping of so much water from the Honokōhau Ditch that a fully running stream flowed through Hahakea/Wahikuli Gulch and out to Hanakaoʻo (Canoes) Beach. Ka Malu o Ka Hālāwai member Kai Keahi took video of water exiting into the neashore area. Up mauka, Wili Wood, another member of the group, supplied video of water freely exiting the Honokōhau Ditch via Wahikuli flume, into and through nearby fields, over cane haul roads, and down into Wahikuli Gulch. Keahi reported sightings of fish swimming through the fields.

"Today, with global warming, sea level rise, and saltwater intrusion occurring in our small island's fragile aquifers, it is very unwise to be wasting such a valuable resource as water," commented Wood, a kalo farmer in Honokōhau Valley. "This imposes a great level of responsibility on the people chosen or hired to be stewards of our future, but unfortunately those stewards are too often shortsighted businessmen."

While the County of Maui pays for transmission of some of the water to the municipal system, the majority goes to the resorts and golf courses in the Kapalua area. Keahi explained the groups' position on the diverted water:

> We don't necessarily disagree with most [of] the use that this water is used for, but MLP who controls the stream intake in Honokōhau Valley is notorious for mishandling and mismanaging the water resource of Honokōhau. Quite often loʻi farmers are left with minimal water to grow their crops, which threatens their harvest. The majority of Honokōhau Stream is taken out of the valley and sent southward towards Lahaina town. The real issue, and the cause of the loss of habitat and the ability to farm kalo, is that MLP when it receives the water at the intake they cannot control how much gets diverted so all of the stream is taken. Because MLP does not need all of Honokōhau Stream water, they dump the unused excess water into various other West Maui streams and areas, such as Honokōwai, Wahikuli, and Hanakaoʻo, thus continuing the dewatering of Honokōhau Stream and hampering the ability of the aquatic life to reproduce and farmers to farm taro.

Honokōhau stream was once lined with over a thousand loʻi kalo. "Allowing water to flow from its sources to the ocean is vital for aquatic life and habitat as well as cultural practice such as lo'i kalo," said Keahi. Wood added, "Now is the time to make sure that tomorrow's streams are still flowing clean and abundant [with] life." The complaint seeks to require ditch operators to upgrade diversion technologies to allow more water to remain in Honokōhau Stream during higher flow periods, and mandate better maintenance practices to ensure gates permitting return of water to the stream are clear of debris and opened at appropriate times.

In November 2019, CWRM took up the complaint at a regular meeting held in Lahaina. Members of Ka Malu o Kahālāwai and Nā Mamo Aloha 'Āina o Honokōhau attended. The Water Commission ordered MLP to submit a permit to replace and upgrade the intake structure to prevent it from diverting more than it needs into Honokōhau ditch. Additionally, the Commission order requires MLP to keep water flowing through taro gate at pre-Hurricane Olivia conditions. While MLP was amenable to a certain schedule of these repairs, the on the ground reality told another story.

In weeks leading up to the Commission meeting, Honokōhau stream-flow to the 'auwai of many of the residents below MLP's diversions was nil to nothing. The 'auwai is supposed to bring Honokōhau stream water to lo'i kalo on the kuleana parcels that line the 'auwai. The stream itself was running sluggishly, stinking with flies drawn to the rotting bodies of native 'o'opu who depended on stream flow to survive.

Honokōhau taro farmer Wili Wood went to investigate the upstream water works to determine the cause of the low flows. When Wood walked up to taro gate, he found it fully closed with a plastic bag filled with sand wedged against it, such that no water at all could get through. The gate was padlocked shut. Hundreds of 'ōpae huddled in the small pool that remained in front of the gate. Honokōhau residents report that MLP contractors admitted to being paid to go up and close and lock taro gate and the county denies that it has anything to do with closing the gate.

Wood, and other former and current Honokōhau residents, have considerable experience with pressing MLP to return water to the stream. Records at the state Commission on Water Resources' Management disclose complaints from kalo farmers against MLP dating back to at least 1991, when the West Maui Moloka'i Taro Farmers Association sought the Commission's help. Over the years, Honokōhau kalo farmers filed more complaints against MLP, a few of which were supposed to be addressed through a guarantee of at least a one million gallons per day (mgd) that would be re-released back into the stream at the "taro gate." From about 2005-2018, however, approximately 2.45 mgd made its way through taro gate. Although it was not enough to sustain the 51.75 acres of loʻi that Honokōhau once supported along its banks, the amount returned by taro gate permitted some loʻi kalo to thrive. After Hurricane Olivia in 2018, however, many of the water works structures were damaged and clogged with debris, such that less water was returned to the stream.

Wood is part of Ka Malu o Kahālāwai, one of two community organizations that filed a water wasting complaint against MLP with the Water Commission on April 23, 2019. MLP not only diverts all of Honokōhau water, which can amount to 40 mgd, but then dumps all but the approximately 5 mgd that can be used offstream into fields and gulches by Mahinahina. This dumping is occurring as of the time of this writing and has gone on for decades. "If they're not going to use the water, leave it in the stream where it is originally from, where it is meant to be. Keeping it in the stream is not just for us, but for the stream's benefit," said Karyn Kanekoa, a leader of Nā Mamo Aloha ʻĀina o Honokōhau. A week later, MLP reopened taro gate without explanation.

Chapter 4

A CYCLE OF HYDROLOGIC FAILURE

Administrative Refusal to Protect Public Trust
Water Rights in West Maui and Hawai'i

VICE CHAIR:... you've described very well that some of the por-
tions of the [Olowalu] stream is gaining and some of it is losing.
Was any calculation done on how much water would need to be
flowing across to get actually continuous mauka-to-makai flow?
WITNESS: I haven't done such a calculation, but I think if—you're
saying you want to be perennial all the way down to the shoreline?
VICE CHAIR: I'm saying some of the people in the Cul-
tural Impact Assessment sought that.
WITNESS: Okay. **If there was zero diversion at Olowalu, I still don't**
think there would [be] perennial flow all the way to the shoreline.
—Transcript of a State Land Use Commission hearing, 2015[1]

The September 2016 flood destroyed the upper Olowalu intake and now
only the lower Olowalu intake is active. Thus, estimates of natural stream-
flow have to take into consideration the approximate 1.1 cubic feet per
second loss between the upper and lower intakes. **Based on the avail-**
able information, the stream reach below the lower diversion is
a losing reach but flows to the ocean 100 percent of the time.
—March 2018 Staff submittal for the Commission
on Water Resource Management (CWRM)[2]

I n late 2015, one of the expert witnesses in a state Land Use Commission
(LUC) proceeding was a well known and widely used water resource engi-

neer who consults on well drilling and other matters across Hawai'i. The expert testified regarding the water availability from the old Olowalu plantation ditch system for a proposed new urban development. On cross-examination, he acknowledged that his work was solely related to the amount of water that existed in the ditch system, not in the stream itself or water for any traditional and customary practices.

However, he later opined, in the quote above, that even if all diversions were removed, Olowalu stream would never reach the ocean. The desire for continuous mauka-to-makai stream flow had been stated by an individual interviewed in the Cultural Impact Assessment for the same project as something sought to help perpetuate traditional and customary Hawaiian practices. The LUC rejected the Environmental Impact Statement (EIS) for that development, and the developer chose not to proceed.

It so happened that less than a year later, in September 2016, a massive flood wiped out the upper intake of the ditch system on Olowalu stream that had been discussed by the LUC. The CWRM's own hydrologist later concluded that with only one of the two ditch intakes removed, the stream now is estimated to flow mauka to makai 100 percent of the time—the exact *opposite* of what the expert witness said would *never* happen even if *both* intakes were removed. Had the development proceeded instead of having been previously withdrawn, considerable pressure could have been brought to bear to reopen the mauka intake and compromise mauka-to-makai stream flow. As it happened, the mauka-to-makai stream flow sought by the cultural practitioner was brought about by flooding rather than state administrative action.

Expert Legal Theft

It has been nearly fifty years since the 1973 *McBryde v. Robinson* Hawai'i Supreme Court decision, wherein historic understandings of water law were restored and decades of plantation-favored jurisprudence were overturned. For almost one hundred years, Hawai'i courts (entirely dominated by plantation interests) increasingly treated water like private property that could be purchased and sold. These claims were largely based on arguments suggesting that when land was privatized in the Māhele (1848–1852, described later in this chapter), water was also privatized as part of those actions. However, in *McBryde*, the court famously declared:

> Thus by the Mahele and subsequent Land Commission Award and issuance of Royal Patent right to water was not intended to be, could not be, and

was not transferred to the awardee, and the ownership of water in natural watercourses, streams and rivers remained in the people of Hawaii for their common good.

Nonetheless, it is still the case in West Maui and across Hawai'i that large landowners and developers, armed with engineers, consultants, well-drillers and attorneys, assert control over water resources in myriad ways. They do so before various governmental panels at the county and state levels. One way they do this, illustrated in the quotes above, is to offer expert witnesses in proceedings before the state LUC, as well as CWRM, who have information on water and other matters supporting their consumptive uses. Sometimes, well after the fact, we discover that the expert opinion was incorrect.

This chapter goes to the heart of how, for the last fifty years in West Maui and across Hawai'i, the control of water has been a way in which ruling classes and governing groups have both drawn their strength and sought their continuing advantage. We look at how this has occurred across Hawai'i in general with examples from West Maui, where that has played out in a way that can be documented.

In Part I, the chapter gives context to how governing groups have had to shift in their methods of controlling water as the current management regime of water in Hawai'i has changed. We review the evolving legal understandings of water from Kingdom rule, through the territorial period, and into the post-statehood modern era. We go into detail to describe the revolutionary court decisions that led to the state Constitutional Amendments of 1978 declaring that water was a public trust resource, and the subsequent adoption of the Water Code in 1987.

Jumping ahead to the present, we next briefly describe (Part II) the key guidance the courts have given over the last two decades in understanding the public trust uses of water that are supposed to have a higher level of protection. This guidance also necessarily describes how state agencies, including CWRM but also all subdivisions of the state (which includes the counties), must prioritize these uses. The protection of these uses is supposed to be a guide star for all of the actions of CWRM and other branches of government.

In Part III, we review the history of CWRM decisions that have been ruled on by the Hawai'i Intermediate Court of Appeals and the Hawai'i Supreme Court. Sadly, CWRM has largely failed to consider public trust obligations to protect water resources and Hawaiian cultural practitioner rights, and these decisions were overturned by appellate Courts in Hawai'i. Indeed, since the enactment of the Code, nine decisions have been so appealed; the CWRM has lost seven of the nine (a failure rate of nearly 78 percent).[3] This review is foundational to an understanding that while the CWRM was set up to protect public trust interests in water, it rarely does so.

The reasons for this failure are myriad. In Part IV we will look at enforcement practices by CWRM in areas of West Maui that illustrate that at least part of the problem appears to be active biases against public trust uses (and users) of water. We look at the fines that CWRM attempted to levy against kalo farmers John and Rose Marie Duey, and compare them to fines sought against larger diverters.

This chapter thus seeks to serve as critical background to understanding the challenges West Maui kama'āina face in protecting water when it flows aboveground (chapter 5) and below ground (chapter 6). It also serves to point to the overall challenges people face when attempting to grow kalo (chapter 7).

THE WATER LAW CYCLE IN HAWAI'I: FROM COMMUNAL TO PRIVATE PROPERTY AND BACK AGAIN

Akin to the diagrams of the hydrologic cycle taught to schoolchildren, it can be useful to think of the evolution of Hawai'i water law from the 1840s to the present as a cycle. Water has gone from being understood as a resource held in trusteeship by the rulers for the people to something quite akin to private property, and now back to the idea of being held in trust.

Water Held in Trust on Behalf of the Gods for the People

From before the first adoption of Western law and through its first codification, water was understood to not be the private property of any one person. Rather, it was held in trust by the governing leaders for the people. Kapua Sproat, in *Native Hawaiian Law: A Treatise*,[4] notes how the leading scholars (Craighill and Elizabeth Handy, with Mary Kawena Puku'i) who reviewed native agriculturalists across Hawai'i in the 1930s captured this understanding very clearly. As they wrote in 1940 when reviewing water rights as part of their larger work:[5]

> Inalienable title to water rights in relation to land use is a conception that had no place in the Hawaiian way of thinking... Water, whether for irrigation, for drinking, or other domestic purposes, was something that "belonged" to Kane-i-ka-wai-ola (Procreator-in-the-water-of-life), and came through the meteorological agency of Lono-makua the Rain-provider... The para-

mount chief, born on the soil and hence first born of the *maka'ainana* of a *moku* (island or district), was a medium in whom was vested divine power and authority... But this investment... was instrumental in providing only a channeling of power and authority, not a vested right... But this was not equivalent to our European concept of "divine right." The *ali'i nui*, in old Hawaiian thinking and practice, did not exercise personal dominion, but channeled dominion. In other words, he was a trustee. The instances in which an *ali'i nui* was rejected and even killed because of abuse of his role are sufficient proof that it was not personal authority but trusteeship that established right (*pono*).[6]

That governance over water continued in law until and through the Māhele. "Māhele" is a Hawaiian word meaning either to divide or to share (Pukui and Elbert 1971). The phrase "The Māhele" is commonly used to refer to a series of laws passed over four years from 1848–1852 that enabled the legal entrance of a Western private property system to the Hawaiian Kingdom. Until that time, all people in the Islands who used land, maka'āinana and foreigners alike, held their lands at the discretion of the King, who was constrained by both tradition, and after 1840, by some law. As reflected in the name, the purpose of the acts was for the King to share management and control of the land so that the kingdom might prosper (Kame'eleihiwa 1992).

While land was privatized, it was not fully divided, and other natural resources, particularly water, were not privatized. The land awards to the King and Ali'i were subject to the rights of kuleana holders to enter into privately held lands for subsistence purposes. Similarly, while the Māhele allowed for the distribution of parcels of land to individual Hawaiians, the waters that were associated with that land were never directly deeded to them as private property. Rather, it was assumed in the legislation that traditional water rights would be guaranteed. As noted earlier Section 7 of the Kuleana Act of 1850 stated (emphasis added):

Where the landlords have obtained, or may hereafter obtain, allodial titles to their lands, the people on each of their lands shall not be deprived of the right to take firewood, house timber, aho cord, thatch, or ki leaf, from the land on which they live, for their own private use, but they shall not have the right to take such articles for profit. *The people shall also have a right to drinking water, and running water, and the right of way. The springs of water, running water, and roads shall be free to all,* on all lands granted in fee simple;

provided that this shall not be applicable to wells and water courses, which
individuals have made for their own use.

The clause explicitly excluded certain items, including flowing water
and springs, from privatization. The small exception—wells and water courses
individuals have made for their own use—would have applied to the individual small domestic wells and irrigation of house holders, as opposed to the few
nascent plantations that existed at the time.

The Judicial Manufacture of Appurtenant, Prescriptive, Surplus, and Correlative Water Rights

Soon after the passage of the Māhele, because of the increasing disputes over
land ownership and water use, dispute management entered into Hawai'i's
nascent justice system. In 1860, the Kingdom's legislature created the Commission on Private Ways and Water Rights in order to settle these controversies. In
one form or another, this commission existed through to the early days of the
Territory, when the duties of the commissioners were assumed by the circuit
courts of the islands.

Disputes settled by water commissioners could be appealed directly to the
Hawai'i Supreme Court. It was the decisions from these appellate court cases
that laid the foundation of Hawaiian water law. While much land passed into
foreign control soon after the Māhele, this change in and of itself did not affect
land and water use practices. The point at which change became dramatic was
when the new tenure was enforced and the lands were put to different uses,
including those that precluded Kanaka Maoli traditional uses.

For approximately the first one hundred years of the court's existence, a
series of cases resulted in the adoption of four doctrines of water rights that
transformed the former trustee system of water: appurtenant rights, prescriptive
rights, surplus water rights, and correlative rights.

The oldest water case reported by the court is *Peck v. Bailey*, 8 Haw. 658
(1867). It helped determine the existence of appurtenant and prescriptive rights.[7]
It was a dispute that involved two sugar cane growers; while Sherman Peck and
Edward Bailey were both sugar planters, both had purchased kalo land and had
diverted some of the water from those parcels to their sugar plantations. Thus the
court used this as an opportunity to rule on the nature of water rights to kalo lands.

APPURTENANT AND PRESCRIPTIVE WATER RIGHTS
The court discussed the idea that riparian rights to water existed in Hawai'i—
that is, that landowners whose properties adjoin a river have the right to make

reasonable use of water as it flows through or over their properties, insofar as they do not harm the rights of other riparian owners.

However, the court also declared that the rights to water for kuleana used to grow kalo and other crops at the time of the Māhele were "appurtenant" water rights; that is, they had attached to the kalo land that was awarded in the Māhele. In doing this, they in a manner endorsed the idea that the Māhele had intended to guarantee the rights of kalo farmers to water. However, while referring to these rights, they claimed that it was not the Māhele that gave Hawaiian rights *per se*, but that the lands had gained them by "immemorial usage" and "prescription."

The prescription of water rights is similar to the way land can be gained by adverse possession—also a common practice against Kānaka Maoli at that time and into the 20th century. In adverse possession in Hawai'i, a person can use someone else's land in an actual, open, hostile, notorious, continuous, and exclusive manner for twenty years and then claim ownership of the land by petitioning a court for settlement. If the court finds that the use was known but not objected to, as well as not permissive, the party claiming adverse possession obtains the land from the former owner. In theory, adverse possession can be initiated by any property owner against any other property owner except the government. In practice, it was nearly always large landholders that adversely possessed the land of small owners. Embracing a similar idea for water, the court declared that water could be prescribed from a former owner by a new user under much of the same criteria, and it was used as a tool by sugar plantations to obtain water rights from kuleana holders.

The court in *Peck* made notice of the fact that Hawaiians were using water to grow kalo across the Islands. However, they opened the door legally to prescription by declaring it was the past use of water that had let Hawaiians claim water rights, rather than stating that the akua, the Māhele, or their rights as indigenous people guaranteed their water. By calling ancient Hawaiian water rights prescriptive, they made rights obtained by newcomers via prescription the equivalent of rights held by Hawaiians. As a result, this legitimized and legalized the recent and future actions of sugar plantations.

Moreover, the court ruled that although water rights were intended at the time of the Māhele to enable kalo cultivation, there was almost nothing to prohibit a landowner with water rights from growing a different crop on that land or even diverting the water from the original parcel to other land on which a different crop would grown. The only restriction was that no harm could come to other users by the changed use, a nod to the riparianism that the judges were familiar with and that they hinted existed in Hawai'i. However, the overall intention of the court to facilitate sugarcane cultivation in the Kingdom is clear (665):

> The court regard[s] this [claim of Peck's that one can not transfer kalo water to sugar cane] as an illiberal construction of the prescriptive right and one which would do infinite mischief... If land has a water right, it will not be contended that the water shall be used forever for the same crop, be it kalo or cane. It may be used for any purpose for which the owner may deem for his interest....

RIGHTS TO "SURPLUS" WATER

From the perspective of a stream, the idea that there could be such a thing as surplus water is absurd; from its low flows to its highest floods, all stream waters are equally a part of their hydrology. However, as sugarcane cultivation expanded, the demands for water by plantations grew beyond what could be provided by the existing rights held by kalo farmers or gained via prescription from them. In a series of cases, the court defined what claims could be made to the "surplus" waters of a stream—meaning to the courts and sugar planters, everything that had to this point not been diverted.

Sugar planters in the Islands may have seen that water not diverted for growing kalo may have been "surplus" and hence available. This ignored, however, what Hawaiian scholar and water commissioner Emma Nakuina noted in 1893 was an intentional practice and a "well recognized rule" that did not divert more than half of the water in a stream:[8]

> No auwai was permitted to take more water than continued to flow in the stream below the dam. It was generally less, for there were those who were living makai or below the same stream, and drawing water from it, whose rights had to be regarded.
>
> Any dams made regardless of this well-recognized rule were leveled to the bedrock by the water rights holder below, and at any rebuilding, delegates from each dam below were required to be present to see that a due proportion of water was left in the stream.[9]

That well-established rule, however, did not survive the period of the sugar planters' thirst or the rule of the Hawai'i Supreme Court they influenced. The court has in that time defined two kinds of surplus. One is the remaining base flow in a stream after all appurtenant and prescriptive rights have been satisfied. The second kind of surplus is from the somewhat common freshets of water that swell streams during storms.

The issue of normal surplus was first raised in *Wilfong v. Bailey*, 3 Haw. 479 (1873). It involved the same Bailey as in *Peck v. Bailey*, and the owners of some kalo lands, the first one named a Chinese man named Wilfong. In that case, the court adopted something fairly close to a prior appropriation rule regarding surplus water. Bailey was diverting more water than he had in appurtenant and prescriptive rights, to which Wilfong et al. objected.

The court did not jump to the rescue of the kalo farmers. Rather, the court stated, "If more water has been used on the appellant's [Bailey's] land than it has been entitled to, that is no reason for requiring him to share it with those who show no better title thereto." In other words they concluded if Bailey was using surplus water and not harming other's rights, the court could not and would not keep him from doing it.

Because of the greater capital and land owned by the plantations, the ability to use so called "surplus" water—water not subject to existing court recognized rights—would much more easily be obtained by sugar plantations than kalo farmers. This rule was definitively made and expanded on in later cases like *Hawaiian Commercial & Sugar Company v. Wailuku Sugar Company*, 15 Haw. 675 (1904).

CORRELATIVE RIGHTS TO GROUNDWATER

As is the case in most areas of the United States, groundwater and surface water have been governed in Hawai'i by different legal regimes. This has persisted despite the fact that in most areas (including West Maui), surface and ground water are intimately interconnected.

The first ruling on groundwater in the Islands adopted the idea of correlative rights—that is, the owner of overlying land owns the water beneath, subject to the claims of neighboring landowners. This decision came from the 1929 case *City Mill v. Honolulu Sewer and Water Commission*, 30 Haw. 912 (1929). This case arose in response to the City of Honolulu's attempt to regulate the groundwater resources of the city. Honolulu is underlain by a huge artesian aquifer that was at the time being heavily drawn down. Two acts passed by the Territorial Legislature in 1925 and 1927 authorized the creation of a commission to regulate water withdrawals and the establishment of a permitting system for new wells.

City Mill Co. applied for a permit to withdraw groundwater for domestic use, specifically to provide for the needs of workers living on its property. The permit was denied on the basis that there were too many existing wells in the area and the aquifer was being over-drafted. City Mill appealed to the Hawai'i Supreme Court, claiming that the denial was unfair as it only restricted them and not their neighbors. The court ruled in favor of plaintiffs City Mill, overturned key parts of the authorizing statute, and declared that the company held correlative rights to the water beneath their property.

Until 1973, the four kinds of rights enumerated above went largely unchallenged in the Islands. By and large, water was understood to be in many ways akin to private property. Water was bought, sold, and leased with no assumption that this was problematic; "surplus water" and other waters were exchanged in business transactions as if their legal foundation was firm.

These legal understandings were enshrined into statute as well. For instance, when Congress passed the Hawaiian Homes Commission Act in 1921, the section of the Act that dealt with water specifically identified how the new homesteading program could obtain rights to "government-owned water" as well as "privately owned surplus water."[10] As the plantations were tremendously influential in guiding the terms of the Act, the inclusion of these ideas is not surprising.

Thus in this era, when parties fought over rights to water they based their claims on the kinds of rights the courts had established—prescriptive, appurtenant, surplus, and correlative. However, this all changed with a series of water battles noted briefly at the beginning of this chapter. They are sometimes referred to as the Hanapēpē cases for the area of controversy, and other times called the *McBryde* cases for the plantiff in the first suit in the series.

Turning the Corner in the Cycle: McBryde

The Hanapēpē area of west Kaua'i was home to two large sugar plantations: Gay and Robinson and McBryde Sugar Company. The Territory (later the state) also held title to land in the area.[11] The parties had fought earlier in the century before the Hawai'i Supreme Court regarding their rights to water *Territory v. Gay*, 31 Haw. 376 (1930). Apparently for a while there was some accommodation among the claimants in the area over how water should be divided.

However, in the early 1970s, a new fight began stemming from Gay and Robinson's diversion of more water from high in the watershed. The two companies again sought a judicial settlement of their water rights. The case first went to the state circuit court that had jurisdiction, and that court settled the dispute by tallying what the various appurtenant, prescriptive, and surplus rights were for each party.

Both parties appealed to the Hawai'i Supreme Court, as did the state of Hawai'i (*McBryde Sugar Co. v. Robinson*, 54 Haw. 174 (1973)). On this appeal, the parties did not question the basic kinds of rights that were understood to exist in the Islands—merely the amount and method of determining the allocations. However, the case was heard by a court now influenced through appointments by Democratic Party officials who had unseated Republican plantation interests, and led by Hawaiian Chief Justice William S. Richardson. Rather than following what the accepted rules of water allocation were, Justice Kazuhisa Abe chose to go all the way back to the Māhele to examine the basis of claims in the case. In the view of many in the Islands, the court stood existing law on its ear, though in reality it merely reversed the decisions that had ignored earlier Kingdom law and precedent. As partially quoted above, the Court concluded that in the Māhele:

> The right to water was specifically and definitely reserved for the people of Hawaii for their common good in all of the land grants. Thus by the Mahele ... right to water was not intended to be, could not be, and was not transferred to the awardee, and the ownership of water in natural watercourses, streams, and rivers, remained in the people of Hawaii for their common good.

This led the majority to make a number of key rulings that overturned the existing regime of water control in the Islands:

1. Water in Hawai'i was never private property; it was held by the King and passed from him all the way to the state.
2. Because water was held by the state, no prescriptive rights to water existed, as one cannot prescribe against the state.
3. Appurtenant rights to water were not severable from the original kuleana they attached to, so that water cannot be applied to other land.
4. Riparian principles had been fully adopted in the Islands, contrary to earlier readings by the court.
5. Because of riparianism, claims to surplus waters were void—they could not exist, as riparianism guaranteed all of the water in a stream to riparian landowners.
6. Also, because of riparianism's prohibition against harm, transfers of any water outside of the watershed of origin were illegal.

Enforcing these conclusions would necessarily deal a harsh blow to most sugar plantations, as they depended on the use of prescriptive, appurtenant, and surplus water rights and the diversion of water outside of watersheds and from former kalo lands. In an opinion that dissented on point 6 above, Justice Marumoto stated that:

> Although I do not have specific information at hand, I presume that, besides the parties in this case, there are other segments in the agricultural economy of Hawaii which depend upon irrigation for the cultivation of their crops, have expended substantial sums in constructing irrigation facilities in reliance upon prior court decisions, and will be adversely affected by the decision announced today.

In mentioning the impacts of this decision, he suggested without saying it that the decision could be viewed as a taking of the parties' property without compensation, thus a violation of the state and federal constitutions.

All parties first appealed to the court for a rehearing (*McBryde Sugar Co. v. Robinson*, 55 Haw. 260 (1973)), but the court upheld what it had found. Perhaps dumbfounded, angered to action, and encouraged by the dissent, the parties then appealed to the US Supreme Court. The sugar planters submitted a motion that they could not obtain a fair hearing in a lower court and needed to be heard by the US Supreme Court. However, the US Supreme Court declined to hear the case (*Robinson v. Hawaii*, 417 U.S. 976 (1974)).

Not wanting to let the issue die, the landowners then brought suit against the State of Hawai'i in federal district court, and named then-Governor George Ariyoshi as lead defendant. They argued along the lines of the Marumoto dissent that the action was a judicial taking of property and sought to enjoin the state from taking steps to enforce the *McBryde* decisions (*Robinson v. Ariyoshi*, 441 F. Supp. 559 (1977)). The federal district court agreed and issued an injunction against the state of Hawai'i.

The State of Hawai'i, however, objected to this ruling. The parties appealed the district court decision to the Ninth Circuit Court. Before they made a decision, the Ninth Circuit submitted six "certified" questions for the Hawai'i Supreme Court to consider. In their response in 1982 (*Robinson v. Ariyoshi*, 65 Haw. 641 (1982)), Justice Richardson reaffirmed the earlier rulings in the two *McBryde* cases.

Following that response, the Ninth Circuit upheld the earlier federal district court decision; while they did not reinstate the injunction, they accepted the Hawai'i court's arguments that riparianism applied in the Islands and held the parties could not be deprived of vested rights pursuant to *McBryde* (*Robinson v. Ariyoshi*, 753 F.2d 1468 (1985)).

The State of Hawai'i then took the issue again to the US Supreme Court. In this case, they argued that the issue was not ripe for judicial review. In order for a "takings" case to be ready for judicial examination and decision, actual injury needs to have taken place and the parties need to have pursued all administrative remedies available to them. The state of Hawai'i argued, quite simply, that no taking had actually taken place and no taking might ever take place if an administrative compromise could be worked out; the court was acting prematurely. The US Supreme Court agreed to vacate the decision and remand the case to the Ninth Circuit for consideration of the "ripeness" issues (*Ariyoshi v. Robinson*, 477 U.S. 902 (1986)). In turn, the Ninth remanded the case back to the federal district court that had ruled on it earlier.

The case ended with an indefinite ruling. The same federal district judge who had issued the injunction against enforcing *McBryde* heard the case again, and strongly objected to the actions of the Hawai'i Supreme Court. He held that the takings had occurred and were therefore wrong; he was ready to issue an injunction if any Hawai'i government official attempted to enforce *McBryde*. The Ninth Circuit court was again appealed to, however, and in 1989—sixteen years after the original ruling in *McBryde*—they overturned the district court, stating that no taking had occurred and so no judicial action was possible (*Robinson v. Ariyoshi*, 887 F.2d 215 (1989)).

After these cases, people involved knew that Hawai'i water policy had changed, but no one knew what the parameters of that transformation were. As a result, policy leaders in Hawai'i were left with a difficult situation. They needed to find a way to manage water in the Islands that would not violate the principles of the *McBryde* cases, which held the state was the Trustee of water resources, and also not raise the taking issues that arose from the subsequent *Robinson* suits.

Clarifying Water Is a Public Trust Resource:
The Constitutional Convention of 1978

When Hawai'i became a state in 1959, it was governed under a constitution developed in 1950 when the Islands were still a territory. In 1968, a new constitution was passed that more directly addressed the needs of state governance. However, ten years later, changing social forces in the Islands led a number of people to call for a new constitution. Particularly strong were calls for environmental protection and the betterment of conditions for Native Hawaiians. In addition to and intersecting both of these issues, one of the long list of tasks that needed to be addressed by the Constitutional Convention of 1978 was how to deal with water management in the post-*McBryde* era.

Many of the key players in water politics in the Islands worked to assure that they would have representation in the convention. The president of the Convention was Bill Paty, a World War II hero and subsequently a well-known sugarcane plantation executive. From the windward side of O'ahu, windward water activists succeeded in electing Charlene Hoe to represent them. Across the Islands, progressive and environmental candidates were elected as delegates to the Constitutional Convention.

The convention had a difficult time crafting a proposed amendment, as the competing interests were split on the issues of water ownership and management. Moreover, while the initial decision in *McBryde* was a few years old, appeals were ongoing and sugar interests were still hoping it could be overturned. To address how this conflict would be managed, they stated that water needed to be managed more effectively to account for differing interests and values. To accomplish this, they mandated the creation of a new agency that could work out compromises. The language, later adopted by the state's voters and included as Article XI, Section 7 reads:

> The state has an obligation to protect, control, and regulate the use of Hawaii's water resources for the benefit of its people.
>
> The legislature shall provide for a water resources agency which, as provided by law, shall set overall water conservation, quality and use policies; define beneficial and reasonable uses; protect ground and surface water resources, watershed and natural stream environments; establish criteria for water use priorities while assuring appurtenant rights and existing correlative and riparian uses and establish procedures for regulating all use of Hawaii's water resources.

The convention also proposed a general statement about the environment of Hawai'i that the voters ratified, which became Article XI, Section 1. That statement clarified that while they were not owned as private property, resources including water were held as a public trust, thus enacting one of the major findings of *McBryde*:

> For the benefit of present and future generations, the State and its political subdivisions shall conserve and protect Hawaii's natural beauty and all

natural resources, including land, water, air, minerals and energy sources, and shall promote the development and utilization of these resources in a manner consistent with their conservation and in furtherance of the self-sufficiency of the State.

All public natural resources are held in trust by the State for the benefit of the people.

In furtherance of Hawaiian interests in water resources, the new constitution specified in Article XII Section 4 that lands held by the state gained in the Admissions Act, with the exception of lands set aside in the Hawaiian Homes Commission Act, were held in trust for two distinct groups: native Hawaiians and the general public. Additionally, the traditional and customary gathering rights of native Hawaiians that had been specified in the Māhele were supported further in an amendment, included as Article XII, Section 7:

> The state reaffirms and shall protect all rights, traditionally and customarily exercised for subsistence, cultural, and religious purposes and possessed by ahupuaʻa tenants who are descendants of native Hawaiians who inhabited the Hawaiian Islands prior to 1778, subject to the right of the state to regulate such rights.

These sections together clarified that water in Hawaiʻi is a public trust asset and cannot be held as private property. However, while the constitution enshrines this idea after years of tumultuous jurisprudence, the public trust in Hawaiʻi does not rely solely on this constitutional provision. Rather, the idea that water is held in trust for the people has been inherent in the law in Hawaiʻi since there was written law.

The Water Code

As noted, Article XI Section 7 of the constitution mandated the legislature to create a water code and a water management agency. However, just as there were significant fights over the language of the constitutional amendment, the same factions fighting at the convention did battle at the state legislature over creating a code. As a result, amid the ongoing appeals of the *McBryde* cases and one other significant water case that ended up upholding the principles of *McBryde* (*Reppun v. Board of Water Supply*, 65 Haw. 531 (1982))[12], the sides were deadlocked for years.

After many failed attempts, the legislature finally passed a code in 1987; then-Governor John Waiheʻe (ally of Bill Paty at the Constitutional Convention) signed it into law. This compromised code did not permanently resolve the differences held by opposing factions; rather, it set out a process for settling these differences, case by case, in a politically charged environment. The powers of the Water Code (Hawaii Revised Statutes (HRS) chapter 174C, more fully described in chapter 2) are administered by a commission weighted toward politically motivated considerations. Of the seven members, the governor appoints all of them. Two serve, as part of their official capacities, as the heads of the Department of Health and the Department of Land and Natural Resources. The five remaining positions appointed by the governor are also subject to confirmation by the state Senate (HRS §174C-7).

This is one reason, according to some, that the code is more of "...a 'crisis management' Water Code rather than a uniform system of water regulation and management."[13] Yet, not all aspects of the code in principle work against comprehensive and logical management. The code does call for each appointee to have "substantial experience in the area of water resource management" (HRS §174C-7(b)), which in theory could de-politicize decision-making. The code also mandates the creation of a State Water Plan in consultation with other state and local agencies, which should provide for comprehensive planning and minimization of controversy (HRS §174C-31). However, the state has not kept up with water planning, and commissioners often do not have qualifications beyond their political connections.[14]

Four characteristics of the code in particular (enumerated more below) prevent it from being a forward-looking and comprehensive management policy. These provisions helped contribute to the contentiousness of water fights in West Maui and elsewhere.

One reason the code is a "crisis management" code is that it does not clearly prioritize the water uses that are given priority in other parts of the law, except for the water claims of Hawaiian Home Lands.[15] Instead, the legislative intent section, clarified in the code's declaration of policy, tries to be all water things to all water-interested people. The Code's "Declaration of Policy" does begin by noting that water in Hawai'i is a public trust resource (HRS §174C-2(a)):

> It is recognized that the waters of the State are held for the benefit of the citizens of the State. It is declared that the people of the State are beneficiaries and have a right to have the waters protected for their use.

But it then goes on to confuse things by having a laundry list of consumptive uses that should be obtained (HRS 147C-2(c)):

The state water code shall be liberally interpreted to obtain maximum beneficial use of the waters of the State for purposes such as domestic uses, aquacultural uses, irrigation and other agricultural uses, power development, and commercial and industrial uses. However, adequate provision shall be made for the protection of traditional and customary Hawaiian rights, the protection and procreation of fish and wildlife, the maintenance of proper ecological balance and scenic beauty, and the preservation and enhancement of the waters of the State for municipal uses, public recreation, public water supply, agriculture, and navigation. Such objectives are declared to be in the public interest.

A review commission that examined problems with implementation of the code suggested setting priorities would be a significant improvement, but that recommendation to the Legislature—which the Legislature requested and funded—has never been followed.[16] They identified four purposes they believed were "priority uses of water": (a) water for conservation (including to thus provide water supporting traditional and customary Hawaiian rights; (b) for appurtenant rights; (c) for Hawaiian Home Lands; and (d) for agriculture. Moreover, they noted that these priorities already exist in Constitutional provision and statutory law—but are unclearly stated in the code[17] itself:

It is the Review Commission's view that the rights that comprise the hierarchy exist in current state law. None of the various rights is intended to be expanded. Gathering these rights in a separate part of the State Water Code underscores their existence and serves as a reminder to everyone that they must be respected when allocation decisions are made. While a balancing of interests is often appropriate when principles are in conflict, it was felt that some structure is needed to ensure that decisions made by the commission on water resource management are reasonably consistent. The establishment of "criteria for water use priorities," it should be noted, is mandated by the State Constitution. To resolve every permit decision as a balance of interests was felt to be inefficient, conducive to excessive disputes, and contrary to law. The commission, therefore, is required to be guided by the hierarchy of water uses when making permit decisions, resolving disputes and citizen complaints, developing the Hawaii water plan, and making allocation and reallocation decisions, including modifications of existing permits.

The second reason the code has failed to help protect Public Trust interests is that it sets up two different processes for water permitting, depending on whether an area has been "designated" or not. Originally, parties trying to pass a water code sought a single statewide system for permitting, but limiting the code's scope was one of the compromises required to enable its passage in the legislature.[18]

As reviewed in chapter 2, the first process for permitting covers most areas in the state. Existing and new wells were required to obtain permits for new wells, well construction and pump installation permits. Changes to surface water diversions require stream channel alteration permits and or stream diversion works permits. In addition, for all water users in all areas, a deadline of one year after the adoption of relevant rules was set for entities to declare their water uses. In response to these declarations, the Commission was required to determine if the uses were "reasonable and beneficial," and that use would then be certified and recognized by the state (HRS §§174C-26, 27).

However, "reasonable and beneficial" as a test is vaguely and tautologically defined: " 'Reasonable-beneficial use' means the use of water in such a quantity as is necessary for economic and efficient utilization, for a purpose, and in a manner which is both reasonable and consistent with the state and county land use plans and the public interest" (HRS §174C-3).

A higher standard for water use exists in areas that are "designated" for management. In general, designated areas are water management units where the water resources in them are in threat of degradation. In designated areas, all water users (including existing users) are required to apply for permits with stricter requirements than just being reasonable-beneficial. The permit cannot be issued unless certain requirements are met. These requirements, while more specific than those for certification of use in non-designated areas, only provide general guidance to the water commission. Permits can only be granted if the use meets all of the following (HRS §174C-49):

1. Can be accommodated with the available water source,
2. Is a reasonable-beneficial use as defined in section 174C-3,
3. Will not interfere with any existing legal use of water,
4. Is consistent with the public interest,
5. Is consistent with state and county general plans and land use designations,
6. Is consistent with county land use plans and policies, and
7. Will not interfere with the rights of the department of Hawaiian Home Lands as provided in section 221 of the Hawaiian Homes Commission Act.

The higher standard for water permitting in designated areas could allow for a greater protection of the resource and forward planning if all of the significant hydrologic areas in the Islands were designated—but few areas are. Two areas of Oʻahu (the Pearl Harbor Aquifer and the Honolulu aquifer) were included as designated areas at the time of the code's passage, as they had already been the subject of special laws governing their water use. Only a few places in the state have been designated since passage of the code: the windward Oʻahu aquifers, groundwater on Molokaʻi, the ʻĪao Aquifer on Maui as well as the Nā Wai ʻEhā surface water management area. Designation has been rare and heavily opposed by development interests and their government allies, which is the third reason the code ends up being a reactive rather than proactive policy.

In order for the Water Commission to designate an area as a groundwater management area, the first mandatory criteria to be examined is that increases in use may cause maximum withdrawals to exceed 90 percent of the area's sustainable yield. Even if sustainable yield could be clearly and conclusively determined (a challenge discussed in detail in chapter 6), by the time that threshold is reached, water controversies are more likely to be contentious then amicable. Moreover, the code lists seven other criteria that must be examined before an area is considered to be designated, including if "serious disputes over groundwater are occurring" (HRS §174C-44). Thus in the design of the code itself, the protections of designation will come too late in the process to prevent battles over water. The criteria for designation of a hydrologic unit as a surface water management area are similarly restrictive (HRS §174C-45).

As was the case with the code's failure to clearly identify existing priority uses of water, the Review Commission on the state water code had a clear and unambiguous first recommendation: "1. Extend the designation of water management areas to include the entire State." (p. 2).

A fourth and final reason that the code fails to avoid controversy and meet its stated intent of protection and management is the manner in which instream uses are treated. The code does acknowledge that a number of instream uses, such as the maintenance of ecosystems and the protection of Hawaiian rights, are presumptively in the public interest. The code also authorizes the Commission to set interim and permanent instream flow standards to assure that instream values are protected. However, the code did not require that interim or permanent standards be set prior to or during certification of uses described above. Thus the interim standards that were set for streams across Hawaiʻi was the status quo—which in nearly all cases were completely dewatered streams.

Interested parties can petition to have interim standards set, but in practice the commission has set these reluctantly, and until recently has only set standards at current levels, which are not clearly high enough to protect instream values (HRS Chapter 174C Part VI). This process is discussed more fully in chapter 5. Until the famous water case, In re Water Use Permit Applications, 94 Hawai'i 97, 9 P.3d 409 (2000) ("*Waiāhole I*"), the Commission never set quantitative instream flow standards.

Thus, while the water code provided a process for resolving disputes over water that allows the inclusion of competing interests in decision-making, it is by no means a model of effective policy. Because of its design as well as its timid implementation, the water code tends to exacerbate crises rather than resolve them, and it fails to settle many of the issues it was designed to address. What it has done is become the setting for the most recent battles over water rights in the Islands, and has the potential to resolve disputes that have been raging since the courts first looked at water issues in the 1850s by determining how the code would be interpreted.

Because of the absence of meaningful leadership at the Legislature, from CWRM members and CWRM staff, and especially the Legislature's complete failure to enact the recommendations of the Review Commission, the courts of Hawai'i have had to provide guidance on how the protection of the public trust in water can be accomplished within the confines of the code. They have done so clearly and succinctly over the past few decades, as well as clarifying what duties the state has to protect these uses.

THE FOUR PROTECTED PUBLIC TRUST USES OF WATER

The landmark *Waiāhole* water case, the first major test of the implementation of the water code, pitted community, Hawaiian, and conservation interests who sought to have stream flow restored in windward O'ahu from a major irrigation system against leeward plantation, large landowner, military, and development interests. After more than eighteen months of hearings, the CWRM allocated most of the water to emerging off-stream users in leeward O'ahu. On appeal, the Hawai'i Supreme Court overruled the decision of the CWRM, which essentially allocated water to off-stream users first, and then gave what was left over to windward streams and interests.

In *Waiāhole*, the Court described the scope of the public trust and specified uses that the trust specifically protected. They specifically rejected the idea that private commercial uses, including water for agriculture, were a public trust use of water. Their next major water decision (*In re Waiola o Molokai*, 103 Hawai'i 401, 83 P.3d 664 (2004)), also overruling CWRM, regarded how a proposed well by a large landowner on the island of Molokai would possibly harm reservations held in a neighboring aquifer by the DHHL. In that case they summarized the public trust uses of water they identified in *Waiāhole*, and added that DHHL reservations were a public trust purpose.

Subsequent cases have cited these precedents, and the most recent clear recitation of these uses was in a case from Kauaʻi: *Kauaʻi Springs, Inc. v. Planning Commʾn of Cty. of Kauaʻi*, 133 Hawaiʻi 141, 324 P.3d 951 (2014). In this case the Kauaʻi Planning commission sought to clarify their public trust obligations when approving a land use permit for a water bottling plant. The Planning Commission first sought information on any potential harm on this use from the CWRM staff, and while the CWRM shared some thoughts, they did not assert any direct claim to jurisdiction because "The Island of Kauai has not been designated as a groundwater management area; therefore a water use permit from the Commission is not required to use the existing source(s) or to change the type of water use."[19] In short, rather than stepping forward as the appropriate and legal trustee for all fresh water in Hawaiʻi, Commission staff dodged the issue.

Where the CWRM declined to act, the Kauaʻi Planning Commission did not, and they denied the permit because they believed the applicant gave them insufficient information to act on the possible impact of this private commercial use on public trust purposes. Unlike the CWRM's sad appellate history, described more below, the Planning Commission was upheld by the Hawaiʻi Supreme Court. The Court used the opportunity as well to provide a summary of guidance on how to apply the Public Trust doctrine:

> To assist agencies in the application of the public trust doctrine, we distill from our prior cases the following principles:
> a. The agency's duty and authority is to maintain the purity and flow of our waters for future generations and to assure that the waters of our land are put to reasonable and beneficial use.
> b. The agency must determine whether the proposed use is consistent with the trust purposes:
>   i.   the maintenance of waters in their natural state,
>   ii.   the protection of domestic water use,
>   iii.   the protection of water in the exercise of Native Hawaiian and traditional and customary rights, and
>   iv.   the reservation of water enumerated by the State Water Code.
> c. The agency is to apply a presumption in favor of public use, access, enjoyment, and resource protection.

d. The agency should evaluate each proposal for use on a case-by-case basis, recognizing that there can be no vested rights in the use of public water.

e. If the requested use is private or commercial, the agency should apply a high level of scrutiny.

f. The agency should evaluate the proposed use under a "reasonable and beneficial use" standard, which requires examination of the proposed use in relation to other public and private uses.

Applicants have the burden to justify the proposed water use in light of the trust purposes.

a. Permit applicants must demonstrate their actual needs and the propriety of draining water from public streams to satisfy those needs.

b. The applicant must demonstrate the absence of a practicable alternative water source.

c. If there is a reasonable allegation of harm to public trust purposes, then the applicant must demonstrate that there is no harm in fact or that the requested use is nevertheless reasonable and beneficial.

d. If the impact is found to be reasonable and beneficial, the applicant must implement reasonable measures to mitigate the cumulative impact of existing and proposed diversions on trust purposes, if the proposed use is to be approved.

In even briefer terms: the duty of state agencies, especially but not only CWRM, is to first protect public trust purposes before allocating any water to a private, commercial use. Moreover, it is the duty of the agency to require that the proposed private commercial user justify their needs and uses. It is not the duty of the agency or trust beneficiaries to justify what their needs are— because their core presumption is supposed to be water for "public use, access, enjoyment, and resource protection."

THE RECORD OF CWRM ON APPEAL

As has been discussed briefly above, CWRM has largely failed to protect public trust uses of water in their decisionmaking, and this observation has been vindicated repeatedly when their decisions were appealed. The chart on the next two pages summarizes the nine times CWRM decisions have been appealed to the Hawaiʻi Supreme Court (HSC) as well as the Intermediate Court of Appeals (ISC), and what the issues and outcomes have been.

CASE	ISSUE	CWRM DECISION	COURT DECISION
Ko'olau Ag, 83 Hawai'i 484, 927 P.2d 1367 (1996)	The Sierra Club petitioned for water management areas (WMAs) on O'ahu.	At their May 5, 1992 hearing, CWRM voted to designate the five aquifers as WMAs. Ko'olau Ag., a commercial water user, appealed.	**HSC upheld** CWRM: "a WMA designation is not judicially reviewable," but a decision to *not* designate may be.
Waiāhole I, 94 Hawai'i, 97, 9 P.3d 409 (2000)	Windward groups petitioned to return water to windward streams that had been diverted to leeward O'ahu for nearly a century.	In December 1997 after a contested case hearing (CCH), CWRM permitted over half the water for ditches and released the "surplus" to two of three windward streams under increased interim instream flow standards (IIFS).	**HSC reversed** because: (1) The new IIFS were not shown to be sufficient for instream uses; (2) "Public Trust" uses are supposed to have priority over private commercial water use; (3) the "precautionary principle" requires protection when science is uncertain.
Waiāhole II, 105 Hawai'i 1, 93 P.3d 643 (2004)	The Agricultural Development Corp. (ADC) and other commercial users sought water use permits (WUPs) for agricultural uses and ditch system losses.	CWRM ruled: (1) IIFS could be half their natural flow because anciently ditches could not divert more than half of streams; (2) Economic impacts on leeward users made groundwater use impracticable; (3) ADC was granted a WUP for system losses.	**HSC reversed** because: (1) CWRM did not show restoring half of stream flow would protect instream uses; (2) economic viability of diversions was not adequate grounds for its decision in light of public trust purposes; (3) ADC's 1.5 mgd losses did not comply with WUP conditions.
Wai'ola, 103 Hawai'i 401, 83 P.3d 664 (2004)	Wai'ola, a Moloka'i Ranch (MR) subsidiary, sought a WUP for development.	Practitioners, the Department of Hawaiian Home Lands (DHHL) and others opposed the WUP. After holding a CCH, CWRM issued Wai'ola an "interim" WUP.	**HSC vacated** the WUP because: (1) CWRM did not protect DHHL's and traditional/ customary rights; (2) Wai'ola had the burden of showing how it would not affect these rights.

(continued)

CASE	ISSUE	CWRM DECISION	COURT DECISION
Kukui, 116 Hawai'i 481, 174 P.3d 320 (2007).	Kukui Moloka'i, Inc. (KMI), a different MR subsidiary, applied for a WUP in a different aquifer than in **Wai'ola**.	In a CCH, DHHL argued water for homesteaders was a public trust use and pumping nearby could affect their reservations. Hawaiian practitioners argued groundwater removal would impact near shore traditional and customary practices. CWRM granted a WUP.	**HSC reversed** CWRM's decision because: (1) DHHL's water reservation was a public trust purpose; (2) KMI had not been burdened with showing an absence of alternatives; (3) CWRM impermissibly placed the burden on DHHL to show how Kukui would impair water quality.
Waiāhole III, 130 Hawai'i 346, 310 P.3d 1047 (App. 2010) (mem.)	Central/leeward users including Pu'u Makakilo, Inc. (PMI) sought WUPs.	Jul. 2006: CWRM granted water to central/leeward users. Windward community groups appealed to the ICA.	**ICA vacated** PMI's WUP because CWRM refused to consider evidence that PMI did not need all water applied for in its WUP.
Nā Wai 'Ehā, 128 Hawai'i 228, 287 P.3d 129 (2012)	Maui community groups petitioned to amend the IIFS for the streams of Nā Wai 'Ehā for instream uses and kalo cultivation.	From 2007–2008, a CCH was held on Hui o Nā Wai 'Ehā's IIFS petition, resulting in a proposed restoration of 34.5 mgd by a hearings officer. CWRM instead chose to limit restoration to only two of the four streams.	**HSC overturned** CWRM's decision for: (1) failing to consider impacts on and protections for practices; (2) incompletely analyzing instream uses; (3) miscalculating alternative water sources, user company's acreage and reasonable system losses.
Nā Moku Aupuni o Ko'olau Hui, 128 Hawai'i 497, 291 P.3d 395 (Haw. App. 2012) (mem.)	A community group petitioned CWRM to amend the IIFS for 27 East Maui streams diverted for Central Maui agriculture.	CWRM amended IIFSs for 8 streams. Oct. 2010: CWRM denied Nā Moku's petition for a CCH on its IIFS petition on the basis that Nā Moku had no "legal" right to a CCH. Nā Moku appealed to the ICA.	**ICA reversed** CWRM's CCH denial. Nā Moku members exercised legally protected traditional and customary practices, including kalo cultivation. CWRM's IIFS decisions on Nā Moku's members' right merited a CCH.
Kukui II, No. SCOT-17-0000184 (2018)	Remand of the **Kukui** case.	CWRM dismissed the **Kukui** remand, at the urging of DHHL and OHA; MR appealed.	**HSC upheld** CWRM: The Commission did not err in finding MR had made a clear and unambiguous waiver.

CWRM Attempts to Punish Public Trust Users and Advocates

As discussed previously in this chapter, the duties of the state of Hawai'i toward the water resources trust, primarily fulfilled CWRM, have been clearly summarized by Hawai'i appellate Courts in the *Kaua'i Springs* case. That case itself was based heavily on the nine cases listed in the table above. These duties can be easily summarized: the state has an obligation to primarily protect water as a resource, and to protect public trust uses of water; the duty "to obtain maximum beneficial use of the waters of the State" (HRS §174C-2(c)) can only be achieved by *first* protecting the resource and allowing for public trust uses, and then only allowing private commercial uses after they have been subjected to a high level of scrutiny.

While it has taken the courts over two decades to fully assemble this guidance, what is striking in the legal history recounted above is the consistency of CWRM's failure at the appellate level. However, determining fault for this consistent failure is challenging, as the responsibilities for code implementation are diffuse. Every Governor has a duty to appoint qualified commissioners, and the state Senate has kuleana to properly vet Commissioners in the advice and consent process. The Commissioners themselves have a duty (and swear an oath)[20] to faithfully implement the constitution and code. The CWRM professional staff is led by a Deputy Director who is to be appointed by the Commission, and that person leads a staff of civil service and other employees; the Deputy and their staff have the day to day duty to implement the code, and in practice have a great deal of discretion in so doing. Success and failure are ultimately shared by all these entities and individuals.

While specific fault for any individual policy failure (as measured by a court reversal) is difficult to determine, what can be observed is that some non-appealed actions of the CWRM have shown a distinct staff bias against public trust users and for private commercial users. This can be especially observed in the enforcement actions brought (and not brought) to the CWRM itself for action.

In general, it is not common for the CWRM staff to bring enforcement actions to the CWRM; monthly agendas are dominated by informational reporting and granting of Water Use Permits in WMAs.[21] Even open and notorious violations of the water code have not been brought up for action. A key example is that of Molokai Ranch—an entity who has lost two of the nine appellate cases cited in the table above. Molokai Ranch continues as of this writing to pump water from its Well 17 in the Kualapuʻu Aquifer on Molokai. Despite designation as a WMA on July 15, 1992, and having no water use permit for Well 17 at all, the Ranch continues to pump and deliver hundreds of thousands of gallons of water a day across the island for largely private commercial uses. The pumping of water without a permit is punishable by a fine of not more than $5,000 for each violation, and the code also specifies that "For a continuing offense, each day during which the offense is committed is a separate Violation." (HRS §174C-15(b)). Yet the CWRM staff have never proposed even a token fine against the Ranch; even one year's worth of violations would equate to a $1,825,000 penalty.

CWRM staff have, however, at times, been aggressive at proposing fines against public trust water users. One of the most recent and controversial instances is located in the Nā Wai ʻEhā side of West Maui. On August 16, 2016 the CWRM took up a staff proposal to fine two kalo farmers $4,500 for putting a pipe into a stream without an issued permit, in order to exercise their traditional and customary rights. The kalo farmers in this case, John and Rose Marie Duey, had also been community leaders of a group called Hui o Nā Wai ʻEhā, calling for the CWRM to enforce the water code against private commercial water users who had been dewatering streams across Maui for decades.

The staff submittal, signed by then Deputy Director Jeff Pearson,[22] alleged that the violation consisted of "Approximately 170-feet of six-inch Driscoll pipe connected to 630-feet of six-inch PVC pipe (Exhibit 2). The diversion, installed after 2001, diverts about 26,600 gpd [gallons per day] of water for domestic uses and agriculture consisting of banana (0.1 acres), breadfruit (0.06 acres), native plants (0.7 acres), and taro (1.0 acre) while returning 22,000 gpd back to the stream. No Stream Diversion Works Permit is on file with the Commission."[23]

In other words, the violation was a diversion which had a net reduction of 4,600 gpd in the flow of the stream. It is notable that it was due to the efforts of the Dueys, over a decade, that the CWRM increased the Interim Instream Flow Standard in the river just above this area from zero gpd to ten million gpd.

The seventeen page staff submittal and additional exhibits, recounted certain times in which the Dueys had applied for permits for this stream diversion and some correspondence from CWRM to the Dueys regarding their application. The $4,500 fine was proposed in part, as noted on page 14 of the submittal, because "Hui o Nā Wai ʻEhā is a party in numerous proceedings before the Commission. Mr. Duey, as President of the Hui, is well aware of Water Code requirements regarding permit requirements in Water Management and non-Water Management Areas."

However, once West Maui and other community members learned of the proposed fine, the plans for Mr. Pearson to smoothly assess a fine against the Dueys with CWRM approval ran into strong resistance. Over five hundred individual pieces of testimony were estimated to have been submitted to the CWRM in opposition to the proposed fine,[24] and sixteen individuals provided additional oral testimony that took over three hours to deliver. Rose Marie Duey and her daughter both testified clarifying that CWRM staff had, years before, orally stated that no permit was needed. They also noted that despite that oral assurance they had consistently responded to CWRM recent staff concerns, though many of these responses were omitted in the staff submittal.[25]

Some submitted testimony called out the apparent divide in approaches taken against the Dueys when compared to to other individual homeowners. One cited case regarded the owner of a lot in the gated Kukiʻo subdivision on Hawaiʻi Island; he drilled and began pumping a well, without a well construction and pump installation permit. The pump installation contractor was unlicensed. The well was used for landscape irrigation in an exclusive, gated subdivision. For a May 16, 2012 CWRM meeting, staff proposed fining a Mr. Pataye $400, and $500 each for the well construction and pump installation contractor.[26] In the end the Commission dropped the fine to only $400 against the landowner. Additionally, CWRM staff did not discover the violation as a result of an active investgation. Rather, the only reason that Mr. Pataye began to seek a permit for the well was that he was selling the property, at which time he supposedly discovered a permit was needed for the well. The home was sold fifteen days later for $11,000,000." CWRM enforcement proceedings were a mere inconvenience in this situation.

Other testimony went into greater detail regarding the apparent targeting of the Dueys for their activism, and the direct contrast of this proposed action to what had happened on the same river when diversions were large and corporate. The longest, most detailed testimony came from a Kanaka Maoli kalo farmer and stream restoration advocate Hōkūao Pellegrino. As included in the minutes:[27]

Hokuao Pellegrino submitted testimony on behalf of the Nā Wai ʻEhā Board Members. Hui of Nā Wai ʻEhā is a Maui-based non-profit organization that advocates for the protection and restoration of Maui's streams and water resources in Nā Wai ʻEhā. It has an engaged membership and support of over 4,000 people, comprised of kuleana kalo farmers, fisherman, native Hawaiian cultural practitioners, educators, agricultural businesses, community leaders, environmental advocates, policy makers, scientists, and concerned Maui residents. Established 13 years ago, Hui o Nā Wai ʻEhā has been successful in providing significant positive solutions to injustices surrounding water rights issues that have affected the Nā Wai ʻEhā community and streams since 1862. A major and historic example of the organization's success was in the 2010 and 2014 restoration of stream flow to all four of Nā Wai ʻEhā streams, three of which are currently flowing mauka to makai. The benefits of restoring stream flow have been tremendously positive within the community and it is continuing its efforts in seeking further justice for its streams. For the first time in over 150 years, the people of Maui can once again enjoy thriving and truly honor the cultural significance of Nā Wai ʻEhā.

None of this would have been possible without the leadership of the Duey ʻohana and Uncle John Duey who is one of the founding members of Hui o Nā Wai ʻEhā. He and his ʻohana have inspired many in the community to engage in one of Maui's most important issues, wai. Historically, Nā Wai ʻEhā was the largest contiguous kalo growing region in all of Hawaiʻi. The water resources of these four great streams sustained a large Hawaiian population and was the royal seat for Maui aliʻi. Two of the largest ʻauwai systems in Hawaiʻi are located within Nā Wai ʻEhā, Wailuku River in particular, and were named in honor of Maui aliʻi (Kama ʻAuwai and Kalani ʻAuwai).

Following the arrival of missionaries and other newcomers, Nā Wai ʻEhā became a focal point for the establishment of the sugar plantation industry in Hawaiʻi, mainly due to its vast water resources and fertile soil. The ripple effect of commodifying and capitalizing on water has led to environmental, cultural and agricultural challenges. Today, Nā Wai ʻEhā provides more than half of Maui's domestic and agricultural water needs and, unfortunately, scientific data has shown signs of distress. Therefore, the protection of the water resources in this region is extremely important and is the impetus behind why the Dueys, along with many others in the community, understood the need to advocate for a resource that cannot speak for itself.

The Commission on Water Resource Management staff has identified and targeted the Duey ʻohana, a native Hawaiian family, exercising its traditional and customary rights by growing kalo. Yet, this same Commission indicates that its responsibility is to uphold the public trust, including supporting rights of native Hawaiian kalo farmers and cultural practitioners protected by the public trust. This selective enforcement is an assault on traditional and customary practices of native Hawaiians. The Duey ʻohana has done nothing but provide positive support for the streams, Maui community and simple justice. In addition, they have worked with Commission staff and staff has relied on Uncle John Duey and his ʻohana in guiding them on best practices and understanding the characteristics of the four great streams.

The Board strongly opposes any and all fines on the Duey ʻohana, a native Hawaiian family with strong genealogical ties to Maui and ʻIao Valley where they reside and cultivate kalo.

The State Water Code states clearly that traditional and customary rights shall not be diminished or extinguished by failure to apply for or to receive a permit. Proposing a $4,500 fine against kalo farmers on kuleana land for failing to receive a permit is a diminishment of their rights.

Equally, important, the Commission does not consistently propose fines against known violators of the Water Code. Five examples and evidence following the Nā Wai ʻEhā IIFS Agreement in which the Commission staff has clearly not chosen nor conducted any enforcement when it was more than deserved:

1. On April 17, 2014, the Commission approved the Hearings Officer's recommendation on the mediated agreement by Hui o Nā Wai ʻEhā, OHA, Maui Tomorrow Foundation, Wailuku Water Company (WWC) and Hawaiian Commercial & Sugar (HC&S) Company and the stipulation of the mediator's report of joint proposed findings of fact, conclusions of law and decision and order. It took WWC over 6 months to implement the IIFS when in fact it described in their implementation plan that it would take anywhere between 6 weeks to 2 months to conduct and finalize the initial work. Numerous correspondences between former Chair Aila and WWC questioned WWC about its restoration plans and timeline dated August 13, 2014. Finally, on October 13, 2014, WWC implemented what was supposed to be a release of 2.9 mgd to Waikapu Stream and 10 mgd to Wailuku River. At both sites, WWC failed to comply, releasing less than the approved amounts. Wailuku River was restored just a little more than half of what was supposed to have been released (5.47 mgd rather than 10 mgd). The Maui community cried foul and rallied to bring attention to the Commission, which should have taken action immediately, especially when WWC had almost half

a year to get this right. Why did the Commission staff not rectify this issue and enforce the law?

2. On both Waikapu Stream and Wailuku River the Commission staff was to ensure that there was connectivity of all points in the stream for biological habitat and that the streams were not diverted 100% at the diversion point. For example, on October 13, 2014, WWC was diverting 100% of the Wailuku River at the 'Iao / Maniania / Waikapu diversion intake and 900 feet below, released the 10 mgd and leaving a 1,000 foot stretch of stream dead. After almost 2 months, outcry from the Maui community, and 2 massive rallies, WWC installed a small metal plate across a small portion of the diversion which they along with the Commission approved as resolving the connectivity issue. In regards to Waikapu, WWC, has not yet notched the South Waikapu intake to ensure biological connectivity and comply with the Commission's implementation plan. There was still a dead stream between the South Waikapu intake and the Kalena Tributary. If it were not for the pressure from the community members of Maui, it would not have come this far. Yet the Commission continues to fail the community on compliance issues.

3. Following the October 13, 2014 IIFS releases for Waikapu Stream and Wailuku River, HC&S, which manages the Spreckels Ditch intake on the Wailuku River, would capture 100% of the 10 mgd released flow and about 100 feet below, would release a portion of that 10 mgd. There were constant communications back and forth with Hui o Na Wai 'Ehā, Commission staff and HC&S and yet nothing was rectified for many months. Once again, the Maui community cried foul and conducted 2 large rallies to bring attention to this issue. Uncle John Duey played a pivotal role by engaging in discussions with Garret Hew of HC&S to hold up its end of the deal for the IIFS. Where was the Commission staff? It was not until March 2015 that HC&S sealed a portion of the Spreckels intake to ensure that there was connectivity of stream flow and that the stream was flowing all the way to the river mouth / ocean. Again, it is clear that the Commission did not impose any fines on HC&S for taking 5 months to weld 2 plates over the Spreckels intake and divert more water than it should have.

4. According the recent Commission monitoring reports on Waikapu Stream, from January 15 through April 5, 2016, WWC has not complied to the 2.9 mgd IIFS and has released well below that amount. Hui

o Nā Wai ʻEhā has no knowledge whether the Commission staff has addressed this issue nor whether it has imposed any warnings or fines against WWC for clearly not being within compliance of the law.

5. Based on what the Commission staff provides via its stream monitoring page online, it only has IIFS compliance data for Waikapu, Wailuku and Waiehu Sreams, Waiehu being somewhat confusing since the Commission staff states that the IIFS is 1.8 mgd yet it is supposed to be 2.5 mgd. In regards to Waihee Stream, no data has been provided as to whether WWC is complying since the IIFS was established in 2010. In order to ensure that WWC is complying and following the law, would it behoove the Commission staff to monitor sites on all streams and consistently report data online so that it is clear and transparent that the law is being followed? Furthermore, there has been no data from the Commission on the IIFS for the Wailuku River in 2016, and now, 8 months later, it is still without any knowledge as to whether WWC is complying or not. The Commission staff can pay closer attention to these kinds of details especially when there is a great negative impact on water flow in the streams. Because staff has mentioned that these pressure transducers are costly, perhaps financial assistance can be sought from WWC, the main diverter of all 4 streams and source of non-compliance issues. These inconsistencies and the resulting inability of the Commission staff to monitor and report the streams manifests itself as a clear breakdown of its responsibility to uphold the law and public trust.

To date Commission staff has never proposed a fine against WWC. This is disturbing and it obviously makes the public believe the Dueys' case suggests selective enforcement. The Commission staff has gone to great lengths on a case against the Duey ʻohana who are consistently and historically excellent examples of those who uphold the public trust and exercise their traditional and customary rights. In effect, the Commission should support rather than cite the Duey ʻohana. Hui o Nā Wai ʻEhā believes that the Commission has failed to protect the traditional and customary rights of Hawaiians, uphold the public trust doctrine and follow through on enforcing the law on those who negatively affect Hawaii's streams, aquatic life, nearshore fisheries, aquifers and traditional and customary rights of kalo farmers. The Commission staff proposes to actively target native Hawaiians who exercise their cultural practices. Clearly Hui o Nā Wai ʻEhā believes that the Commission has created an unlevel playing field. The Commission should reject the proposed fine and issue the Duey ʻohana a permit and enforce real and serious issues.

Following the extensive testimony of Mr. Pellegrino as well as subsequent testifiers, in this instance the Commission overruled the staff and wholly rejected the fine. They went on to approve a new permit for the Duey ʻohana to divert 410,000 gpd, the amount that would allow full kalo production on their family lands.

The Commission also appended to the motion a request that the staff prepare for CWRM approval an expedited permitting process for traditional and customary uses of water. As of January 2020, the staff has yet to present any briefing or proposal in response to the request. They did, however, at their May 15, 2018 meeting approve a staff recommended $1,500 fine against a large landowner who constructed a new dam and spillway across Olowalu stream and diverting over 2 mgd without authorization.[28]

The Commissioners' last-minute correction of its staff's plan to penalize the Dueys was hard won. The correction is owed to the efforts of Maui community members, many who had to fly to Oʻahu and take hours away from work and family, who called attention to the very wrong proposal to impose fines on Hawaiian cultural practitioners. The system should not be one in which the community is taxed this way by the very agencies that are supposed to affirmatively protect their rights.

Chapter 5

ONGOING ISSUES WITH INTERIM INSTREAM FLOW STANDARDS

If a stream was meant to be dry it wouldn't be a stream.

—Keone Downing, Board member, State of Hawai'i Board
of Land and Natural Resources, December 7, 2017.

On December 7, 2017, the Board of Land and Natural Resources (BLNR) considered and renewed revocable permit no. S-7340 to the Kaua'i Island Utilities Cooperative (KIUC) for surface waters from the North Fork of the Wailua River and Waikoko Stream in the Puna moku of Kaua'i. KIUC's diversions fully dewatered these streams for significant stretches, in order to run small hydropower operations. The temporary permits had been renewed for approximately thirteen years by December 2017. Community groups, including Hui Ho'opulapula Nā Wai o Puna and Kia'i Wai o Wai'ale'ale, and Kānaka Maoli who sought stream water restoration for lo'i kalo practices, long complained about KIUC's operations. Many of these community members testified at the meeting, but a majority of board members allowed the permit to be renewed yet again.[1]

In parallel proceedings, the Commission on Water Resource Management (CWRM) was considering amended Interim Instream Flow Standards (IIFSs) in several streams across Hawai'i, including West Maui's Ukumehame, Olowalu, Kaua'ula, Launiupoko, Kanahā, Kahoma, Honokōwai, Honolua, and Honokō-hau streams. Unlike the revocable permit renewal and water-leasing process before BLNR, IIFS proceedings are directly concerned with ecological and instream uses of surface waters. CWRM sets the IIFSs after considering these uses and setting a flow standard intended to protect instream public trust uses of water.

"Do they mean we get more or less water?" asked a community member with generational ties to Olowalu. Her question arose in reference to the technical Instream Flow Standard Assessment Report for the newly proposed amended IIFSs, and was concerned about whether the IIFSs would mean that her community in Ukumehame, Olowalu, Kauaʻula, and Launiupoko would see restored consistent stream flow. The answer is "more, in theory" especially in regard to Kauaʻula stream. As of this writing, Launiupoko Irrigation Company continues to divert more streamwater than is permitted under the amended IIFSs. Her question cogently comments on the effectiveness of the processes through which CWRM manages water.

This chapter tracks the community response to, and engagement with, the Water Commission's efforts to amend IIFSs in West Maui, which currently promises to restore a significant amount of water to most West Maui streams. West Maui has a Hawaiian history of highly curated agriculture based on careful management of surface water resources, which was disrupted in various ways by settler colonialism. Although the usual story of this disruption focuses on plantation agribusiness's diversion of the streams for sugar monocrops, that diversion was only the most direct impact on West Maui streams. The decimation of the population through disease, displacement of native tenants from kuleana lands, famine, and environmental change, and even generational shifts in which a postwar generation of Hawaiians sought a way of life away from subsistence agriculture were all intertwined with the dewatering of streams, practices, and landscapes. This chapter focuses on the history of surface water resource distribution and current restoration efforts, but with an emphasis on the interests of a new generation that is seeking to return to kuleana lands and restore streamflow in order to farm kalo.

The story of Kānaka Maoli in West Maui reopening loʻi and seeking stream restoration is not a one dimensional story of returning to the land but a chronicle of navigating disinvestment from traditional structures of mālama ʻāina. This means defending claims to kuleana lands, fighting for restoration of streams, and negotiating for access to these lands, in addition to the work of actually farming loʻi. The IIFS amendment process does not incorporate all of these efforts, but is an important arena in which they are made more visible. All of these—kuleana lands, water rights, and rights of way—are specifically and specially protected under Article XII, §7 of the Hawaiʻi Constitution and Section 7-1 of the Hawaii Revised Statutes (HRS). Because of this when the disinvestment of traditional structures of mālama ʻāina starts to become visible, the disconnect between state law and on-the-ground practice becomes glaring.

Kekai Keahi, a West Maui community member and teacher who closely follows many of CWRM's processes, noted the blatant disjuncture between Hawaiian water rights and the reality of West Maui water resource distribution. Keahi testified to CWRM on proposed IIFS amendments:

> I look at the laws, and it's pretty cut and dry and clear, somewhat. I under-stand you guys gotta do your studies to validate uses and stuff, but tradi-tional and customary usage, appurtenant, the whole gamut, from water in the stream for instream life... Looking at that, and then I look at the river in Lahaina, except for Ukumehame after they went stop the plantation, I looking at the rivers in Lahaina. Ho, 100 percent dry. So where was the pro-tection, where's this protection, for all these things that is stated in the law and that's supposed to be protected? Nobody protecting ʼem.[2]

Keahi and his family have lived in the area for generations and have a kuleana parcel in Kanahā valley. He often speaks out at community meetings, sharing the collective memory of West Maui's dry streams and the stark contrast of that memory with the strong legal protections for instream use, including and especially for native Hawaiian traditional and customary practices. Those legal protections for instream uses, while only starting to be implemented in this area, have nonetheless already been in statute for four decades. We begin by reviewing one aspect of managing surface water—the determination of "certified" existing uses—that was meant to set the stage for meaningful IIFS and IFS regulations.

CWRM "CERTIFICATION" OF WATER USES

Chapter 4 discussed the dilemmas faced by the state when it wanted to adopt a regulatory scheme that managed water in the islands that would not violate the principles of the *McBryde* cases—that the state was the trustee of water resources—but would also not raise the taking issues from the subsequent *Robinson* suits. One of the challenges this raised was to document and eval-uate existing uses of water after passage of the code. Thus, under the code as adopted, all water users would have to declare their water uses and then have them "certified." From 1988 to 1989, approximately 2,600 firms and individuals filed 7,600 forms declaring their water use. CWRM compiled these into two volumes available on their website.[3]

Many others, however, did not register or declare their uses, and were likely unaware of the requirement. Of those who did declare their uses, CWRM often did not follow through on a certification process for their uses. Very few declared uses were able to be certified, which meant that their water uses are not presumptively "reasonable and beneficial" under the Water Code.

Certification of water uses was meant to apply in all areas regardless of whether they were designated as water management areas. Certification was intended as a means of accounting for historic and ongoing water uses. HRS §174C-27, titled "Issuance of Certificate," set forth the process for certification:

1. When a declaration has been filed in accordance with this section and the commission has determined that the use declared is a reasonable, beneficial use, the commission shall issue a certificate describing the use. The certificate shall be deemed to constitute a description of the use declared. With respect to certificates for water use, the confirmed usage shall be recognized by the commission in resolving claims relating to existing water rights and uses including appurtenant rights, riparian and correlative use.

2. The commission shall hold a hearing upon the request of any person adversely affected by the certification or the refusal to certify any water use.

3. Whenever a certified use of water is terminated, the owner of the certificate shall file a report with the commission, providing all information prescribed in the rules of the commission.

However, as mentioned, many did not register or declare their surface water uses. This hampered the State's process of setting IIFSs and IFSs, which was meant to follow certification.

IIFS in West Maui, 1988–2018

The CWRM failure to certify uses properly did not result in staff being granted an extension of time in setting IIFSs. Thus, while CWRM staff lacked even the most basic information on existing flows and diversions, they needed to act to recommend IIFS for West Maui. Unfortunately, they and the appointed CWRM members chose to act in a manner that privileged existing diverters, whether or not those uses had been certified.

As noted and is widely known, Lahaina gets little annual rainfall. Instead, it relies on stream water originating deep within the West Maui Mountains. "[O]rographic precipitation (warm ocean air moving up the steep mountains into cooler altitudes) is created in the center of the mountains and valleys and produces some of the highest average daily precipitation in the world at Puʻu Kukui."[4] The dearth of rainfall across Lahaina is thus mitigated by the concentration of upper-level supply to its mountainous watershed. The concentration of water in these mauka areas, however, has also allowed especially large landowners to exert power over Lahaina's communities through surface water source control.

The Water Commission's IIFS process was meant to address the public's interest in water resource allocation. In the context of Lahaina's unique hydrologic conditions, the IIFS process is even more important for safeguarding non-commercial and non-municipal public interests and even more fraught. As the plantations have continued to divert water but not used it to irrigate fields, the impacts on West Maui communities have gone beyond immediate instream impacts. The closure of Pioneer Mill meant that the fields were no longer irrigated; during droughts, the fallow fields have caused dust storms and loss of topsoils from wind erosion on the western slopes of West Maui at Lahaina and Olowalu.[5]

The Water Commission is tasked with protecting seven recognized instream water uses: (1) maintenance of fish and wildlife habitat; (2) outdoor recreational activities, (3) maintenance of ecosystems, (4) aesthetic values such as waterfalls and scenic waterways, (5) maintenance of water quality, (6) the conveyance of irrigation and domestic water supplies, and (7) the protection of traditional and customary Hawaiian rights. Large-scale ditches and diversions of West Maui streams challenge protected in-stream uses of surface water, yet such ditches and diversions continue well beyond the plantation era.

As noted, the principal tool used by CWRM to protect instream uses is the establishment of "instream flow standards" (IFSs), which characterize the amount of flow necessary to protect the public interest in stream water balanced against existing and potential water developments.[6] On October 19, 1988, IIFSs were established for West Maui. These IIFSs were not quantitative characterizations, but rather described the status quo of water flowing in the streams on the effective date of the IIFS, "as that flow may naturally vary throughout the year and from year to year without further amounts of water being diverted offstream through new or expanded diversions, and under stream conditions existing on the effective date of the standard."[7]

Specifically, CWRM's current IIFS for West Maui and its procedure for amending that standard is governed by rule. HAR §13-169-48 provides:

The Interim Instream Flow Standard for all streams on West Maui, as adopted by the commission on water resource management on October 19, 1988, shall be that amount of water flowing in each stream on the effective date of this standard, and as that flow may naturally vary throughout the year and from year to year without further amounts of water being diverted offstream through new or expanded diversions, and under the stream conditions existing on the effective date of the standard, except as may be modified by the following conditions:

1. Based upon additional information or a compelling public need, a person may petition the commission on water resource management to amend the standard to allow future diversion, restoration, or other utilization of any streamflow.

2. The commission reserves its authority to modify the standard or establish new standards, including area-wide or stream-by-stream standards, based upon supplemental or additional information.

3. In any proceeding to enforce the instream flow standard, the commission, its delegated hearing officer, or a judicial officer may abate the enforcement proceeding if, under the circumstances and weighing the importance with the importance of the present or potential uses of the stream's water for noninstream purposes (including the economic impact of restricting such uses), the enforcement of the instream flow standard would:

   a. Create a substantial hardship on a use existing on the effective date of this standard; or

   b. Impermissibly burden a right, title, or interest arising under law.

4. Projects under construction or projects that have secured all discretionary permits required by appropriate federal, state, or county agencies prior to July 1, 1987 shall not be affected by the standard.

This rule provides that any person may petition for IIFS amendments upon additional information or a compelling need, which has generally meant bringing forward information about stream diversion impacts on ecosystems and traditional loʻi kalo practices. It also provides for those showing a substantial hardship consequent to IIFS amendment to raise those concerns in a proceeding to enforce the IIFS.

If it is not clear from the rule how much water was set aside for West Maui streams, it is perhaps because the truth was awful. Because the IIFSs for West Maui streams were set to be "that amount of water flowing in each stream," along with the 1988 effective date, meant that IIFSs largely reflected ongoing diversions by large landowners. Pioneer Mill was still operating in 1988, and other large landowners already had their diversions in place as of that date. Pioneer Mill Co. did not stop its sugar cultivation operations until 1999. Effectively, CWRM's rule required, ironically, that the IIFS meant to protect instream water was zero—that no water be present in many streams.

This regulatory approval of complete diversion of streams has meant that in West Maui and across Hawaiʻi, following the closure of plantations, there have been increasingly incongruous situations. By rule, an assumption was made that all waters in a stream were being diverted by uses existing at the code's passage, thus leaving nothing for public trust uses. On the ground, however, without the presence of sugar as the Islands' thirstiest crop, there was a need to cease or modify diversions or justify—in actuality or appearance—their continued existence. This justification was provided operationally and by university academics.

Diversion Operator and Academic Support for Non-protective IIFSs

After the demise of the sugar plantation, less water was needed to irrigate fields. However, large landowners had every incentive to keep IIFSs at their established level rather than allowing them to be amended to reflect actual water needs of stream ecosystems and kalo farmers. Across Hawaiʻi, historic water diverters turned to the derided practice of "water banking," which is more accurately described as "water wasting." To justify their continued level of diversions and avoid amended, increased IIFSs, these diverters employed various tactics. In central Oʻahu, after the closure of Oʻahu Sugar, water from the diverted windward streams of Kahana, Hakipuʻu, Waikāne and Waiāhole continued to be fully withdrawn from streams and then dumped in dry leeward gulches. In Nā Wai ʻEhā, the Wailuku Water Company took to dumping water at night into fallow "sand fields," which were considered too thirsty to irrigate during the height of sugar in Hawaiʻi.[8]

In their study of optimal allocations of ground and surface water, economists James Moncur, Jim Roumasset, and Rodney Smith obliquely referenced this but characterized it as a failing of the water code. "The code does not permit, let alone encourage, temporary reallocations such as might be undertaken under water 'banking' or 'leasing' arrangements [citation omitted.] Similarly, there is no incentive to install bulkheads, revive groundwater storage capacity, and rationalize its use. Water allocated to instream flow standards, once established, will be extremely difficult to transfer."[9] In the view of Moncur et al., providing a means whereby accumulated water rights could be leased or banked would better accord with the economic rationale that prevents water diverters from merely releasing that water back into its native ecosystems and streams.

Such an argument cogently points to a failure in the architecture of the State Water Code from the point of view of a capitalist actor. However, it fails to consider that a reduction of diversions and a return of waters to the streams was anticipated upon the demise of sugar plantations. Regardless of the legislature's intentions, amendment of IIFSs has proven contentious and water "banking" (i.e., wasting) continues to occur in West Maui. Much work is left to be done to restore West Maui's streams and the communities they support.

SCIENTIFIC BACKGROUND ON WEST MAUI STREAM FLOWS

One manner in which the state and other actors have attempted to address some of the contentiousness associated with setting IIFSs has been to bring additional scientific research to bear on existing flows. In West Maui, this was in particular stimulated by an initial attempt by Maui Land and Pine (MLP) to address long-standing conflict over their diversions.

MLP filed a petition to establish amended IFSs or IIFSs for Honokōhau and Honolua streams in August 2006.[10] MLP sought to have the instream flow standards account for diversions existing on October 19, 1988, with the clarification that 1.5 cubic feet per second (cfs) of continuous flow is returned to the stream at the "taro gate" near elevation of 400 feet and a flow of 1.5 cfs is returned to the stream from Aotaki Gate at elevation 835 feet as of 2004.[11]

From its headwaters at Puʻu Kukui, Honokōhau stream descends for 9.5 miles into Honokōhau Bay and drains into a watershed area of approximately eight miles. Honokōhau is one of West Maui's three perennial streams. MLP admitted that the release of this portion of the diverted stream had significant positive impact on native stream biota.[12] In 2011, CWRM entered into a $648,000 cooperative agreement with the United States Geological Survey (USGS) to conduct a low-flow study for ten streams in West Maui, noting MLP's IIFS petition as background to the request.[13] The study was to take place over a three-year span. As in other areas of Hawaiʻi, however, study of West Maui streams was handicapped by a lack of gauges to provide needed flow information. In 2014, USGS finally published its Lahaina Stream low-flow study[14] of diversions that are used by the State Water Commission to regulate surface water use.

West Maui has ten stream valleys, from Honokōhau in the north to Ukumehame in the south. These valleys hold surface waters, including:

1. Honokōhau Stream
2. Honolua Stream
3. Pāpua Gulch (tributary to the Honolua stream)
4. Honokahua Stream
5. Mokupeʻa Gulch (tributary to Honokahua Stream)
6. Kahana Stream
7. Amalu and Kapāloa Streams (tributaries to Honokōwai Stream)
8. Wahikuli Gulch and tributary
9. Hāhākea Gulch (tributary to Wahikuli Gulch)
10. Kahoma Stream
11. Kanahā Stream (tributary to Kahoma Stream)
12. Kauaʻula Stream
13. Launiupoko Stream
14. Olowalu Stream
15. Ukumehame Gulch.

Of these, Honokōwai, Kahoma, Kanahā, Kauaʻula, Launiupoko, Olowalu, and Honokōhau Streams, and Ukumehame Gulch, have been diverted at the upper reaches. Without diversions, Honolua Stream, Kahoma Stream, and Kanahā Streams supported mauka-to-makai water flow between 80 to 95 percent of the time. Kauaʻula Stream, Olowalu Stream, and Ukumehame Gulch have water flowing in them at least 95 percent of the time.[15] Pāpua Gulch, Honokahua Stream and its tributary Mokupeʻa Gulch, Kahana Stream, and Wahikuli Gulch and its tributary Hāhākea Gulch are "ephemeral" streams, which means that they flow less than 50 percent of the time. The Wahikuli Ditch and a portion of the Honolua-Honokōhau Ditch systems are currently integrated into the MLP/PMIS, which is discussed as part of the State Department of Agriculture's agricultural water use and development plan (AWUDP), which is part of the Hawaiʻi Water Plan.

Honolua Stream was not reported as having been diverted in the USGS study area.[16] However, an abandoned intake structure is located at around the 800 ft. elevation mark. Between 1903 and 2004, this intake diverted approximately three million gallons of water daily into the Honokōhau Ditch. In 2004, MLP voluntarily closed the intake. While the diversion structure remains operational, the water flowing through it is currently returned downstream. MLP, however, has petitioned the Water Commission to amend its IIFSs for Honolua streams based on 2006 findings by its consultant, SWCA Environmental Consultants, that Honolua stream flow is intermittent. [17]

The 2014 USGS low-flow study was meant to provide peer-reviewed information that could be used by policy makers, including for the setting of IIFSs. Yet, as of the date of this writing, the Water Commission is overdue on its plans to adopt amended IIFSs for all West Maui streams. The lag time illustrates how scientific information alone is insufficient to allow CWRM to navigate the competing legal, cultural, and political dynamics that characterize water use across Hawaiʻi.

CWRM Efforts to Revise IIFSs in West Maui

The central role that IIFSs are supposed to play in the management of surface water and protection of public trust interests is difficult to overstate. In its historic *Waiāhole* decision, the Hawaiʻi Supreme Court concluded, "instream flow standards serve as the primary mechanism by which the [Water] Commission is to discharge its duty to protect and promote the entire range of public trust purposes dependent upon instream flows."[18]

This conclusion is borne out by the ample authority CWRM is afforded for stream water management under the Water Code. HRS § 174C-71 (1993) provides, "[t]he commission shall establish and administer a statewide instream use protection program." In furtherance of this mandate, the water code states CWRM "shall" "[e]stablish instream flow standards on a stream-by-stream basis whenever necessary to protect the public interest in the waters of the state," HRS § 174C-71(1); "[e]stablish interim instream flow standards," HRS § 174C-71(2); and "[e]stablish an instream flow program to protect, enhance, and reestablish, where practicable, beneficial instream uses of water," HRS § 174C-71(4); see also HRS § 174C-5(3) (1993) (same); HRS § 174C-31(i)(1) (Supp.1999) (requiring CWRM to establish "[a]n instream use and protection program for the surface watercourses in the area" within each hydrologic unit).

CWRM's IIFS amendment process is initiated by CWRM or a petition for the amendment. CWRM staff then conduct an inventory of best available information, and generally seek agency review and comments. In recent practice, staff have assembled this information into reports that are publicly available. Then, staff issue a public notice of a public fact-gathering meeting. CWRM staff then compile the information gathered and prepare a recommendation for IIFS amendment on which CWRM will vote.

For Lahaina's four southernmost streams: Ukumehame, Olowalu, Launi-upoko, and Kauaʻula, IIFS amendments were approved by CWRM on March 20, 2018. A significant number of the West Maui community members turned out for the hearing.[19] The following discusses testimony from the earlier Water Commission's December 6, 2017 "Public Fact Gathering Meeting" in Lahaina-luna Intermediate School.

Olowalu

Although there is a sizable stream bed and deep valley here, there is no visible evidence of wet taro cultivation, and the Hawaiian planters at Olowalu say that loʻi never existed in Launiupoko. It is possible that there may have been a few terraces on the level land at the base of the valley, but this is wholly arid land now and covered with dense brush.

—E. S. C. Handy.[20]

Olowalu is the largest and deepest valley on the southwest side of Maui and used to support extensive terraced cultivation. The lower ranges of terraces have been completely obliterated by cane fields; but just where the sugar cane ends and the valley begins there is a little spot where five Hawaiian families, all of them intermarried, raise several varieties of taro in flourishing wet patches. Some of it is sold, but most is pounded by hand for family poi. There are said to be abandoned terraces far up in Olowalu.[21]

Proposed IIFSs were 3.6 cubic feet per second (2.33 mgd) near altitudes of 130 feet, which would allow 3.36 mgd at the upper diversion and 2.65 mgd at the lower diversion, with accounting for system seepage losses of 0.71 mgd.[22] CWRM staff specifically noted that the proposed IIFS for Olowalu Stream would allow "Olowalu Water Company to meet their 0.196 mgd agricultural water demand and 0.141 mgd landscaping water demand at least 50 percent of the time."[23]

Rosemarie Duey, who also farms in Olowalu, spoke on behalf of the Olowalu Cultural Reserve, which leases 74 acres of land from [West Maui Land Company's] WMLC's Olowalu Elua Associates for kalo growing and other mahiʻai practices. Duey commented that 40 kuleana on 100 acres existed in Olowalu.

Frankie Caprioni, a resident of Olowalu, raised the important question of whether and how an amended IIFS would be enforced. Since 2008, complaints had been issued by community members against Olowalu Water Company's unauthorized alterations to the streambed.[24] Caprioni had earlier reported Olowalu Water Company's unpermitted diversions, which led to CWRM investigations into the matter. However, his citizen enforcement actions were also technically illegal because they involved trespassing onto Olowalu Water Company lands.

Kaua'ula and Launiupoko

Approved IIFS amendments returned a significant amount of water to Kaua'ula stream and triggered the ire of West Maui Land Company (WMLC). WMLC owns Launiupoko Irrigation Company (LIC), which delivers surface water to gated subdivisions and most kuleana in Kaua'ula Valley as well as farmers on Kamehameha Schools land. The Kaua'ula stream IIFS specified 0.4 mgd would be available for Kamehameha School's agricultural uses 100 percent of the time. The Launiupoko Irrigation Company supplies non-potable water to customers in the Kaua'ula and Launiupoko hydrologic units, while the Launiupoko Water Company supplies potable water to customers in the Kaua'ula and Launiupoko hydrologic units.[25]

Every stream has stories of its communities. U'ilani Kapu pointed out that WMLC was transferring water from Kaua'ula to Launiupoko. She testified, "Kau'aula water is for Kaua'ula, for all the kuleanas that live there. We have over, I would say, 50 to 75 people within that area now. All the families have come home, and we depend on this. We depend on it for our household. We depend on it for our farming."[26]

Charlie Palakiko, also a kalo farmer, hunter, and resident of Kaua'ula Valley and just below U'ilani Kapu's property, testified:

> There's water that's reaching the ocean right now in Kaua'ula, but it's from ... They're dumping it like maybe mid-way, not even mid-way. It traveled a lot. It took it 10 years for this thing to reach the ocean. Now we started in 2000. In 2001 we started cleaning the land, opening up our auwai, which is the Waimana auwai. That's the name of it. But we started at the 2000/2001. By 2002, I was putting water already into the ditch to run these patches. A few years later, we already were seeing 'o'opu in the stream, along with crayfish and clams, which were from the reservoir. Had prawns, everything in there. And even now after the 2016 storm, all the 'ōpae that was in the mountain all came down. So now I'm finding 'ōpae all below the diversion. And I've seen them in my auwai—they're probably in my patches; they're in the stream. So I'm saying there is life in that stream. I've been running, I'm talking years already, so basically all we gotta restore is a small section of dry stream to connectivity. You know? And there's life in there already.

…That's where you guys took…I know. Later on I figured it out, 1990 was the study, but this is what you guys going give to the Board. This right here, right? Here Board, read this; see if Kauaula is…you know? It's like you telling them no more nothing in there, when there is….[27]

Another Lahaina resident, Kanoelani Steward, also attested to native biota in West Maui streams. Steward testified:

> I'm currently working for The Nature Conservancy as an assistant marine coordinator in their Marine Conservation Fellowship Program, and in collaboration/partnership with the Division of Aquatic Resources, working with Uncle Skippy Hau over here. We've been collecting native fish and invertebrate data that includes all five species of ʻoʻopu, ʻōpae kuahiwi or kalaʻole, ʻōpae ʻoehaʻa, and hīhīwai, and hapawai. And we're doing this research to look at the presence and absence, and abundance of these species in the middle and upper regions of Ukumehame, Olowalu, Kauaʻula, Kahoma, and hopefully Honolua as well.[28]

In describing the Hawaiian families of Kauaʻula Valley, Kapali Keahi noted that they had been struggling against water diversions installed by Peter Martin for a long time. Martin established his West Maui Land Co. in the mid-1990s. "Water goes hand in hand with land issue," Keahi said.[29] The conflict is not only with distribution but also with efforts to educate new developers, including Martin, on water laws in Hawaiʻi, which emanate in large part from Hawaiian Kingdom law. As of this writing, Martin's Launiupoko Irrigation Company continues to divert Kauaʻula stream at levels that do not comply with IIFSs.

Kahana Kuleana and Streams

Kai Keahi also testified at the Water Commission's December 6, 2017 meeting. Kai Keahi provided perhaps the most comprehensive overview in his testimony on the renaissance of Hawaiian kuleana owners and their descendants in West Maui:

> We was the last family for raise taro in Lahaina. But then Charlie was the first family to restart taro in Lahaina also. So a few years after we stopped farming in Kanaha, when we was in high school, we went back to Kauaula where Charlie's guys was and we opened up two patches, eh, brah? And we went use one hose, one green garden hose, and you know, to us, that

was everything, even if it was from one hose. And, um, I was going to UH, later on when I graduated and went to UH and I got different taro species, we brought 'em back, we tried all kind different stuff. Was like one mad scientist type of experiment going on. And just looking back at that time, we never really think about, whoa brah, you the only guy raising taro in Lahaina. Yeah? And we never thought was something that was that great.

Until you get older and you start looking around, and it's like ho brah, you the only taro farmer in Lahaina. And then you start looking at why. And then you get frustrated. You get mad. Then we start trying to find solutions to the problem, which was basically not having water. And so, you know, we start to read up and you start to do studies and you look at the laws when it comes to water in the streams. I look at the laws, and it's pretty cut and dry and clear, somewhat. I understand you guys gotta do your studies to validate uses and stuff, but traditional and customary usage, appurtenant, the whole gamut, from water in the stream for instream life....

Looking at that, and then I look at the river in Lahaina, except for Ukumehame after they went stop the plantation, I looking at the rivers in Lahaina. Ho, 100 percent dry. So where was the protection, where's this protection, for all these things that is stated in the law and that's supposed to be protected. Nobody protecting 'em. And so now, OK, we gotta figure out how we going get more water. And in Kauaula, here comes Peter Martin. Peter Martin wasn't even in the picture at the time we started. He's one rookie, but he pilau. [...]

[I]n Kahoma we got the opportunity to kind of work with Kamehameha Schools, which was ... they crooks too, straight up ... but to find out that Kamehameha Schools leasing out that area in Kahoma, the intake, to Pioneer Mill to dewater Kahoma and then Pioneer Mill having that opportunity to steal land like you seen in every other place. Was one shock to find out was one Hawaiian entity that allowed that to happen.[30]

Keahi has been active in water rights and stream restoration issues across West Maui—from Honokōhau to Olowalu. His testimony referred to the struggles of the Palakiko and Kapu ʻohana to restore Kauaʻula Stream and maintain their loʻi kalo. Keahi powerfully recounts some of the first resurgences of kalo growing in a region once famous for its loʻi terraces. "Charlie" is Charlie Palakiko, a Hawaiian kalo farmer from Kauaʻula Valley. Keahi mentions that his family stopped farming in Kanaha Valley, but has since sought to return to those lands.

[Y]eah Charlie [Palakiko], summertime they struggling for water and they get the whole river. One more thing. Charlie never mention, but as long as I could remember, every week he calling the developer, "no more water." Calling the developer, "no more water." We not supposed to be calling him. He's not the guy in charge. We're not supposed to be calling him.

If our rights are supposed to be protected, then we should be calling you guys. But then when we call you guys, ah kind of like shucks brah, not going happen. You know what I mean? And then you get the process. You gotta go through a process. I happy you guys doing this, and I happy you guys putting all that stuff together, yeah? But for the rest of you community, you guys gotta watchdog, read close.[31]

Foster Ampong, who has familial ties to West Maui, testified:

But I have children that are interested. And so, I would like to see the Commission address and look at how much water each taro farmer would need based upon the taro patches that's in the stream. So if you have one family that's using one or two patches, you can't say that, OK, that's all he's going to need. When in his whole ʻili ʻaina, or his kuleanas, he may have 23, 25, 30 patches. So the determination should be based upon that. That's the rationale that I want to see implemented. And the other rationale I want to see implemented is that plan for the taro farmer, not just for the tourists. Not just for the malahini that's going to move here in 10, 15, 20 years. Because it seems like the state moves a lot faster for them than they do for the taro farmer. And, you know, like it or not, taro farmer was here before anybody else. Mahalo.[32]

Proposed amended IIFSs for Ukumehame were an estimated flow of 4.5 cubic feet per second, or 2.9 mgd, with at least 0.13 mgd supplied to loʻi kalo.[33] CWRM staff, however, noted that the 4.5 cubic feet per second flow standard may not be sufficient to meet the instream habitat needs due to uncertainties concerning the hydrogeologic conditions.

Victoria Kaluna-Palafox was the only individual testifier to submit her comments in advance of the public meeting. Kaluna-Palafox and her family have lived on the same kuleana lands along Ukumehame stream for generations. Today, Kaluna-Palafox and her husband continue to grow kalo on their small lot, which is encompassed by a larger parcel that is recognized by the county and CWRM as belonging to the county.

Post-IIFSs Pushback

Months after the Water Commission approved the IIFSs for Kauaʻula Stream, "homeowner groups" that utilize Launiupoko Irrigation Company (LIC) delivered water sought contested cases on all four of the West Maui IIFSs at the regular CWRM meeting on June 19, 2018. Three groups that grew out of subdivisions built by Peter Martin's companies—Mahanalua Nui Homeowners Association, Inc., Makila Plantations Homeowners Association, Inc., and Puʻunoa Homeowners Association, Inc.—along with the Steve Strombeck and the Strombeck Family Revocable Trust, formally requested contested cases. Their requests were denied. At issue for these water users was the threat by Launiupoko Irrigation Company, an affiliate of West Maui Land Company, that their water service could be cut off due to the implementation of the IIFSs.

The issue cited by the LIC was a claim that the State Public Utilities Commission had imposed requirements upon the irrigation company that the company would be unable to meet under the IIFS distributions. Thus, the subdivision groups sought relief from the Water Commission on the poorly articulated basis that their water "rights" were somehow at issue. The subdivision groups contested case requests were curious for several reasons, not the least of which was that the irrigation company itself had not sought a contested case.[34]

On the other side, many in the community as well as others concerned with potential implications for Water Commission IIFS processes generally, weighed in through public testimony at the June 19, 2018 meeting. Some of the points raised included the propriety of the Kauaʻula IIFS itself. CWRM staff conducted seven years of monitoring, analysis, research, and outreach in developing the IIFSs that were approved months ago in March 2018. The IIFSs recognized public trust priority given to natural resources, cultural practices, other reasonable beneficial instream uses, and expressly considered offstream uses.

Second, testifiers argued that the petitioning groups from the subdivisions should be treated like everyone else. The rules were clear that a request for a contested case has to come before the end of the March 20, 2018 meeting. The chair announced this requirement at that meeting. Diverters, including Launiupoko Irrigation Co., were present on March 20th. CWRM held a public fact-gathering meeting prior to March 20th and issued many public notices. No special exception should be made for the petitioners' belated request, they argued.

Third, testifiers pointed out that the contested case requests were incomplete. They do not provide any verifiable evidence of their actual water needs, efforts to obtain alternative sources, water conservation efforts, or that their water uses are reasonable and beneficial, or would not impact public trust uses of water. Despite their claims to need water for "small-scale farming," a significant number of petitioners listed addresses located in North America, or did not describe their farming activities, acreage of crops, or production of crops. Testifiers brought in photographs downloaded from Google Earth, showing mansions and pools with very little, if any, agricultural development in the homeowners' agricultural subdivisions.

Others, including the authors, raised the question as to the propriety of seeking relief from the Water Commission as opposed to filing a request for declaratory orders from the Public Utilities Commission, which could clarify whether and how the IIFSs would impair the irrigation company's ability to meet their obligations as a public utility. To date, no such petition for declaratory orders has been filed.

The requests for contested cases also exacerbated a widespread impression that many of the wealthy homeowners were not committed West Maui residents with firm stakes in the community. The 2018 Water Commission actions were not a surprise to many longtime community members, as they had actively participated in public engagement related to these CWRM efforts for many years.

However in response to these concerns, West Maui legislators also tried to get involved. On June 6, 2018, Maui legislators held an informational meeting on both the proposed IIFS amendments and the Lahaina Flood Control Project, which had been in the works for decades. First proposed in 1960,[35] it was not until 1991 that the US Department of Agriculture's Soil Conservation Service issued its environmental review documents for the proposed Lahaina Flood Control Project, consisting of construction of a 6,824-foot-long water diversion channel from Lahainaluna Road to Kaua'ula Stream and a series of debris basins designed to reduce sediment discharge into the ocean.[36] The project's long history began in 1960, when Lahaina suffered a major flooding event.

Despite its 1991 determination that the project would not have any environmental impacts, construction was halted due to lack of funding and the state's determination that it needed to review the environmental assessment.[37] In 2004, the National Resource Conservation Service (NRCS) prepared a full environmental impact statement (FEIS) for the project.[38] Community members seeking to restore streams raised concerns about interruption of mauka-to-makai flow and native biota habitats. The 1991 documents prepared for the project evaded the issue by concluding, "There are no undisturbed natural areas in the lower part of the Lahaina Watershed that will be affected by project installation."

Likewise, the Lahaina flood control project FEIS concluded, "fish rearing habitat of the lower reaches of Kauaula Stream" would not be affected because that section of the stream consists of a concrete channel bottom that is dry throughout the year except during periods of heavy rainfall.[39]

This conclusion may well change in light of the amended IIFSs for Kauaʻula Stream, which will permit regular mauka-to-makai flow. As discussed further in chapter 7, the channelization of streams, Kahoma Stream in particular, has been a source of controversy between the county, kuleana water users, and large landowners who seek to maintain control over water resources as a legacy from Pioneer Mill.

CHANNELIZED STREAMS AT KAHOMA

Stream restoration has as its ideal goal natural mauka-to-makai flow as well as upstream movement of ʻoʻopu and other native species. Yet much of Lahaina's development has been along the coast, and accordingly, much of the flood control efforts have been constructed in this area. The situation has led to the replacement of natural stream flow by channelized streams in the lower reaches. This is true of Kahoma, where Kapali Keahi and many others, including Archie Kalepa, Tiare Lawrence, and Kai Keahi have been working with Kamehameha Schools, the landowner of Kahoma Stream watershed and appurtenant lands, to restore streams. Kamehameha Schools operates an upstream diversion, but agreed to release two mgd. Kahoma Ranch, also owned by Peter Martin, posed another issue because they had not developed an agricultural plan for its use of the water. Instead, the water was going back into Kahoma Stream, where it eventually flows to a cement channel and into the water.

The lower reaches of Kahoma Stream were once adjacent to the ʻAlamihi fishpond. This lower part of Kahoma stream was called "Kapaʻulu" or, roughly translated, "an enclosure of breadfruit," and it was from Kapaʻulu that freshwater fed into the ʻAlamihi fishpond.[40] The ʻAlamihi area had once been owned by Kamehameha III after an important battle, but later passed to David Malo. As early as 1853 the fishpond itself was owned by P. Nahaolelua, governor of Maui.[41] By 1889, Pioneer Mill entered into a fifteen-year lease for the ʻAlamihi land. In 1953, however, the Territory of Hawaiʻi issued a revocable permit for ʻAlamihi fishpond to Shizuko Suehiro.[42] Given the importance of the area, surveyors concluded that the existence of cultural deposits in the area was likely. The historic importance of the area compounds the concern with the impacts of further construction in these sensitive areas.

The Kahoma Stream Flood Control project was completed in 1990. The project was authorized under Section 201 of the Federal Flood Control Act of 1965 at a considerable cost of $18,500,000 (federal: $10,840,000; non-federal: $7,660,000). The drainage basin extends over 5.4 square miles. The project consists of a 5,415-foot concrete channel, a debris basin, an offshore rubble apron, three pre-stressed concrete bridges, and related utility relocations. The project, sponsored by the County of Maui Department of Public Works, was designed for standard project flood level protection with a discharge of 15,200 cubic feet per second at the stream mouth.

The cement channel has a grate system through which at least 500,000 gpd of streamwater is allowed to flow to the ocean. Oʻopu are returning to the upstream areas. DLNR Aquatics Specialists at one time opined Kahoma was a "dead river," but have since reconsidered their opinion. In August 2016, Kahoma Stream was restored sufficiently to see three kinds of oʻopu. Despite nearly a mile of cement channel, oʻopu are getting up through the basin and into the valley. As of this writing, the county indicated its interest in shutting down the stream restoration in order to clean out the grate system for a week every month. Under the county's plan, Kamehameha Schools would divert the water to the Kahoma reservoir owned by Peter Martin once a month in order to clean the grate. This, however, would kill native species that require constant water flow to survive. In October 2016, despite community protests, the county took a month to clean the grate system due to a storm that moved 60,000 yards of dirt.

Instead of constantly shutting down streamflow, community members suggested that the channelized areas and basin may not be needed. When the storm runoff basin was constructed, no one had factored into the analysis the existence of a living stream, which is here now. Community members have been meeting with the County Public Works director to develop a plan other than cleaning the basin in ways that will kill oʻopu.

The mouth of Kahoma stream is blocked by a 150-foot sand berm that was installed as part of a stream flood control project. The purpose of the M-3 Kahoma Stream Flood Control project was to collect stormwater from a drainage channel and convey it towards agricultural irrigation to the north. The M-4 Lahaina Flood Control Project similarly sought to collect stormwater from a drainage channel and detention pond and convey it for agricultural irrigation to the north, south, and east. However, these flood control projects were developed prior to the restoration of streamflow to Kahoma Stream and renewed efforts by Lahaina communities to restore the loʻi kalo that depend on those flows.

Keoki Freeland commented that Kahoma is "interesting" because water from down the valley, and a development tunnel drilled laterally into the valley, goes into the stream as well. Approximately 1.5 mgd of freshwater was developed through the installation of the tunnel. Because that water is not "naturally flowing," it seemed fair to give the "development water" to Martin's Kahoma Ranch and "leave the natural water to kalo people."[43]

NEW IIFSs FOR HONOKŌHAU STREAM

An urbanizing Lahaina has long had its eyes set on Honokōhau and Kahakuloa surface waters. In 1974, the legislature appropriated funds to conduct a feasibility study on development of surface and high-level waters on the northern end of West Maui. In December 1975, DLNR's Division of Water and Land Development published an Environmental Impact Statement for the Kahakuloa Water Project, prepared by Wilson, Okamoto, & Associates. The study considered installing surface water diversion and dam structures at Kahakuloa and Makamakaole watersheds. It also considered installing vertical wells, Maui-type wells (consisting of a mine-like shaft with a horizontal infiltration tunnel that would skim water from the basal lens), and Lanai-type wells (tunnels or shafts used to develop high-level water behind dike barriers), and further tunnels for groundwater development. Water development of Kahakuloa, Honokōhau, and Makamakaole watersheds was proposed "to meet the needs of the Lahaina District."

The only mention of kalo farmers was made in reference to development of Honokōhau stream waters above the existing ditch intake. "If all of the high-level ground water at elevation 600 feet were lifted to the Honokōhau Ditch, downstream use of surface flow water by farmers and residents might be affected; however, existing water rights for taro cultivation will be observed."[44] The authors did not explain how reduction of upstream flows and high-level water sources would avoid affecting existing water rights held by kalo farmers. The EISPN rejected desalination and water reuse alternatives, deeming them both too expensive to be "competitive."[45] The "no action" alternative was also rejected on the basis that water development—"if the Lahaina District is to experience further urbanization envisioned by the report, *A General Plan for Lahaina District, County of Maui*, additional water sources need to be developed."[46] "No action" was rejected because it was not "responsive to the water needs for maintaining a viable agricultural industry necessary for a balanced economy."[47]

Although Honokōhau stream will likely be the last of West Maui's streams to receive amended interim instream flow standards, as noted, they were also the subject of an earlier IIFS petition from MLP. In August 2006, MLP submitted its petition to CWRM to establish amended IIFSs for Honokōhau and Honolua Streams, and these petitions were accepted as complete on October 2, 2006.[48] In November 2008, CWRM notified MLP that its petitions were being delayed because CWRM's energies were being directed rather to the Nā Wai 'Eha IIFS contested case hearing and IIFS proceedings in East Maui. In March 2011, however, CWRM approved a funding agreement with the US Geological Survey for low-flow studies of the main streams within the ten watersheds of the Lahaina District. While not specifically responsive to MLP's petition, the low-flow studies would provide information needed to amend the IIFSs.

In 2014, USGS provided an update on West Maui stream flows, inclusive of a description of ongoing diversions. Those descriptions relied nearly exclusively on water diverter accounts of their use of surface water.[49] Honokōhau Stream is currently diverted to support a plethora of uses running from Honokōhau Stream through Wahikuli. According to MLP, after the closure of their pineapple operations in 2009, they continued to use Honokōhau Ditch waters for irrigating smaller-scaled diversified agricultural lots, golf courses, raising livestock, providing water for domestic needs, and supporting reforestation efforts.[50] Honokōhau ditch diversions provide potable water for MDWS systems supporting residences from Nāpili to Honokōwai. Ditch water is treated at the MDWS Māhinahina Water Treatment Facility, which produces on average 1.5 mgd.

In 2003, Pioneer Mill Company, Limited merged and became Pioneer Mill Company, LLC, a Delaware corporation based in Chicago. Pioneer Mill, LLC has an affiliate, Kaaanapali Land Management Corporation (KLMC), which was registered on May 13, 1999—the same year that Pioneer Mill closed its sugar operations in West Maui. KLMC owns portions of the Honokōwai Stream bed, Wahikuli Gulch and the Honokōwai diversion, which diverts an average of 2.779 mgd of streamwater from Amalu and Kapāloa streams.[51] KLMC reports that these waters are used to irrigate its coffee plantation fields on the lower slopes of Wahikuli Gulch and for providing nonpotable water to a KLMC subdivision. KLMC is indeed installing coffee crops in West Maui. KLMC is the innovator of "Kā'anapali Coffee Farms," which entices "pleasure-seekers from around the globe" to purchase five- to seven-acre farm plots, many replete with infinity pools and a "veteran team of local farmers" that "grows, harvests, and markets the coffee crop on your estate[.]"[52] Far from the large-scale industrial agriculture of the Pioneer Mill plantation days, KLMC's coffee plantation promises the fat of the land to wealthy non-residents and wage labor to the non-landowning sharecropper.

Honokōhau Stream is completely diverted into Honokōhau Ditch at an upper level intake. As a "gaining stream," Honokōhau Stream regains some flow downstream. Maui Land and Pineapple's diversion takes Honokōhau Stream water and water from Honokōhau development tunnels into the Honolua and the Honokōhau Ditch. That ditch flows past copious arid agricultural lands and expanding development in Kāʻanapali and Kapalua and towards Lahaina town. Today, Maui DWS diverts water from the Honokōhau Ditch to serve its two domestic water systems: the Honokōhau system and the Lahaina-Alaeloa system, both within the Lahaina District.[53] The Maui DWS's Lahaina-Alaeloa system is bifurcated into Northern and Southern subsystems.

Honokōhau communities and those supporting the protection of instream uses and Hawaiian traditional kalo growing are critical of any potential IIFS that might seek to satisfy offstream claims to water. Several have asked why the recycled water from the Lahaina wastewater reclamation facility might not be repurposed to at least water DHHL-planned agricultural developments in Honokōwai. Currently, the county has a higher capacity to produce recycled wastewater than is needed or claimed by others in Honokōwai. Resorts use some of this recycled water in Kāʻanapali for golf course irrigation. The hope is that the county can increase recycled water production capacity such that, at minimum, the public trust uses of water needs in Honokōwai can be met without need for further diversion from Honokōhau Valley. Public trust uses of diverted Honokōhau surface water do not trump the instream uses, but would be given higher priority than commercial and new water uses. With a dozen or so more development projects proposed across West Maui, however, it is likely that the Water Commission will allow much of the water to remain diverted to existing water users, including the Kāʻanapali Land Management Company's coffee estates, and other offstream uses.

Conclusion

At the time of this writing, the Water Commission staff are currently determining recommendations for IIFSs for Honokōwai and Honokōhau streams. Recommendations for Honolua and a water wasting complaint regarding Honokōhau stream went before the Water Commission in November of 2019. IIFSs for Honokōwai were deferred pending potential Water Commission action to designate the area as a surface and/or ground water management area. Honokōhau Stream standards, which will likely be the most contentious of all the IIFS-setting actions in West Maui, were also deferred due to grave concerns from MLP, community groups, and the Kapalua Plantation Estates homeowners' group. Ka Malu o Kahālāwai opposed the proposed portions of the recommendation for Honokōhau IIFSs because it included a "development reserve" and did not prioritize restoring streamflow.

Historically, 51.75 acres of loʻi kalo were cultivated in the valley, which would require more than 10.65 mgd of stream flow. Incorporating such potential instream water uses into the formulation of the IIFSs accords with the Commission's mandate to "reestablish, where practical, beneficial instream uses of water[.]" HRS §174C-5; HAR §13-169-1; see also HAR §13-169-22.

The CWRM IIFS proposal references 5.15 acres of kuleana parcels in Honokōhau valley requiring 1.11 mgd. Yet, review of Land Commission Awards show approximately 128 acres of kuleana parcels line Honokōhau stream. Although all of these kuleana are not actively farmed today, this figure offers a horizon for the reestablishment of beneficial instream uses of water based in a historical reality. Complainants have worked with Honokōhau valley residents and Nā Mamo Aloha ʻĀina o Honokōhau on loʻi restoration in view of a larger call to kuleana owner descendants to return to the valley to farm and reestablish their community.

The "reestablish[ment]" of beneficial instream water uses include Native Hawaiian traditional and customary practices of growing kalo, ecosystem uses necessary to the thriving of ʻoʻopu, limu, and ʻōpae, and domestic uses associated with Hawaiian communities who are returning on live on kuleana parcels. The Water Code prohibits abridging or denying Native Hawaiian traditional and customary rights through the operation of this chapter. HRS §174C-101(c). Taken together, the mandate to reestablish beneficial instream uses and the prohibition against abridging or denying Native Hawaiian rights demonstrates an intent to establish IIFSs that provide for historical and future water uses that support these rights and practices.

Reserving needed instream waters for future (as opposed to existing) offstream development inverts the priorities of the water code. Rather than allowing amounts in excess of 8.6 mgd to flow to offstream uses, all water not clearly established to be needed in amounts certain for offstream use, should be remain in Honokōhau stream. The Water Code anticipates that the Commission's acts of "preserving, enhancing, or restoring instream values" to impact existing uses, but those impacts may be "avoid[ed] or minimize[d]" through a range of water management tools including "uses of water from alternative sources[.]" HRS § 174C-71(1)(E). "The clear implication of these provisions is that the Commission may reclaim instream values to the inevitable displacement of existing offstream uses." *In re Water Use Permit Applications,* 94 Hawaiʻi 97, 149-50, 9 P.3d 409, 461-62 (2000) (*Waiāhole*) citing Comm. Whole Rep. No. 18, in 1 Proceedings, at 1026 ("[T]he agency should have the flexibility to regulate existing as well as future water usage of Hawaii's water resources....").

HRS Chapter 174C is quite clear that instream uses that are currently suffering must be satisfied before even considering new offstream diversion uses. The Water Commission indicated that it would take up the Honokōhau IIFSs again in the spring or summer of 2020.

CHAPTER 6

PROTECTING WATER WHILE IT IS BELOW GROUND
The Unsustainability of "Sustainable Yield"

*The Honokowai Well will pump groundwater from the Honokowai Aquifer,
which is the same aquifer that the Mahinahina Well will pump from. As
discussed previously, the CWRM has established a sustainable yield of 6
million gallons per day (mgd) for the Honokowai Aquifer ... Approximately 3.41 mgd from the Honokowai Aquifer has been in use by private
source developers. The combined amount of ground water used by private
source developers and drawn at the Mahinahina Well and the Honokowai Well will be within the sustainable yield of the Honokowai Aquifer.
It is noted that the CWRM regulates well development and groundwater resources in the State. As such, the proposed action is not anticipated to
result in significant adverse cumulative impacts to the Honokowai Aquifer.*

—Draft Environmental Assessment for the Proposed
West Maui Source Development Project [1]

*Accounting for groundwater pumped by several private water
systems in the area, the total demand for groundwater is expected
to increase from 5.8 Mgal/d in 2007 to 11.1 Mgal/d in 2030.
However, the amount of groundwater that is available in the
Lahaina area to meet future water demands is uncertain.*

—Groundwater availability in the Lahaina District, West Maui, Hawai'i:
US Geological Survey Scientific Investigations Report 2012–5010 [2]

Can we know if the management of West Maui's groundwater will be sustainable by simply comparing two numbers, as if we were balancing a checkbook? Do we only need to know if the number of gallons that will be pumped from existing and new wells is smaller than a specific number? Or, as the USGS has suggested in examining West Maui groundwater, is there considerable uncertainty in knowing what amount of water is available and sustainable?

How can West Maui kama'āina know which of the above approaches to understanding groundwater sustainability is closer to the truth? How can we engage in policymaking to ensure a sustainable future for groundwater?

In West Maui and across the Islands, the State of Hawai'i claims to protect public trust uses of groundwater through the use of "sustainable yield" (SY). Developers, public and private, rely on and defend this method. It sounds good—sustainable, even.

However, as we will show, the only thing SY possibly sustains, if it is implemented perfectly and all of its embedded assumptions are met, is the quality of water pumped for consumptive uses. These uses include water for irrigation, resort and hotel needs, luxury homes and water features, and other commercial uses. The four public trust purposes of the water resources trust in Hawai'i are not explicitly protected in the state's management scheme, and can be directly harmed through uses that are not prohibited by the state. If sustainable management of groundwater is understood to protect and sustain these public trust uses—water left in its natural state supporting ecological functions, water used for the traditional and customary practices of Hawaiians, the domestic needs of the general public, and water for homesteading under the Hawaiian Homes Commission Act—then management by SY is not sustainable.

The Imitation of Sustainability in "Sustainable Yields"—An Overview

To begin to understand why what the state claims is sustainable is not, we start with an oversimplified and favorable description of Hawaii's SY management approach. First, the state CWRM divides each island in the whole archipelago into hydrologic units that represent, as near as possible, distinct groundwater basins. Second, a range for groundwater recharge in a given hydrologic unit is determined. This is the estimate of the quantity of water that flows into the aquifer from precipitation like rainfall and fog drip, irrigation and wastewater return, reduced by the amount not adding to recharge due to processes like runoff and evapotranspiration. Third, the CWRM chooses a low end of recharge estimates, and further chooses only a percentage of that recharge that will ultimately be allowed to be pumped. That number is set as a target that should never be exceeded—the SY. Because they choose the lowest estimates they have for recharge, and do not choose to set SY at 100 percent of that number, they claim that management by SY due to its method of determination follows the precautionary principle.[3] Fourth and finally, when actual and planned pumping reaches 90 percent of that SY number, the state should designate the aquifer as a groundwater management area, and thus subject new users to more rigorous reviews of their withdrawals and proposed uses, thus purportedly ensuring protection of the resources in perpetuity.[4]

This simplified description matches well what decisionmakers and writers of environmental documents report as our approach to managing groundwater.[5] However it is inaccurate due to oversimplifying the approach and incompletely describing what is actually done by CWRM, which obscures the significant complexities and uncertainties that groundwater presents. In truth, if the goal of groundwater management is the sustainability of the resource and public trust uses of water, the SY approach in Hawaiʻi is flawed in both design and application. We now briefly review why this is so, points we will expand on greatly throughout this chapter.

First, the boundaries chosen for hydrologic units by CWRM are largely based on surficial features—what one can see above ground. Because of this choice and other reasons, CWRM, acting on the recommendations of staff, separate some areas that are hydraulically connected,[6] and they manage other areas with significant hydraulic barriers as a single hydrologic unit.[7] As every management choice that follows after this point assumes that the unit is working like a single aquifer, these errors confound every subsequent decision.

The errors do not stop here, however. For these areas (where boundaries are not set in any consistent fashion and inflows and outflows are incompletely known), CWRM then uses a simple mathematical equation to set the SY, based on the amount of estimated recharge and a large number of assumptions of questionable fit to actual hydrological and development conditions. For instance, for this simple equation to accurately describe available water for pumping, it would have to be for a place where recharge is uniform throughout the aquifer unit. Any tourist newly arrived in West Maui who stands in the sun of Lahaina or Kaʻanapali and looks at the cloud-covered summit of Mauna Kahālāwai can readily realize that assumption is false.[8]

Because following the precautionary principle requires choosing presumptions that protect the resource,[9] and there is no evidence that the percentage of recharge CWRM chooses to leave in the ground sufficiently protects resources, the mere fact they do not allow the full pumping of their estimate of recharge cannot accurately be called precautionary. Thus the method for calculating SY generates a number with a veneer of scientific basis, precaution, and conservation value—but those appearances are illusory.

Finally, the water code states when the CWRM or a party asks for an area to be designated for water management, the CWRM must examine "whether an increase in water use or authorized planned use may cause the maximum rate of withdrawal from the ground water source to reach ninety percent of the sustainable yield of the proposed ground water management area."[10] This sets an arbitrary point for determining when management is needed. There is, for instance, no guarantee that the future domestic water uses of the general public can be adequately met with the remaining 10 percent of the SY for a given hydrologic unit. Similarly, there is no guarantee that other public trust uses can be satisfied after better capitalized interests have already captured most of the SY.

Even this flawed criterion has been implemented in a completely inconsistent manner by CWRM over time. Sometimes CWRM staff seems to treat the 90 percent pumping level as a trigger for management when that threshold has *not* been met.[11] However their own documents note aquifers that are undesignated, and yet pump far above the set SY. In the case of the Kahului aquifer in central Maui, the SY is set at one mgd for this dry area, and according to the 2018 draft update to the WRPP, pumping is at 5,257.5% of SY.[12] The Waiʻanae, Oʻahu aquifer is pumped at 92.3% of SY, with no CWRM action in progress to designate.[13] In the same document it notes the Waimea, Hawaiʻi Island aquifer is currently being pumped at 86.4% of SY, and the same plan proposes not to initiate designation, but to combine it with a nearer aquifer, therefore raising the SY—thus somehow protecting the resource from over-pumping without moving a single well or reducing their withdrawal rates.

The way that groundwater is purported to be managed sustainably through the use of SY is an imitation of sustainability—and should be seen as a poor imitation to anyone familiar with Hawaiʻi and its protected public trust uses of water. This unfortunately applies to West Maui just as it does to the rest of Hawaiʻi.

In this chapter, we expand on this brief summary of the current groundwater management approach, its significant limitations, and describe how it applies to West Maui. We first, in Part I, discuss the ways in which management of groundwater is kept administratively separate from surface water management, despite the unitary nature of the hydrologic cycle. This can result in policy outcomes where resource impacts are merely shifted, rather than resolved. We next describe how that separate management, combined with the management assumptions embedded into the SY approach, reverse the protective management inherent to surface water regulation by design. Then we describe the methodology of determining SY—through the determination of hydrologic units, recharge, and the mathematical equation employed to calculate SY. We fourth explicitly examine all the assumptions that must be true for SY to be a reliable tool to protect future pumping, which is the only specific goal of the management tool. Fifth and finally we will raise potential remedies that West Maui kamaʻāina could consider pursuing to overcome the limitations of current management regimes.

Surface and Groundwater: We Gotta Keep 'Em Separated

The Los Angeles rock band Offspring had a 1994 hit, "Come Out and Play," that alluded to ongoing yet also sensationalized violence between gangs the Bloods and the Crips. The tagline "You gotta keep 'em separated" rings throughout the track, underscoring the message that when you do not, violence erupts, and inevitably after a clash, "One goes to the morgue and the other to jail / One guy's wasted and the other's a waste."

The lengths to which the CWRM tries to keep ground and surface water management separated suggests they envision an outcome just as dire. This is odd, at first blush, as groundwater and surface water are inextricably intertwined—two tightly woven parts of the overall hydrologic cycle. Yet the CWRM and the State Water Code manage surface and ground water nearly completely separately.

This disconnection is clearly seen in policy implementation. One area is in the water management area designation process. For instance, if a community wishes to have their water resources more carefully managed by seeking to have their area designated as a Water Management Area, the CWRM has required that they seek designation for surface and ground water separately. This requires two different filings and legal proceedings, has different criteria to consider, and any associated legal costs would increase.

This was required by CWRM in the Nā Wai ʻEhā area of West Maui. After more than two decades of support for better water management, the community succeeded in their urging for CWRM to designate the ʻĪao Aquifer as a Ground Water Management Area in 2003.[14] Yet when the same community wished to have the private Wailuku Water Company stop draining streams completely dry, including the Wailuku River[15] that runs above and is interconnected to the ʻĪao Aquifer, CWRM staff required that a separate petition and process for surface water designation be prepared and filed.[16]

After stream restoration to the Wailuku River in ʻĪao, these separate management approaches continued. Even after mauka-to-makai flow was returned to the Wailuku River, which contributes to groundwater recharge, the CWRM staff have not proposed changing the amount of groundwater available for pumping. This is a good thing from a conservation and public trust perspective, as certain legendary springs have begun to run again as stream flow has returned and groundwater levels have risen,[17] and increased pumping could reverse this. However, relevant to how groundwater and surface water management are separated, the current draft WRPP does not ever address the relationship between restored stream flow and aquifer water levels for ʻĪao.

Areas where surface and groundwater separation led to contradictory policy actions occurs elsewhere in West Maui. In March 2018, as discussed in chapter 5, CWRM took steps to restore stream flows to four West Maui streams (Ukumehame, Olowalu, Launiupoko, and Kauaʻula). This was notable for being the first time that CWRM staff began initiating amendment of Interim Instream Flow Standards (IIFS) as opposed to communities driving the process through petitions (as occurred in Waiāhole on Oʻahu, and Nā Wai ʻEhā). In the staff submittal recommending the IIFS amendment, staff even meaningfully discussed the relationship between surface and groundwater flows:[18]

> In West Maui, streams generally have losing reaches in the lower elevations and have considerable groundwater gains from springs and development tunnels in the upper elevations. A common misconception is that flow restoration from diversion ditches is immediately followed by continuous flow downstream from the point of release all the way to the coast (analogous to turning on the faucet). When sufficient flow is restored to a stream that normally gains groundwater from the point of release to the mouth, streamflow will increase and the stream will probably flow along the entire length. For a stream that is losing, restored flow infiltrates underground once it reaches the losing section. In this case, flow is oftentimes absent downstream of the losing reach. In some cases, flow will become continuous after enough water has infiltrated the streambed and raised the water table, allowing base flow to be maintained by groundwater input. In other cases, the restored stream will remain dry at low-flow where the water table cannot be raised high enough to allow groundwater discharge to the stream.

This analysis sets up an excellent informational basis for making policy rec- ommendations that integrate ground and surface water management. However, in the final recommendation from staff, adopted by CWRM, the taking of additional groundwater was recommended as an alternative to now-curtailed surface diversions, without any analysis of whether current groundwater man- agement regimes would result in the dewatering of streams over the long term. This occurred despite guidance from the CWRM in the current draft WRPP, that "from a regulatory perspective, CWRM is primarily concerned with ground and surface water interaction issues as they affect surface water resources and estimates of ground water availability."[19] While the restoration of streamflows was undoubtedly a good thing for public trust purposes, these positive effects could be temporary; no analysis was done to show the possible interactions.

The distinction and gulf between surface and groundwater management even pervades the organizational charts at CWRM. In the implementation of the Water Code (which does not require this separation), CWRM maintains separate ground and surface water branches. They are staffed with different staff members and managed under different managers.

Merely withdrawing the water through a well rather than a surface-water diversion, when the stream pays for it, makes little difference to surface water public trust uses. Water itself does not know different individuals are manag- ing it when it is above ground or below ground. To a cultural practitioner who depends on mauka-to-makai flow, the impacts of flow disruption can exist despite the method of water extraction. The continued managerial separation of surface and groundwater in Hawai'i is not serving public trust uses of the water resources trust. However, this is just one way in which separate is not equal.

SEPARATE BUT UNEQUAL BY ADMINISTRATIVE DESIGN

This administrative distinction and separation between surface and groundwa- ter management also flies in the face of indigenous knowledge and management practice in Hawai'i, which clearly understood the unity of the hydrologic cycle. The famous chant "Aia i hea ka wai ā Kāne?" which calls forth the water god's presence in ground, surface, clouds, springs, and rain, shows an understanding of the continuity of the hydrologic cycle that does not exist in Hawai'i water law and management practice.

Another matter quite problematic with CWRM's separate manage- ment of surface and groundwater is the inequity in protection of public trust uses of groundwater. This particular circumstance is not due primarily to legislative drafting or design, but rather comes from CWRM and CWRM staff implementation.

The CWRM record of protecting public trust interests in surface water is abysmal, as discussed in chapter 4. But, at least in theory, the administrative process protects public trust uses of surface water first. As described fully in chapters 4 and 5, the Water Commission is supposed to first set IIFS[20] on streams to protect public uses of water before considering the continuance or increasing of off-stream, private, commercial uses. In plain language, they are supposed to first make sure there is enough water left in the stream so that public trust uses can be accommodated—including water left in the stream, mauka to makai, for its entire length, sufficient for fish and wildlife and for the exercise of related traditional and customary Hawaiian practices. Until that analysis is done and protections put into place, private commercial users are not supposed to have any opportunity to take water from streams.

However, the way the CWRM and its staff have chosen to manage groundwater turns that presumption for public trust uses of surface water on its head. In their rigid and convoluted interpretation of the simple legal requirement that they set "sustainable yields" for aquifers, they have relegated public trust concerns to an afterthought. As described briefly at the beginning of this chapter and more fully below, SYs, as implemented by CWRM, are actualized in a way that is only explicitly concerned with maximizing the long-term extraction of water. It is as if streams were managed by first choosing how much water could be diverted over the long term, and then public trust uses would be forced to show how much they need. This is of course how the private sector, with legal support, developed surface water during the pre-water-code plantation era—draining every single drop of base flow, with only larger storms allowing some water to flow freely.

For these reasons alone, it is clear that the SY approach in design is not meant to protect public trust uses of water, in West Maui or elsewhere. However, the somewhat complex process by which SYs are set further obscures this problem, because there are so many significant problems with the approach beyond this fundamental one.[21] Understanding these other policy design flaws requires unpacking the entire methodology of how SYs are determined.

THE WATER CODE REQUIREMENTS AND THE IMPLEMENTATION OF "SUSTAINABLE YIELD"

"Sustainable yield" is defined in the code as "the maximum rate at which water may be withdrawn from a water source without impairing the utility or quality of the water source as determined by the commission."—HRS §174C-3 (Definitions). The code further stipulates that the Commission develop a Hawai'i Water Plan, and that the plan contain two critical components as they relate to groundwater management and setting SYs.

The Code specifies, "The Hawaii water plan shall divide each county into sections which shall each conform as nearly as practicable to a hydrologic unit." (HRS §174C-31(h)).[22] Hydrologic units are defined as "a surface drainage area or a ground water basin or a combination of the two"—HRS §174C-3 (Definitions)—which makes it clear that the CWRM has discretion to define a unit as comprising both surface and groundwater. For each groundwater unit a "sustainable yield" needs to be developed (HRS §174C-31(i)(2))—but beyond the definition above, staff and commissioners are left considerable flexibility in how they accomplish this. They exercise this flexibility in many ways, including the definition of hydrologic units—but not in a manner that emphasizes protection of public trust uses of water. These critical decisions are made in an appendix to the Water Resources Protection Plan (WRPP), in its current draft a 739-page tome.

To describe how the WRPP does this, we next review how boundaries are set, recharge is estimated, and what kinds of aquifers are assumed when setting SYs. We then describe the Robust Analytical Model (RAM), the simple mathematical equation used to calculate SY.

Hydrologic Gerrymandering: Aquifer Sector and System Boundaries

In the WRPP, the CWRM formally adopts the boundaries of hydrologic units and sets sustainable yields. The setting of surface water hydrologic units can be somewhat straightforward, as elevation maps can be used to define drainages. Across-unit transfers of waters regularly occur in surface water units, either through natural groundwater flow that later contributes to surface water, or through human transport of water. Nonetheless, surface boundaries have a relationship to surface water flow.

Groundwater units are far more complicated. Because they are supposed to be the basis of determining how much water can be safely withdrawn from an aquifer, it could be presumed that the mapped boundaries represent some underlying geological or hydrological reality; however, this presumption would be wrong. Some of the boundaries are claimed—without provided evidence—to represent geologic separations. Other boundaries are specifically only designed to distribute pumping, though how they do that is also not justified nor explained. As the 2019 draft update to the WRPP states (Appendix F, page 20):

In general, each island is divided into regions that reflect broad hydro-geological similarities while maintaining hydrographic, topographic, and historical boundaries where possible. These divisions are known as Aquifer Sector Areas. Smaller sub-regions are then delineated within Aquifer Sector Areas based on hydraulic continuity and related characteristics. These sub-regions are called Aquifer System Areas, which are the basic ground water hydrologic unit. In general, these units allow for optimized spreading of island-wide pumpage on an aquifer system area scale.

Indeed, the WRPP admits, "It is important to recognize that Aquifer Sector Area and Aquifer System Area boundary lines were based largely on observable surface conditions (i.e. topography, drainage basins and streams, and surface geology) and limited subsurface geological data such as water level characteristics. In general, only limited subsurface information (i.e. well logs and well cores) is available. Hydrogeologic features and conditions at the surface may not adequately or accurately reflect subsurface conditions that directly affect ground water flow." (WRPP 2018, Appendix F, Page 21.)

In simpler words, while there are lines on a map that are used to delineate aquifers and regulate pumping, those lines are by the CWRM's own admission what was easily visible on the land's surface, not actual underground conditions. Therefore, a core legal premise of the code, that these lines should represent hydrologic units, is not followed, even for the Aquifer Sector Areas.

This is as true in West Maui as it is anywhere else in Hawaiʻi. West Maui is divided into two Aquifer Sector Areas. If the line that separates the Wailuku and Lahaina Aquifer Sector Areas is based on observations of actual pumping or any knowledge of underground conditions, no evidence is given in the WRPP. That applies just as well to the subunits, the Aquifer Systems. For instance, the line between the Honokōhau and Honolua Aquifer systems is not necessarily anything more than a line drawn on a map, as opposed to being an actual hydraulic barrier.

Within these system units, however, there is also heterogeneity. The 2018 draft WRPP notes that all of the Aquifer System areas comprise at least basal and high-level aquifers, and the Honokōhau Aquifer system is also known to have perched groundwater. (The different kinds of water bodies are reviewed more below.)

This boundary-making that does not reflect hydraulic connectivity or obstruction is critical for a number of reasons, but two in particular. First, these boundaries become the basis for setting SY, and the CWRMs sometimes pay slavish adherence to only designating an area for management when pumping exceeds 90 percent of that SY. Second, the way in which SYs are calculated in this area assumes all of the water is in a basal aquifer—which has implications for what impacts pumping can have on coastal ecosystems, which is a protected public trust use of water.

We will next look at how, after these arbitrarily drawn lines are reified, the CWRM calculates SY. Sustainable Yield cannot be calculated, as implemented by CWRM, without first knowing the boundaries of the hydrologic unit (discussed above) and the amount of groundwater recharge, which is covered next.

Recharge

Recharge, simply stated, is the amount of water that enters into groundwater from the surface or any other aquifer boundary. Not all precipitation turns into recharge; water can directly run off beyond aquifer boundaries, evaporate, be taken up and transpired by plants, or be captured as soil moisture.

Beyond that simple statement, however, estimating historic recharge can be challenging, and the amount of water calculated to recharge a given aquifer can vary significantly depending on data availability and calculation method. Recently on Hawai'i Island, work by John Engott of the United States Geological Survey (USGS) resulted in estimating significantly higher rates of recharge for most areas of the island, and significantly lower rates for some parts of the island, when compared to previous peer-reviewed studies.[23] For Maui in 2014, Johnson, Engott, et al. similarly found recharge estimates different than estimates previously used in the WRPP; some areas were wetter, and others drier.[24] The differences stemmed from a few methodological changes, including the methods used to estimate runoff, evapotranspiration, and the inclusion of fog drip. These changes can have significant potential consequences, depending on how they are included in calculations of SY.

The WRPP itself admits that recharge calculations are highly dependent on data availability and calculation method. They discuss different variables, including spatial data coverage (the number and location of data measurement points), time steps (the periods for which data is available and comparable), estimates of total direct runoff, and how evapotranspiration is deducted from total possible recharge. Variance in any one of these methods can result in significantly different results in estimates of recharge.

Prospective examinations of recharge amounts have additional uncertainty due to climate change. There are two broadly different methodological approaches to modeling how the changing climate will effect precipitation and other factors in Hawai'i that play a significant part in influencing estimated recharge amounts. One method, statistical downscaling, looks at local long-term historic climate data and projects trends forward. Another takes global climate models and "downscales" them to local conditions. Both methods have advantages and disadvantages: there is no obvious long-term (year 2100) confluence of projections in some areas, and a very limited number of runs of dynamic models. For some areas, including areas of West Maui, significantly drier futures are possible.[25]

Despite the estimates that exist for lower rates of precipitation due to climate change, and hence recharge, these changes are not yet incorporated into setting SY in Hawai'i. The current WRPP update merely states, "Climate change and data from the last 25 years should also be included into recharge analysis."[26] In other words, when it comes to calculating recharge (and hence SY), CWRM is not considering any climate change impacts whatsoever.

Even if SY were a management tool that fostered sustainability, this issue of not considering climate change-driven possible reductions in recharge would be significant for West Maui Aquifers. Current SY figures range from 20 mgd ('Iao) to as low as two mgd (Olowalu and Ukumehame), and they are relatively small compared to common municipal well sizes and demands. For instance, there are two new proposed county wells in the "West Maui Source Development Project"; the Environmental Assessment (EA) for that project is one of the quotes at the beginning of this chapter. The EA describes, "The Mahinahina Well will draw 0.672 million gallons per day (mgd) from the Honokowai Aquifer, based on an operational schedule of 16 hours pumping per 24-hour period, and the Kahana Well will draw approximately 0.96 mgd from the Honolua Aquifer, based on an operational schedule of 16 hours pumping per 24-hour period."[27] The current SY for Honokōwai is six mgd and Honolua is eight mgd; each of these wells will capture about 12 percent of the current SY.

This is of concern because, even ignoring all else discussed in this chapter, there is supposed to be a linear relationship between what the state calculates as recharge and how it calculates SY. Thus, if recharge is reduced by 20 percent, the SY is reduced by 20 percent if all other methods remain unchanged. Some climate modeling predicts a 28 percent decline in recharge in Honolua and a 27 percent decline in recharge in Honokōwai.[28] At 28 percent less, if the CWRM did nothing else but follow their stated process, the SY would be reduced from eight mgd to under six mgd; the proposed impact from this new well would go from approximately 12 percent of SY to almost 25 percent; and the overall pumping would rise from approximately one-third of the SY currently to over

50 percent—without any new groundwater development from any other party. This could presumably change the assessment of the significance of a proposed well, both individually and cumulatively.

Furthermore, when CWRM assumes that the future will look like the past when it sets SY, public and private well developers will rely on those assumptions. Water developers must assume the infrastructure they are building to capture, store, and deliver that water will have water available to it over the anticipated economic life of the infrastructure—usually at least thirty years. If climate change drives significant changes to precipitation, these reliances could prove to be significant financial barriers to adaptive capacity in West Maui.

With this tenuous foundation—an estimated future amount of recharge over a geographically defined area without uniform geology and hydrology—the state then chooses to assume away some of this complexity by describing what kind of water bodies exist in each aquifer system area, for the purposes of calculating SY.

Not as Dense as Some: Assuming Everything is a Basal Aquifer

Determining what kind of groundwater body holds the resource—or assuming such for modeling purposes—is an essential step for the state's approach to using SY. In the current draft of the WRPP, CWRM describes the many types of aquifers known to occur in Hawai'i: basal, dike-impounded, perched, caprock, brackish, and deep confined freshwater. Across West Maui, all except deep confined freshwater aquifers are known to occur. The two most relevant to water management in West Maui are basal and high-level dike aquifers.

The USGS describes these two kinds of aquifers clearly in an important 2018 overview report, "Volcanic Aquifers of Hawai'i—Hydrogeology, Water Budgets, and Conceptual Models" (citations omitted): [29]

> A general conceptual model for Hawai'i, especially O'ahu, emerged in the early to middle 20th century…In this conceptual model, the freshwater lens was commonly referred to as "basal" groundwater. The dike-free lava flows were generally regarded as having high permeability, thus the basal water table sloped gently from a few tens of feet above sea level in inland areas to near sea level at the coast. Low-permeability coastal-plain sediments and rejuvenated-stage volcanics formed the semiconfining caprock that resisted groundwater discharge to the ocean and caused the freshwater lens to thicken, but even so, the basal water table in this conceptual model was nowhere more than about 50 ft above sea level. Higher

groundwater occurrences—in some cases hundreds to thousands of feet
above sea level—were referred to as "high-level" groundwater. High-level
groundwater included water impounded by dikes and groundwater perched
on buried low-permeability horizons formed by ash, soil, weathered rock,
or unusually dense lava flows.

In other words, in West Maui and in many other areas of Hawaiʻi, nearer to
the coast and a few miles inland, if you drill you can find a lens of fresh water
floating on saltwater. If there is a confining structure, such as the ancient coral
reefs on the south shore of Oʻahu, this slows water flow into the coast and
water levels are higher than they would be otherwise, but no more than a few
tens of feet high. More inland and in mountainous areas, water levels can be
much higher when they are held in lava dike compartments or other structures.
These areas can be of varying and often unknown size. These high-level water
bodies can also have varying kinds of hydraulic connections to neighboring
aquifers. A typical presumption is that when these high-level water bodies are
not developed by either wells or tunnels (which can pierce the lower reaches of
one or more dike-separated water bodies), the water in the system will slowly
percolate through lower, less pervious structures, and also emerge from where
the dike systems intercept the land surface in mountainous areas, as springs
or seeps. It is one critical way in which ground and surface water systems are
interconnected.

A groundwater management scheme that was focused on protecting public
trust uses in West Maui would first try and reliably describe the complex geology
and hydrology of the area along with natural and manmade features effecting
hydraulics, in addition to estimating short- and long-term recharge patterns and
overall aquifer capacity. It would then identify current and future public trust
uses with some geographic specificity, along with information on water quantity
and quality needs for those uses. Such a management approach would also be
concerned with economically significant non-public trust uses, including the
location, quantity, and quality of their needs. Modeling efforts would try and
run different development scenarios against the specific needs and values that
development should serve and protect.

However, in part because they lack staffing and sufficient hydrological
data, a core assumption made by CWRM for most SY calculations is that the
aquifer in question is an unconfined lens of fresh water floating on saltwater at
sea level—a basal aquifer. This does not reflect reality—as they readily admit,
their hydrologic units hold multiple kinds of aquifers. However, it does allow

them to calculate an SY figure when little else is known other than recharge, and they focus their concerns solely on whether existing or future wells will begin to draw up saltwater that lies below the fresh water lens.

Putting aside for a moment the accuracy of the inputs to the equation and its applicability to complex hydrologic units, the RAM equation described below works in part because of the different densities of fresh water and seawater. These densities lead to a predictable relationship (known as the Ghyben–Herzberg ratio), wherein for every foot of fresh water above sea level (something known as the head), there will be forty feet of fresh water in the aquifer below sea level.

That numerical relationship is core to understanding how the state chooses to calculate SY. As a new theoretical well or wells are allowed to draw off fresh water in a basal aquifer, the height of the lens lowers above sea level, and the bottom of the lens rises—forty feet for every foot the top of the lens lowers. This physical relationship, incorporated into RAM, allows CWRM to choose how much it will allow the lens to shrink—above and below sea level—with the only goal being to protect existing and future wells from the impact of seawater rising below the fresh water lens. As stated in the CWRM's first WRPP in 1990, "Sustainable yield refers to the forced withdrawal rate of groundwater that could be sustained indefinitely without affecting either the quality of the pumped water or the volume rate of pumping."[30] The only goal of SY is consumptive pumping, and the equation that allows the current calculation of SY is the Robust Analytical Model, or RAM.

1980—The Year of the RAM

The Robust Analytical Model (RAM) methodology utilized by CWRM to calculate the sustainable yield of many aquifer systems is not well understood by decisionmakers and the general public. This is odd, as the equation is fairly simple, it has been in existence for almost forty years, and its use is critical to our water future. In 1980, Hawai'i hydrologist John Mink published his work developing the RAM in application to the groundwater of southern O'ahu.

A simple equation, RAM has four main variables: (1) groundwater recharge; (2) the height above sea level of the basal lens before any wells were developed (its initial head); (3) the height above sea level that a manager is willing to accept after development has occurred and a new balance has been created (equilibrium head), and (4) SY.

There are different ways of presenting the RAM equation. If you are solving for SY, the equation can be presented as follows:

$$Sustainable\ Yield = Groundwater\ recharge\ \times \left\{ 1 - \left(\frac{Equilibrium\ head}{Initial\ head} \right)^2 \right\}$$

In plain language, here is how the equation is used: when an unconfined basal aquifer is pumped, it shrinks in all directions. Of concern to someone who wishes to pump fresh water, and whose well is near the inland (thickest) area of the aquifer, is the lowering height of the top of the fresh water and the rising bottom of the lowest part of the lens. If too much water is withdrawn, the well will begin to pull up salty water.

To prevent this outcome for a well, the manager—like CWRM—chooses how low they are willing to draw down the head from initial conditions. Thus if it is guessed that initial head was at four feet above sea level, CWRM could decide that they are willing to let the head lower by one foot—or 25 percent. This is the exact ratio CWRM chooses when they think initial heads were between 4–10 feet high.

When you add those numbers into RAM, you can calculate for SY if you also know or have an estimate of recharge. Quite simply, for a basal aquifer from which you are willing to decrease its height by 25 percent, you calculate an SY that is 44 percent of recharge.[31]

Thus, if you have a known area that represents a hydrologic unit, and it is a basal aquifer, and future recharge is reliably estimated, and you know how thick the basal aquifer was initially, and you are concerned only about future wells—you can use RAM to calculate your SY to try and protect future consumptive uses. Unfortunately—as CWRM itself acknowledges—even if these conditions are all true, there are still significant limitations in use of the RAM due to other critical assumptions.

RAM ASSUMPTIONS VS. REALITY

A significant hallmark of the current public review draft of the WRPP is how clearly it states its limitations while simultaneously taking no action to address those limitations. The previously quoted statement from the current WRPP draft that "Climate change and data from the last 25 years should also be included into recharge analysis" is one example. Another is the extensive information they provide about the limitations of RAM. Table 6.1 summarizes the assumptions in and limitations of RAM, as stated in pages 63 and 64 of the WRPP Appendix F. It also then relates them to the aquifers of West Maui that ecosystems, public trust uses, residents and visitors depend upon.

Table 6.1 RAM Assumptions versus Reality

ASSUMPTIONS AND LIMITATIONS OF RAM	RELATION TO WEST MAUI
Fresh water occurs as a basal lens floating on top of seawater	Fresh water occurs in basal, dike-confined, and perched aquifers
A sharp interface exists between the fresh and sea water	A gradual transition zone exists between the fresh water and underlying saltwater
The aquifer is unconfined	Aquifers can contain confining structures
Aquifer properties are homogeneous	Aquifer properties are heterogeneous
Aquifer thickness is constant	Aquifers are thickest at their inland boundary
Groundwater flow is uniform and laminar	Groundwater flow can vary
Wells are optimally placed throughout the aquifer system area	Wells are placed based on land ownership, proximity to infrastructure (roads, power)
RAM ignores the spatial distribution of recharge	Recharge is spatially heterogeneous, changing with elevation, land cover, and other factors
RAM ignores the spatial distribution of actual well placement and pumpage	Wells are not optimally placed to maximally extract water across the aquifer
Many "initial heads" used in RAM calculation were estimated due to the absence of data	Incorrect estimation of initial heads can result in significant damage to resources
RAM does not account for convection and dispersion	Convection and dispersion can alter flow and salinity
RAM does not account for variability in the transition zone	Transition zones can vary within and between aquifers
RAM does not account for flow between aquifer system areas	Aquifer system area boundaries do not reflect hydraulic separation
RAM does not account for boundary conditions (e.g. caprock)	Unit boundary conditions can alter groundwater flow and aquifer head
RAM does not account for the needs of groundwater-dependent ecosystems	Existing and historic GDEs, like the Mokuhina fishpond surrounding Moku'ula, are critical public trust resources
RAM does not model groundwater flow in three dimensions	Groundwater flows in three dimensions

The implications of all that has been discussed to this point in the chapter should be clear; the SY numbers that public and private well developers rely on and repeat as clear guideposts to sustainability are no such things. At best they are rough approximations of how much water can be consumptively developed now and used into the future, without rising chlorides in these consumptive uses, if wells are optimally placed. As has been seen in Lahaina, one can be pumping well below SY and still have dramatically rising chlorides in wells when pumping is not optimally placed. The same USGS report quoted at the beginning of this chapter noted (citations omitted):[32]

> The chloride concentrations of water pumped from wells in the Lahaina area increase in response to increased withdrawals on a monthly basis. Chloride concentrations in water pumped from several MDWS wells has exceeded 250 mg/L, which is the recommended secondary standard for drinking water. Chloride concentrations in the pumped water have been as high as 877 mg/L in 1992 and were recently as high as 349 mg/L in 2006. Data are insufficient, however, to determine whether a long-term regional change in the transition zone has taken place.

The SY numbers for West Maui have been briefly described in chapter 2, and compared to pumping rates. However, kama'āina of this area, along with all interested landowners and investors, should no longer simply accept a checkbook-like approach, comparing one column to another as an assessment of sustainability. Rather, more nuanced and local approaches to defining what should be prioritized for protection is necessary—something that is compatible with the language of the water code, no matter how different it is in the code's implementation to date.

Other Methods for Managing Groundwater and Estimating SY

As noted near the start of this chapter, all the state water code requires is that hydrologic units be defined and an SY be developed for them; the code further allows that units can combine ground and surface water bodies. And while the law suggests that these units "conform as nearly as practicable to a hydrologic unit," it is clear that sub-unit creations are allowed, at least by current practice.

A new approach to managing groundwater sustainably in West Maui then could begin with citizen and stakeholder participation and advocacy to identify sub-aquifer sector units that reflected a unified approach to managing ground and surface water, along with clearer and more diverse criteria of sustainability beyond the availability of fresh water for consumptive uses. These could identify areas where groundwater development might be restricted because of its impact on groundwater-dependent ecosystems (like limu beds), on stream flow, significant springs, or other factors. The long-sought restoration of Mokuʻula and intertwined restoration of Mokuhina, dependent on surface and ground water flow, is a prime candidate for such an approach.

Other approaches to managing groundwater sustainably need not directly take on the current identification of groundwater units and their SY numbers. Because designation allows individual well proposals to be scrutinized, and specific concerns over sustainability to be identified and protected, the existing approach of seeking designation of ground and/or surface water resources can be pursued. This pursuit could be done in full knowledge that proposed or existing pumping at 90 percent of SY for a given unit is merely one criterion that must be considered. Another is that "serious disputes" over water future exist; this criterion has been clearly met in West Maui from before the existence of the code itself, and continues to this day.

CHAPTER 7

CARRYING KULEANA

In the context of water resource management, kuleana is a way of describing both a property and a property right. A kuleana is a land parcel claimed under the 1850 Kuleana Act, which allowed "native tenants" to claim fee simple title to lands they worked under a specific and sometimes burdensome process. The need to register claims to these lands was consequent to the 1848 Māhele, which created a formal system for real property claims and recognitions. All lands granted under the 1848 Māhele were also "subject to the rights of native tenants" that govern water rights as discussed further below.

"Kuleana" has meanings beyond its use in this property regime. Chancellor, professor, activist, and musician Jonathan Kamakawiwoʻole Osorio described the concept of kuleana:

> Kuleana is a word that survived the attempt to eradicate the Hawaiian language.... Kuleana means an obligation, a responsibility. So, when somebody says this is your kuleana, it means you have some work to do. It means you are shouldering some kind of obligation and you are responsible for it. But, it's not seen in a negative sense because it is also a privilege. When you have been given a kuleana, it means essentially that you have been trained to do a certain thing and do it well enough that you get to do this work. And you get to decide how it's done. And that's why in Hawaiian families, when you hear a dispute among children, you'll hear the phrase, "Eh, that's not your kuleana. That's my kuleana." So, I love the word. I love what it means.[1]

Osorio's statement was offered as testimony in the context of the state BLNR's decisionmaking on a permit for construction of the Thirty-Meter

Telescope on Mauna Kea. Kuleana is not only a value or a concept, but also a relationship to land, community, and a personal property. It is no accident that the parcels claimed by native tenants were governed under the Kuleana Act.

Many in West Maui are returning to kuleana lands for which they have obligations and which come with specific privileges. Those privileges include certain rights to access water and to defining the uses of that water. Their ability to fulfill their kuleana, however, often depends on a complex negotiation with state, county, and landowner assertions of rights under a settler colonial regime.

This chapter addresses intersections between water resource rights and kuleana in the sense of the term applied to both obligation and responsibility described by Osorio as well as the proper term for lands registered and patented under the Hawaiian Kingdom's Kuleana Act of 1850. We describe some current controversies amongst West Maui communities in their attempts to assert and implement water rights associated with West Maui's kuleana lands and describe two areas where kuleana holders struggle to exercise those rights.

THE MĀHELE OF 1848 AND THE KULEANA ACT OF 1850

The following is a brief recitation of Hawaiian Kingdom and native Hawaiian traditional and customary laws that was more comprehensively set forth in chapter 1. The 1848 Māhele divided the vested land rights of the Mōʻī King Kamehameha III and the aliʻi, including 245 chiefs. Until that time the mōʻī, aliʻi, and the makaʻāinana held an undivided interest in lands. In the Māhele, King Kamehameha was granted 1 million acres (Crown Lands), the aliʻi obtained 1.5 million acres (aliʻi lands), and the government was granted 1.5 million acres (government lands).[2] Whereas the mōʻī and aliʻi were able to quitclaim their interest to each other and record them in the *Māhele Book*, makaʻāinana were required to file claims, provide testimony (their own and witnesses), pay for a survey and commutation tax, and obtain a Royal Patent. The aliʻi also submitted their claims to the Land Commission, but these claims were already identified in the *Māhele Book*; therefore they only lost their lands if they failed to file the claim or pay the commutation tax. Only approximately half of the Kānaka Maoli who were expected to file claims did so by the initial February 14, 1848 deadline.

The Kuleana Act was implemented on August 6, 1850 and authorized the Land Commission to award fee simple titles to native tenants who were working on Crown, government, and aliʻi lands. However, most makaʻāinana did not claim their kuleana lands; only 8,205 makaʻāinana received kuleana awards, accounting for 28,600 acres of land. This constituted less than one percent of the Kingdom of Hawaiʻi's land.[3] However, many such eligible makaʻāinana would later exercise an option to purchase government lands, greatly increasing the 28,600 acres under Native tenant ownership to 195,000 acres.[4]

The rights of native tenants in land existed prior to the 1848 Māhele and Kuleana Act, were recognized in those laws, and continue to this day. These "kuleana rights" include rights of access, traditional gathering of food resources, and fresh water for household purposes. These rights are recognized in the Hawaiʻi Constitution and statutes, including HRS §7-1, which provides:

> Where the landlords have obtained, or may hereafter obtain, allodial titles to their lands, the people on each of their lands shall not be deprived of the right to take firewood, house-timber, aho cord, thatch, or ki leaf, from the land on which they live, for their own private use, but they shall not have a right to take such articles to sell for profit. The people shall also have a right to drinking water, and running water, and the right of way. The springs of water, running water, and roads shall be free to all, on all lands granted in fee simple; provided that this shall not be applicable to wells and watercourses, which individuals have made for their own use.

This statute adopts Section 7 of the 1850 Kuleana Act, which section was included to preserve the rights of makaʻāinana to continue traditional and subsistence lifestyles. In 1978, Hawaiʻi's state constitution was amended to mandate protections for Native Hawaiian traditional and customary practices. Article XII § 7 of the Hawaiʻi Constitution provides, "The State reaffirms and shall protect all rights, customarily and traditionally exercised for subsistence, cultural and religious purposes and possessed by ahupuaʻa tenants who are descendants of native Hawaiians who inhabited the Hawaiian Islands prior to 1778, subject to the rights of the State to regulate such rights."[5]

The State Water Code also recognizes that kuleana rights to water are to be preserved and not infringed upon through its water resource management. HRS § 174C-101 provides in relevant part:

> d) The appurtenant water rights of kuleana and taro lands, along with those traditional and customary rights assured in this section, shall not be diminished or extinguished by a failure to apply for or to receive a permit under this chapter.

The water rights associated with native tenants and kuleana lands thus have a strong basis in Hawaiʻi law. These may form a basis for the preservation of those lands and native Hawaiian traditional and customary uses of water. In 1860, the legislature created the Commission of Private Ways and Water Rights to settle controversies concerning water rights attached to allocated lands. Most of the disputes concerned water used for domestic purposes and loʻi kalo irrigation. The commissioners applied ancient custom and usage in determining water rights, often using oral testimonies of those kamaʻāina to the area. In 1907, the duties of the commission were transferred to circuit court judges.[6] Kepā and Onaona Maly's *He Wahi MoʻOlelo No Kauaʻula a Me Kekāhi ʻĀina o Lahaina i Maui: A Collection of Traditions and Historical Accounts of Kauaʻula and Other Lands of Lahaina, Maui* (2007) compiled claims and awards made pursuant to the Māhele in Kauaʻula and the near vicinity. The Malys reviewed and translated pages from the *Native Register, Native Testimony, Foreign Register, Foreign Testimony,* and the *Māhele Award Book* in tabulating 425 claims in 24 ahupuaʻa or land areas of Lahaina that were recorded in 1,189 documents.[7]

Public Trust Lands

Water rights were never completely separate from land, historically and now. This section reviews the histories of the un-ceded Hawaiian Kingdom lands that were transferred to the U.S., and are to be held in trust. These histories and lands are central to kuleana as an organization of relationships, in which water plays a critical, albeit often overlooked, role.

Today, "public trust" lands, approximately 1.8 million acres, derive from the 1848 Māhele, which transformed Native Hawaiian traditional land tenure systems to private land ownership under the Hawaiian Kingdom. Acting pursuant to Māhele enactments, the Land Commission "settled and established the inception of private land titles" under the authority of King Kamehameha III, the sovereign owner of all of Hawaiʻi's lands.[8] The Commission's awards and patents are considered the "foundation of all titles to land in this Kingdom."[9]

During the Māhele process, King Kamehameha III divided his lands into government and private ("Crown") lands. "Crown" lands consisted of approximately one million acres, or a quarter of the ʻāina, that Kamehameha III retained for himself from the Māhele. When Kamehameha III's successor, Kamehameha IV, died in 1863, Kamehameha V (and not his widow, Queen Emma) received these lands in a court ruling that determined that Kamehameha V as monarch needed to have lands to fulfill his responsibilities to his people. In 1865, the

Hawaiʻi legislature passed a statute that made Crown lands inalienable. From this point, a Board of Commissioners of Crown Lands managed the Crown Lands and used the revenues to support the monarchy.

"Government" lands, approximately 1.5 million acres, were transferred to the government itself in the Māhele, to be used for public purposes. Substantial amounts were sold during the Kingdom era, with about 800,000 acres remaining at the time of the 1893 overthrow. Both Crown and Government lands were considered "public lands" under the Land Act of August 15, 1895, which repealed the 1865 statute that made Crown Lands inalienable. These lands were later merged into government lands.[10] Between 1865 and 1898, governments of Hawaiʻi (the Kingdom, and after the 1893 overthrow the Republic of Hawaiʻi), sold 46,594 acres of Crown and Government Lands.

Seizing power in the wake of the overthrow of the Hawaiian Kingdom's last reigning monarch, the Republic of Hawaiʻi usurped property consisting of: 1) government lands that had been surrendered by Kamehameha III; 2) lands ceded by the chiefs in lieu of a commutation fee required to establish their fee-simple ownership; 3) lands purchased by the government; 4) lands forfeited by certain claimants; and 5) pursuant to an 1894 act of the Republic of Hawaiʻi, "Crown" lands that had been the personal property of the King.[11]

In 1898, the US annexed Hawaiʻi, and the Republic of Hawaiʻi "ceded" these government lands to the US. The instrument of that annexation, the 1898 Newlands Resolution, states that the Republic of Hawaiʻi:

> cede[s] absolutely and without reserve to the United States of America all rights of sovereignty of whatsoever kind in and over the Hawaiian Islands and their dependencies, and also … the absolute fee and ownership of all public, Government, or Crown lands, public buildings or edifices, ports, harbors, military equipment *and all other public property of every kind and description belonging to the Government of the Hawaiian Islands, together with every right and appurtenance thereunto appertaining.*[12]

In 1982, the Hawaiʻi Attorney General opined that the broadly inclusive language of the Newlands Resolution extends to all public property that the Republic controlled.[13]

Lands ceded to the Republic of Hawaiʻi, and to the US government thereafter, "include all of the rights reserved by the King at the Māhele, by the Government in Land Commission Awards and Patents, and all other property rights accruing to the Government of Hawaiʻi prior to 1898."[14] These "ceded" lands retain the "reserved rights of...all mineral and metallic mines of every kind and description," and all other natural resources in the public domain in 1898, which have not been subsequently transferred.[15]

The 1898 Newlands Joint Resolution, the 1900 Organic Act, and the later 1959 Admissions Act, provided that revenues and proceeds from public lands should be used for the benefit of the inhabitants of the Territory of Hawaiʻi for educational and other public purposes.[16] In both the 1898 Joint Resolution of Annexation and the 1900 Organic Act, the United States recognized the unique status of Hawaiʻi's public lands and stated that the laws governing US public lands generally should not apply to them and that the revenues from these lands should go to the people of Hawaiʻi.

An 1899 opinion of the US Attorney General clarified that these lands should be considered to be "a special trust." This trust was separate from 200,000 acres set aside for the Hawaiian Home Lands Program in 1921, and the federal government retained approximately 350,000 acres for military bases and national parks.

The 1959 Admission Act transferred approximately 1.4 million acres to the new State of Hawaiʻi, recognized the trust status of these lands, and stated that land revenues should be used for public purposes, including "for the betterment of the conditions of native Hawaiians."[17]

Under the Admissions Act's §5, public trust lands consist in all 5(b) lands that were ceded by the Republic of Hawaiʻi to the US, excepting lands that were 5(c) set aside by federal actors or the state governor as of Hawaiʻi's admission on August 21, 1959, or 5(d) lands that the Territory of Hawaiʻi conveyed to the State.[18] Section 5(f) of the Admissions Act established a special public trust from lands transferred from the US to the State upon admission in 1959 and is the basis for the public trust established in Section 4 of the state constitution. Section 5(b) of the Admissions Act specifies that public trust lands are those public lands and other public property that the Republic of Hawaiʻi ceded to the US federal government by Joint Resolution of Annexation.[19]

In 2003, the Hawaiʻi State Attorney General stated, "[c]eded lands... includ[e] the water, minerals, plants, and other things connected with the lands, and every species of title inchoate or complete."[20] This reference to 'ceded lands' indicates those lands that constitute 5(b) public trust lands. In coming to this conclusion, the Hawaiʻi State Attorney General reviewed *State v. Zimring*, 58 Haw. 106, 566 P.2d 725 (1977), in which the Hawaiʻi Supreme Court determined that newly formed lands as a result of lava flows are part of the public trust.[21] The *Zimring* court found the lava flow question a case of first impression and applied equitable doctrines to balance between the relative "windfall" coastal property owners would enjoy against the overall public "benefit of all the people of Hawaii."[22] *Zimring* looked to the language of the Joint Resolution, which conveyed rights to the US that were then conferred to the state upon the passage of the Admissions Act. The court found that the Hawai'i Republic's voluntarily cession of "all other property of the Hawaiian Islands together with every right and appurtenance thereunder appertaining" included property "real, personal and mixed, choate and inchoate, corporeal."[23]

Because the *right* to these lava flow land extensions vested in the trust in 1898 with the Newlands resolution, the fact that the actual land did not form until 1955 did not remove them from the state's public trust. "Since the right to future lava extensions was conveyed to the United States at the time of annexation," the court found, "any lava extension thereafter created should be considered to be among the "lands and properties that were ceded to the United States by the Republic of Hawaii under the joint resolution of annexation."[24] Lava flow land extensions, existing and in the future, were part of the 1898 cession and returned to the state in section 5(b) of the Admission Act.[25]

A later decision, *Napeahi v. Paty*, 921 F.2d 897 (9th Cir. 1988), used the *Zimring* rationale to find that the lands that *become* submerged through natural processes after 1898 also thereby become public lands subject to the section 5(f) trust. The Ninth Circuit also drew from *County of Hawaii v. Sotomura*, 55 Haw. 176, 571 P.2d 57 (1973), which held that the state may acquire title to newly eroded submerged lands.

In 1978, Hawai'i residents ratified Hawai'i Constitution Article XII, Section 6, which established a state agency, the Office of Hawaiian Affairs (OHA), and its right to receive a "pro rata portion" of the revenues generated from the use of public trust lands for the betterment of the conditions of Native Hawaiians. Hawai'i Constitution Article XII, § 6 further empowers the OHA board "to manage and administer the proceeds from the sale or other disposition of the lands, natural resources, minerals and income derived from whatever sources for native Hawaiians and Hawaiians, including all income and proceeds from that pro rata portion of the trust referred to in Section 4 of this article for native Hawaiians."

The Hawai'i Constitution, Article XII, § 4 describes this public trust as "lands granted to the State of Hawaii by Section 5(b) of the Admission Act" and excludes Hawaiian Home Lands.

Through Act 273, Session Laws of Hawai'i (SLH) 1980, which was codified as Hawai'i Revised Statutes (HRS) §10-13.5, the state legislature defined

OHA's pro rata portion as "twenty percent of all funds derived from the public land trust." Initially, the state interpreted HRS § 10-13.5 to include only revenues generated from lands controlled and managed by the Department of Land and Natural Resources (DLNR). An Attorney General Opinion dated Sept. 23, 1983 upheld the state's practice of not including within OHA's pro rata portion revenues from lands that had been set aside or leased to agencies other than DLNR for public use, such as harbors and airports, or revenues generated by private businesses managing or operating on public lands or facilities. Using this methodology, between 1981 and 1990, the state transferred an average of approximately $1.4 million annually to OHA. HRS § 10-3(1) further specifies that the public trust consists of:

> all proceeds and income from the sale, lease, or other disposition of lands ceded to the United States by the Republic of Hawaii under the joint resolution of annexation, approved July 7, 1898 (30 Stat. 750), or acquired in exchange for lands so ceded, and conveyed to the State of Hawaii by virtue of section 5(b) of the Act of March 18, 1959.

Under HRS § 10-13.5, OHA should receive twenty percent of these public trust revenues. Act 178, Session Laws of Hawai'i 2006, sets aside HRS section 10-13.5 "until further action is taken by the legislature," and establishes OHA's interim pro rata portion as a specific dollar amount ($15.1 million per year). Accordingly, Act 178 is an interim determination of OHA's pro rata portion of public land trust revenue going forward.

Currently, Executive Order 06-06, authorized by then-governor Linda Lingle, requires agencies to transfer twenty percent of revenues from public trust lands unless such a transfer conflicts with other laws.

PIONEER MILL AND KULEANA LANDS

West Maui's plantation era lasted longer than in other areas of Hawai'i. Although Pioneer Mill, Amfac, and MLP took over much of West Maui's privately held lands, at least 425 people claimed kuleana ownership of individual plots in West Maui's region from Launiupoko to Paunau (Kahoma) alone.[26] Of these claims, only 286 were awarded. Thousands of small parcels across the land were not awarded and left unaccounted for. This meant, in part, that although more than 1,700 lo'i were claimed in the mid-1800s, many traditional places of residency and agricultural usage were abandoned.[27] Kepā and Onaona Maly documented several native families who continued working their loʻi kalo at Kauaʻula, Paunau and Kahoma through the 1940s. But after 1940, few loʻi kalo were maintained due to factors including a lack of water, an aging population, and the dearth of economic opportunities for younger generations.[28] For example, Kauaʻula Stream, now diverted by West Maui Land Company and its subsidiaries, once flowed perennially from mauka to makai. Pioneer Mill's near monopoly of surface water resources had a precedent as a war tactic in West Maui.

Pioneer Mill acquired crop and ditch lands in West Maui, as well as the water rights of kuleana. It leased 1,000 acres from Kamehameha Schools/Bishop Estate (KSBE) at a rate of $465 per year in 1911.[29] In a sampling of the years 1906 and 1907, Pioneer Mill recorded its lease rights to it had been acquired from Qualau Pelapela for kuleana award no. 11293 and water rights in Kauaʻula Valley, Lahaina for $200;[30] Kualau Pelapela for kuleana lands and waters in Kauaʻula, Lahaina for $225; from Helena Kalawela for ʻāpana 3 of kuleana award no. 9822 for $50; from Malie Kupanihi for ʻāpana 1, 2, and 3 of kuleana award no. 2866 in Kapewakua, Lahaina for $50; from Geo Stephenson for ʻāpana 4 and 5 of kuleana award no. 6872 and water rights in Kauaʻula, Lahaina.[31]

Former Pioneer Mill workers were aware of tensions between Pioneer Mill and other large water users and Hawaiian tenants. James Higuchi said in a 2003 interview:

> There used to be some Hawaiian families living way up toward the mountain side. You know, because many of them, they owned [their property]. Still living by Olowalu section. Like Kauaʻula. They get families living up there. That's why you get this big controversy over there. They [outside developers] tried to develop and they tried to dig wells and all that. Because plenty of them, they get the water rights. So even guys living Olowalu, plenty of them, they get water rights. Those families include families such as the Palakiko, Kapu, and Dizon ʻohana in Kauaʻula Valley, the Kaluna ʻohana in Ukumehame, the Kalepa ʻohana in Kahoma, and the Keahi ʻohana in Kahana.[32]

These families are highly engaged in West Maui communities and public processes affecting their kuleana. Significantly, and despite his thirty-four years of experience in Hawaii's sugar industry, former Pioneer Mill Vice President Keoki Freeland did not remember any conflicts with other water users while he was with Pioneer Mill. Nor did the enactment of the Water Code in 1987 seem to disturb any of Pioneer Mill's operations, "I don't even remember it. The civil engineering took care of it," commented Freeland.[33] While he was with Pioneer Mill, Freeland recalled people cultivating kalo, but not on a large scale such that the water that came down past diversions or through gaining streams was sufficient. "Now they want to cultivate more than when I was there, so they want more water." The relative quiescence concerning water issues in the 1980s may have less to do with the absence of conflict than with the intergenerational, comprehensive process through which the Hawaiian Renaissance is taking root in Hawai'i.[34]

During a public forum on Hawaiian self-governance at the William S. Richardson School of Law, an audience member noted that he had lived in Hawai'i for a long time and did not remember Hawaiians in his youth agitating for return of water and land and asked, why are "they" demanding it now? Panelist Jon Osorio replied, "Because it's logical."[35]

Kapali Keahi pointed to the competitive relationship between economic uses of water stating, "Industry is a veritable vaccuum for everyone. A lot of people backed off of farming taro." Many of the older generation were no longer physically able to farm. Younger generations that want to farm are faced with title, access, and water resource issues.[36] Keahi recalled an effort by Wesley Horcajo, a former Maui Land and Pine (MLP) manager who was putting on workshops to get taro farmers in Honokōhau to raise dryland kalo instead of lo'i kalo. Many in Honokōhau Valley saw Horcajo's purpose as a means to restrict their water use. Their distrust of water managers, landowners, and county water management has a long history, and persists today. Keahi noted that a huge volume of water had historically been taken from Honokōhau water to "feed the whole west side all the way to Ukumehame." Yet, after the decommissioning of Crater Village/Kahoma reservoir, the water stopped going all that distance. He asked, "If the diversions are continuing to take the same amount of water without all the farming, where is the water going?"

As discussed in chapter 3, Honokōhau Stream and other waters that are diverted into the Honokōhau Ditch and irrigation system are being stored, wasted, and delivered to new agricultural and other lands. Some of these uses predate the cessation of sugar and pineapple cultivation but others do not. Privately, water managers have blamed unnamed "trespassers" and houseless persons for creating an unpermitted diversion from the ditch into Honokōwai. Large landowners, such as the Kaanapali Land Management Company (KLMC) and West Maui Land Company, seek to maintain diversions and merely store water in anticipation of construction of new residential and agricultural sub-

divisions. Some new agricultural enterprises have already been developed in
Kāʻanapali and are served by ditch waters.

HISTORICAL SHIFTS IN KALO FARMING IN WEST MAUI

Kalo farmers have long defended their rights to Maui water resources. As discussed in chapter 1, in the late 1890s, kuleana tenants and kalo growers actively
defended their rights in *Horner v. Kumuliilii*:

> Alleging a controversy between plaintiffs and defendants in respect to the
> amount of water, method and time of its use upon lands owned or held by
> both parties... The entire stream [Kauaʻula] is taken up and used upon land
> in the valley on both sides of the stream for irrigating crops of kalo and on
> the flats below for sugar cane... Doubtless the stream itself has diminished
> somewhat in quantity during the last half-century from reasons that are con-
> jectural. Mr. James Campbell says that the freshets or storm waters which
> everyone could use at will to fill all their patches are much less frequent now
> than when he was a resident of Lahaina from 1851–1876.[37]

While recognizing the need to address the decrease in kalo production
and impacts on especially Hawaiian communities, mainstream commentators
and "experts" shied away from addressing redistribution of water resources. In
1903, the *Maui News* reported, "Maui Natives are Short of Taro" and on the
"Taro Rot Remedy."[38] Mauians were producing poi from breadfruit. Poi was
short in supply "owing to the many diseases which of late years have attacked
the plant[.]"[39] The causes of taro root rot were identified with soil conditions,
lack of drainage, and "planting of diseased hules."[40] No connection between
the shortage, the rot, and the plantations' diversion of needed surface water
flows was made at the time. Rather, the "remedy" prescribed sought to have
kalo farmers use only the amounts of water they received:

1. A supply of good hules, free from disease.
2. A patch so laid out as to secure the most economical use of the irrigation water.
3. The application of proper fertilizers at the right time.
4. A constantly running stream of water circulating over the fields, or
   when this is not possible, a frequent change of water.

5. An occasional change in the variety of the taro planted.
6. An entire change of hules from one patch to another, or a rotation of crops, using taro land for rice or bananas, at least two years in every five.[41]

Conveniently for diverters like Pioneer Mill, methods such as crop rotation and "a frequent change of water" are methods that would not require kalo growers to petition against the plantations' monopoly of water resources.

In 1906, the case *Aheong v. Haiku Sugar Company* was initiated by a taro planter, A. J. Aheong, who filed suit for damages on account of alleged loss incurred by the taking of water claimed by Aheong for lands said by him as being ancient taro lands but denied by the Haiku Sugar Company.[42] The *Maui News* headlined it as a "case of considerable interest." It came before Judge Robinson of the First Circuit Court on the bench in place of Judge A. N. Kepokia, who was disqualified. W. A. Kinney represented Aheong, and W. O. Smith and W. J. Warren the defendant company. A large number of witnesses were called on both sides, and the case was closely contested.[43] Kinney closed his address with an appeal to the jury on the ground that so much was at stake that it was a case of life and death to the plaintiff, Aheong. "This called W. O. Smith to his feet, and a lively tilt ensued."[44] The judge returned with a verdict for the plaintiff Aheong in the sum of $1,500.

We cannot easily insert Aheong's legal victory into a narrative about Hawaiian kalo growers facing off against settler plantation agribusinesses. Newspaper archives did not indicate whether Aheong was Hawaiian. Rather, at the time, there was a perception that Chinese taro growers were seeking to oust Hawaiian kalo farmers in Wailuku.

A peculiar condition of affairs exists among poi dealers and taro growers in the district of Wailuku. Two months ago taro was selling at $2.25 a bag and was a scarce article at that figure. Poi was also selling at a correspondingly high figure. A few days ago native taro planter was unable to find a purchaser for his crop of taro, and, after selling a few bags of taro at $1.50, is quite willing to sell the rest or his crop, rather than see it spoil on his hands, at any figure even if it is only sixty cents a bag. Yet an offer at so advantageous a figure to poi dealers goes begging on a short market with no takers.

Another planter with a small crop of taro can find no purchaser for his crop at any figure short of making a present of it to poi dealers.

For taro to be selling at $2.25 one month [*sic*] drop to sixty cents a bag with no takers savors of a corner in the market or of the methods of Wall Street.

That such staple food articles as poi and taro, so generally used by all classes of our cosmopolitan population, can become unsaleable at a time when the taro crop itself is short is ascribed by several Hawaiian planters to the fact that Chinese planters who control much taro land rented from Hawaiians are working in combination with poi shop men.

Chinese poi dealers have agreed to buy all the taro they need from the Chinese taro planters only, and other taro planters not in the favored circle can find no purchaser for their crops even at a time when poi is still selling at a price way above what would be normal at times when taro is scarce.

As an [*sic*] Hawaiian planter puts it, poi may lie selling at a price, but if you do not belong to the combination your crop of taro will rot in the patches and yet no poi dealer will buy it from you at any figure.[45]

In 1918, the best four specimens of wetland taro were produced by Wong Nin and the best collection of dry land taro came from Loo Fat Kun.[46] In an op-ed extolling taro as "one of the best foodstuffs known to the human race," a Jas. W. Givrvin wrote:

> Formerly, the raising of taro and manufacturing it into poi for home or market was entirely confined to the natives. Today the Chinese have encroached on even the native industries to such an extent that they culti-vate the majority of this staff of life and sell it from door to door, either as taro for the housewife or as poi to the native.[47]

Chinese settlers were not the first to seek to exploit Hawai'i's taro market. Earlier, in 1886, the Alden Fruit and Taro Company of Wailuku, Maui announced their new enterprise: "Taro flour! Taro flour! Every Body Can Make Their Own Poi at Home."[48] Alden's poi was "free from all impurities which exist in the Poi commonly made" and the flour could be used to make cocktails, muffins, rolls, bread, griddle cakes, pudding, and taro mush.[49] The emphasis on purity in poi milling was racialized:

> Poi, as commonly made, can scarcely be free from impurities of various kinds, some of them of a most deleterious character, owing to the filthy process of handling and the latent diseases prevalent among natives and Chinamen, who are usually employed to pound and manipulate the same.

By the substitution of the machinery above described for hand labor, all these objections to the use of Poi are removed.[50]

Beginning in 1912, kuleana owners in Wailuku, specifically those farming kalo, were accorded opportunities to obtain "free water" from Wailuku Sugar Company under an agreement between Maui County, the territory, and the sugar company.[51] By letter dated July 10, 1922, however, Wailuku Sugar's manager, H. B. Penhallow, complained to the county engineer of the arrangement. While professing the sugar company's interest in "the granting of free water to water users," Penhallow asserted,

> We would ask that we be notified so that we may have an opportunity to be heard, in case we have objections to offer. In this way, it will save embarrassment, both to the County of Maui and the Wailuku Sugar Company, should we make a protest, as it is much easier to clear up such matters ahead of time before third parties become interested than after.[52]

Penhallow's assertion was belied by the identity of the water users as kuleana owners and kalo farmers, whose interests in the water resources doubtless existed long before the sugar company arrived. The county engineer responded:

> Mr. Penhallow's contentions are well taken, and before any one is granted free water he should be required to show: (1) That the applicant is the undisputed owner of the land for which he is applying free use of water. (2) The kuleana on which the land is situated, by map or other satisfactory data. (3) Proof that the land in question has taro land up to the amount for which application is made, and in accordance with the agreement entered into between the county, territory, and the Wailuku Sugar Company. (4) That the land is not drawing any water from open auwais. The preparation of these data, particularly item 2, in most cases will require considerable time and work and neither the county nor the plantation should be called upon to produce the evidence. A sample of what is required is herewith submitted.[53]

Here, we see how even the rights associated with kuleana were eroded by burdensome surveying and data compilation requirements. Kuleana owners face multiple challenges to their assertion of water rights, including the need to navigate their claims to the kuleana parcels themselves.

Ukumehame Stream and Displacement
of Kuleana Owners

*Above the Pioneer Plantation reservoirs, terraces cover the flatland just
below the entrance to Ukumehame Canyon. Only a few of these are now
under cultivation. The upper terraces have been long abandoned, and
those just above the reservoirs are only half used—that half unsuccessfully,
because of insufficient water for flooding. The terraces used to extend well
down over the land below the valley, but, with the exception of one tiny taro
plantation standing like an island in the midst of the cane, all vestiges of the
ancient cultivation have been plowed under. This is excellent wet taro soil.*

— E. S. C. Handy[54]

Traveling towards Lahaina town, just after passing Ukumehame Beach Park,
drivers on Honoapiʻilani Highway pass a narrow strip of green amidst the otherwise arid mauka lands. That area indicates Ukumehame Stream, which is currently diverted by West Maui Investors towards several reservoirs and through
to Ukumehame Gulch.

For many generations, Victoria Kaluna-Palafox's family has lived and
farmed kalo along Ukumehame Stream under a kuleana land awarded under
Land Court Award No. 6408. Kaluna-Palafox's claim to kuleana lands is linked
to one of the Land Court Awards (LCA No. 6408) held by Kaleleiki. In 2015,
another of Kaleleiki's awards, LCA 7779, was at issue. In 2014, Mehrdad and
Gina Shayefar sued to quiet title of their ownership of approximately eight acres
in Ukumehame under a warranty deed they obtained from West Maui Investors
in about 2008.[55] In 2014, Samuel Houpo Kaleleiki, Jr. recorded a quitclaim deed
to the same 7.846 acres of land, conveying his interest to his children, defendants Von-Alan Hinano Kaleleiki and Sarah-Therece K. Kaleleiki. The Kale-
leikis, proceeding pro se, defended against the Shayefar's claim. The Shayefar's
attorneys contended that they had obtained good title insurance and opposed
the Kaleleiki's evidence. Defendants Von-Alan Kaleleiki and Sarah-Therece
Kaleleiki stated that Lot 32 is located within a large parcel of land that was
awarded to their ancestor by Land Commission Award Number 7779 in 1848.
(Def.'s Opp. filed June 26, 2015, at p. 4, ECF No. 41.) Defendants claim they
are "direct lineal descendants of the original grantee, Aleiamai Kaleleiki, who
fathered Kahaunaele Kaleleiki, birth mother of Samuel Kekuaokaalaaualailiahi
Houpo Samuel Kaleleiki, father of Hopou Samuel Kaleleiki, Jr., father of Von-
Alan Hinano Kaleleiki and Sarah Therece K. Kaleleiki." They contended that

none of their ancestors ever sold the land and claim that the Kaleleiki family "has maintained their presence in these lands for all time to present day." In 2016, however, the Shayefars prevailed in their suit to quiet title to the Ukumehame lands.[56]

In May 2018, the large-scale and commercial real estate brokerage the Commercial Real Estate Exchange, Inc. (CREXi) advertised "24 entitled, residential estate lots along with five supporting parcels situated on ±216 acres of land[.]"[57] Current entitlements permit a prospective developer to build up to 48 single-family homes (a main house of unlimited square footage, and an ʻohana (cottage) of up to 1,000 square feet) on large agricultural lots. Another 21 lots were already sold on an individual basis between 2006 and 2009. None of the entitlements or government approvals for the Ukumehame land permits have an affordability component.[58] Real estate agents advertise Ukumehame lots as a "rare opportunity" for development in part due to its "dedicated freshwater stream[,]" which "produces water year-round and provides the agricultural subdivision with a low-cost water source."[59] The sales pitch for Ukumehame lands are silent on the issue of significant kuleana that continue to be farmed in traditional ways by people like Thomas Lindsey and Victoria Kaluna-Palafox.

Kaluna-Palafox, whose family has lived in Ukumehame for generations, offered written testimony, dated December 26, 2017, to CWRM on proposed amendments to Ukumehame Stream IIFSs that went immediately to the point.

> Area Ukumehame (6004) since May 23 & 24, 2009 and continuance til today December 26, 2017 and on. Total Length of pipes, which follows the old [auwai] is 1540 Feet. 6 feet header with 6 inch pvc pipes, more or less are set in the river above water fall. 1540 feet is for Kuleana usage. Water traditionally used for kuleana, home and agricultural usage. Water for domestic use for Kaluna-Palafox Ohana, approx . . . 1000 gal. per day. Kuleana 4 taro patches and more to open. Home use and agricultural usage. Total [acreage] 9.1. Lcaw 6408:1, R.P. 5124; T.M.K. 4-8-01-057, Ahupuaʻa o Lahaina moku puni o Maui.[60]

Kaluna-Palafox's testimony was notable because she drew direct connections between her rights as a kuleana owner and her highly specific claims to water resource needs, which were broken out into categories and measurements with which CWRM staff would be conversant.

Māhele records show kalo cultivation in Ukumehame as early as 1826. Ukumehame Stream has been running continuously from mauka to makai since 1995, when sugar cultivation was terminated. The stream splits into two sections. The flow on the right bank has no diversion. On the left, waters naturally flow past an 18-foot diversion. Depending upon the stream flow, the water will flow into the ʻauwai without any kind of diversion. Both the diversion and ʻauwai are made from river stone.[61]

The main diversion is the Ukumehame Ditch, which supports Maui Cultural Lands' loʻi and another loʻi, and also fills at least two reservoirs owned by West Maui Investors. Very little of the water diverted by the Ukumehame Ditch is returned to the stream. Some water is also diverted via the Kaʻakua ʻAuwai, which supplies approximately 16 loʻi, after which the water is returned to the stream below the Ukumehame Ditch diversion. Of the four streams recently targeted for amended IIFS, Ukumehame was the subject of the most complaints.[62] Since 2006, kuleana users have filed complaints against the proposed Ukumehame subdivision, specifically due to the impacts that it may have on their water rights. Other complaints also concerned kuleana water rights, including a complaint against the removal of a pipe from the stream and the developer's alteration of the stream channel in May 2014.[63]

A significant amount of land appurtenant to Ukumehame Stream is owned by West Maui Investors, LLC (also called Uka, LLC), whose owner is located

Ukumehame stream ʻauwai. Source: CWRM Staff Submittal, SDWP.4646.6 Ukumehame Stream, Maui Item B-1 (Nov. 21, 2017). Kaluna-Palafox testified that her family dug the ʻauwai.

in Beverly Hills, California.[64] They own and operate Ukumehame reservoir numbers 2 and 3, which are earthen embankment dams constructed side-by-side along the bottom of the western slope of the Ukumehame Gulch. The reservoirs receive water from a small diversion off of the stream in the Ukumehame Gulch and which has historically been utilized for agricultural water to irrigate sugar and pineapple croplands. The reservoirs, which have a total storage capacity of 11.4 mgd, have not been used to supply downstream users in many years. DLNR regulated them as a dam and reservoir facility until 2017.

In 2008, a large leak of greater than 100 gallons per minute was found in Ukumehame reservoir no. 3. DLNR ordered West Maui Investors to reduce the water level in both reservoirs to eight feet. In 2012 and again in 2016, the legislature approved special purpose revenue bonds of up to $850,285 to "assist" West Maui Investors with the two leaking reservoirs at Ukumehame.[65] The 2012 measure failed because it preceded amendment of the Hawai'i Constitution in 2014 to allow the issuance of special purpose revenue bonds. In 2017, however, BLNR approved removal of the reservoirs, which would result in a new 200-foot-long channel that would effectively escape the definition of a "dam" and associated permitting requirements.[66]

Hawaiian kalo farmers in Ukumehame, including Kaluna-Palafox's 'ohana, have been concerned about general rumblings regarding West Maui Investors' plans for development of an agricultural subdivision in Ukumehame. West Maui Investors now appears to work under the business entity Uka, LLC, which operates out of Beverly Hills. Uka, LLC plans to develop up to 45 private farm lots in Ukumehame.[67] Such development would tax the infrastructure of the area and challenge the ability of those caring for their kuleana to continue their cultural practices. In March 2018, however, CWRM staff recommended an amended IIFS for Ukumehame stream of 4.5 cubic feet per second to allow Uka, LLC to meet their 0.045 mgd agricultural water demand and 0.004 mgd landscaping water demand at least 50 percent of the time.[68]

For the state's part, it has facilitated West Maui Investors' development. In 2016, the legislature determined to float revenue bonds for "Ukumehame reservoirs two and three." DLNR supported the revenue bond proposals without comment on how these would impact kuleana owners along the stream.[69]

Access and Water for Kanahā Kuleana

Kanahā Stream is approximately seven miles long, with a perennial flow in its upper elevations and intermittent flows at its lower elevations. The contributing watershed lands are five square miles at a maximum elevation of 4,500 feet in the West Maui mountains. Kanahā and Kahoma Streams once merged and flowed together into the ocean. Beginning in the nineteenth century, they were instead used to irrigate extensive sugar plantations. Kanahā is a perennial stream, but two intakes above the kuleana parcels divert water from the stream.[70] The first diversion is a three-way split that previously delivered water to Pioneer Mill's boiler plant operation, the county, and Lahainaluna High School. The second upstream intake took the overflow from the first diversion into Pioneer Mill's irrigation ditch and to its cane fields.[71]

Until at least 2015, Maui DWS diverted 1.6216 mgd of Kanahā Stream waters deep in the valley above the many kuleana in the valley.[72] Much of Kanahā Valley was subject to Land Court Application No. 403, which meant the lands were part of the Torrens System, or Land Court system. Under the Land Court system, a claimant petitions to register the lands in her name and if successful, the state issues a certificate of title. No notice of prior encumbrance or adverse possession can defeat a certificate of title. The kuleana along Kanahā Valley stream, including that of Keahi, were exempted from the Land Court system registration due to a singular history.

Land Court Application No. 403, which is available online thanks to the North Beach West Maui Benefit Fund,[73] holds an interesting story for Kanahā. Bishop Estate and the Territory of Hawai'i each claimed adjacent ahupua'a that overlapped in part. At issue in the overlap was the constitution and ownership of the ahupua'a of Paunau. The territory claimed to have gotten the entirety of the Paunau ahupua'a, including section numbers 1–8 from the American Board of Commissioners for Foreign Missions (ABCFM), a missionary organization. ABCFM reportedly obtained the ahupua'a via adverse possession, but the Land Court examiners found that ABCFM had returned it to the kuleana owners for an unspecified reason. The Territory said it had held onto the lands anyway after ABCFM disclaimed ownership and so the Territory got the land via adverse possession themselves. However, the Land Court examiner decided that the conflict raised between Bishop Estate and the Territory was a novel situation. The examiner had not seen this overlap in his 40 years of surveying or 16 years as a Boundary Commissioner. The examiner therefore decided the most ancient description of the Paunau ahupua'a would govern. This description included "1428[.]10 acres more or less"[74] of the steep valley mauka lands and was "Exclusive of Kuleanas." The examiner therefore excepted Sections 1–8 from Land Court Application No. 403. These exceptions from the Land Court certification were recognized in at least two orders, dated 1985 and 1987.

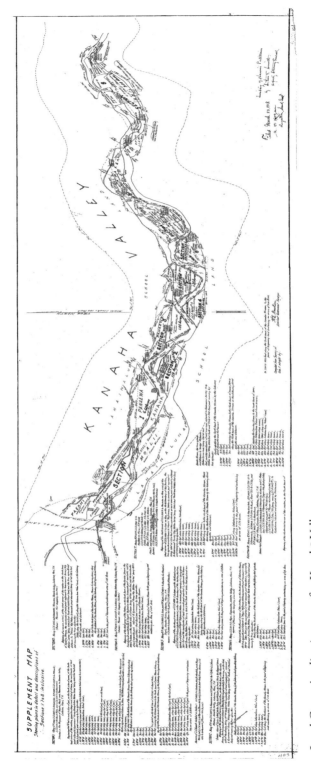

Land Court Application map for Kanahā Valley.

Map 3 of the Land Court Application identifies the kuleana on both sides of Kanahā stream as Lot D-1 Section 1–8 and states, "Portion of the northerly boundary and the area of Lot D-1 as shown hereon have been cancelled by Order of the Judge of the Land Court dated July 12, 1985." Map 13 identifies the same exclusion of those 16.8 acres of Lot D Section 1–8 and shows this was approved by Land Court dated December 2, 1987.

Kanahā Valley has been informally called "Hans Valley" owing to Hans Michel's claim to own approximately nearly all of the kuleana that line Kanahā Stream. On October 12, 2010, the county Water Resources Committee heard testimony on an agenda item concerning access through the Michel's property for maintenance and operation of the Kanahā Valley stream intake, operated by the county Department of Water Supply.[75]

Glenn Au testified on behalf of a nascent nonprofit organization dedicated to helping Native Hawaiians, as well as kupuna and keiki. Au raised concerns that the county was making decisions about Kanahā Valley stream access while new laws and community awareness were creating a new context in which "there's a cloud on all kuleana lands today."[76] Au continued:

> We're finding out there has been fraud committed by the big plantation owners, and they were in cahoots with the . . . konohikis of our ancestral chieftains and all that business. But I'd rather you know that it's coming and it's gonna happen and when and where and why. Like you said, you'd probably be gone in 20 years, but our ancestors will be here, my children will be here. But the problem now exists making you aware of who did what to whom.[77]

The committee asked Au no questions and moved on to Hans Michel. Michel testified to multiple conflicts with the county water department since at least 1975 when wells were drilled in Kanahā Valley.[78] In 1972, however, Michel began charging Pioneer Mill, the county, and Lahainaluna High School $30 a month for use of the intake on property he claimed to be his. Later, that amount was raised to $120 per month.[79] In exchange, Michel removes debris from the intake.

In the mid-1990s, the county Department of Water Supply entered into an agreement with Michel for access to the intake at the back of Kanahā Valley. Michel's complaints concerned water from diversions overflowing onto a trail, other malfunctions with the county diversion, the county's reticence to repair the trail that winds through Kanahā Valley and over properties claimed by

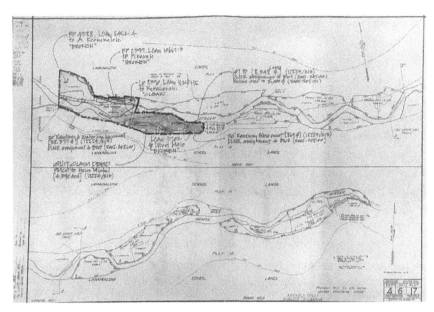

Map submitted to the county by Hans Michel indicating state of titles to Kahana kuleana.

Michel, and his unreimbursed attorneys' fees.[80] The committee pointed to broken title issues with some of Michel's claims, to which Michel responded that his attorney was working on them at that time.[81]

The county's intake for the Lahaina water system lies on a kuleana parcel owned in common with many others of a long-time Lahaina family, the Keahis, including Moses "Moke" Keahi, his son Kai Keahi, and his cousin, Kapali Keahi. Kai Keahi, amongst others, have been making efforts to restore lo'i in the back of Kanahā Valley. Keahi has been working with the state Water Commission, county Department of Public Works, county DWS, and landowners in order to gain both access and water flow to their lo'i. Water diverted from Kanahā Stream is subject to a three-party water source agreement between the state, county, and Pioneer Mill Ltd., which was executed in 1982. The agreement establishes priorities amongst the parties for a flow of up to 2.7 mgd from Kanahā Stream, and also provides for flows to Lahainaluna High School.[82] A ten-inch pipe conveys surface water from Kanahā Stream intake to a screen box below, from which water is distributed to Lahainaluna School, Maui DWS, and, previously, Pioneer Mill. The Lahaina Water Treatment Facility tapped into this system.[83]

Currently, Kanahā Stream does not meet Kahoma Stream, although this may change when CWRM imposes its new IIFSs. Kai Keahi has expressed the hope that the IIFS for Kanahā allow it to merge with Kahoma stream, while still allowing for certain household and other municipal uses of Kanahā waters by Maui DWS.

Prior to the plantation's diversions, loʻi lined Kanahā Stream. Kuleana owners towards the back of the valley could access their lands by walking or riding donkeys over the loʻi banks. Another access existed on the mountainside, but that trail has since been eroded due to overgrazing by goats and other ungulates. Today, the only viable access lies through the road to which Michel lays claim and through which other kuleana owners have not been able to obtain regular access. The issue remains disputed.

Kahoma Loʻi Restoration

On July 30, 2017, Lahaina community members including Kai Keahi, Archie Kalepa, and Tiare Lawrence put together an event for the opening of loʻi that they and others had just completed. "Taro has not grown in that valley for 130 years. For us to do the first planting in 130 years…was really amazing," said Lahaina resident Archie Kalepa.[84] Most kalo farming had dropped off by 1887, after which a few families had been cultivating kalo in scattered, irrigated plots in the back reaches of Kanahā and Kahoma into the 1930s–1940s.[85]

Kalepa made clear that their efforts in Kahoma were directed at cohering a community around a practical project of imagining how life might be possi-

Kahoma stream flowing, July 30, 2017.

ble despite and against environmental collapse. He stressed that his work was a product of learning—not only about aquatic biology, hydrology, and traditional agriculture, but the traditional history of the place. Kahoma had once fed many acres of loʻi.

"Building a future for the children" and "drawing on the wisdom of ancestors" can come across as mere banal tropes, but the work of putting these into practical directives is far from cliché. For eight years prior to the July 30, 2017 event, Kalepa and others worked with Kamehameha Schools to restore this streamflow. This work meant building trust between and amongst the West Maui communities who would imbue the loʻi with meaning, negotiating with various landowners to obtain rights of entry, persuading Kamehameha Schools to restore the water, meeting with Maui County's Department of Public Works concerning the flood control sand berm at the mouth of Kahoma Stream, guarding against new West Maui Land Company developments, and, of course, building loʻi.

The event was made possible by Kamehameha School's release of water into Kahoma Stream, which, as Kai Keahi pointed out in a half-joking tone, was made possible by Kamehameha School's previous permission that allowed Pioneer Mill to divert the water away. Watershed lands from which Kahoma stream originates are owned by Kamehameha Schools. In 1882, Pioneer Mill had earlier made arrangements with the trust to lease the land and, once leased, used the Kahoma Ditch to divert the water to one of its reservoirs on a parcel owned by the plantation.[86] When the lease ran out and Pioneer Mill shut its doors, Kamehameha Schools had to find new water sources for its parcel. It is from those other sources that Kahoma waters were restored. As an aside, with Kahoma Stream waters no longer diverted, flows to the Crater reservoir ceased. This has meant Kahoma Ranch Company is unable to continue to sell "water flume" rides as part of their ATV tours.

Many who attended the Kahoma loʻi opening were working to reopen or sustain loʻi in other of West Maui's valleys. Wili Wood had reopened a half-dozen loʻi in Honokōhau Valley. Charlie Palakiko was working on loʻi in Kauaʻula Valley. Skippy Hau, an aquatic biologist with DLNR's Division of Aquatic Resources, enthusiastically reported that Kahoma Stream was full of ʻoʻopu nākea. And it was not only loʻi for which community members were fighting.

On July 18, 2018, Kahoma Valley saw its first harvest of kalo in 120 years. Ka Malu o Kahālāwai, a local nonprofit organization headed by Archie Kalepa and Tiare Lawrence, amongst others, celebrated its first harvest. Many called it a historical event and celebrated the return to ancestral lands to grow food

West Maui community resident and organizer, Tiare Lawrence, addresses the group assembled to honor the reopening of loʻi in Kahoma. July 30, 2017.

Archie Kalepa, a famous waterman and community organizer native to Kahoma, opened the celebration. July 30, 2017, Kahoma, Maui.

Participants each planted huli in the newly opened loʻi kalo, July 30, 2017, Kahoma, Maui.

and reconnect with the Native Hawaiian culture. Loʻi in the valley were dry for decades because Kahoma Stream water had been diverted to irrigate sugar plantation lands. "Veins of the earth that are fertile with water, allow our earth to heal," said Kalepa. "We are beginning to practice our cultural rights once again. This is how we're going to build our community so that the Western way can understand our way, and the importance of what that means and how it needs to be part of our life."[87] For the two years preceding the celebration, Tiare Lawrence had led community organizing and workdays. "We want the restoration of Kahoma Valley to be a template for future restoration projects across the state that proves how resilient mother nature is when we give her a chance to recover. When we talk about food security, we should talk about restoration. The agriculture infrastructure created by our kupuna still exists in many of our valleys. We just need to restore them," said Lawrence.[88]

Honokōhau Valley Water Struggles

Under normal conditions, Honokōhau Stream is dry between the Maui Land and Pineapple Company (MLP) intake and a natural spring located approximately 1.5 miles downstream. A "taro gate" was installed in the Honolua Ditch Tunnel to release 1 mgd of water diverted by MLP back to Honokōhau Stream about two miles downstream from the diversion point. MLP controls the taro gate and adjusts the gate according to overall water flows. The taro gate requires maintenance and periodic cleaning due to debris blocking water flow. About a half-mile further downstream, additional water is returned to Honokōhau from Jerrold MacDonald's hydroelectric plant through a six-inch pipe. At this point downstream of the hydroelectric plant contribution, approximately two mgd flowed in the stream. Members of the West Maui Molokaʻi Taro Farmers Association (WMMTFA) maintain an intake (the "WWMTFA intake") located much lower in the valley, at approximately 70 feet elevation. The WWMTFA intake was a dam across the channel constructed from stone and concrete. Leakage and the low height of the WWMTFA dam means that less than half of the streamflow is diverted into the ʻauwai to feed loʻi kalo.

In the early 1990s, kalo farmers organized to exercise water kuleana that are supposed to be upheld by CWRM. Honokōhau communities and kalo farmers requested additional water, CWRM, in turn, requested that MLP return two mgd to the stream. MLP refused to comply. MLP-diverted Honokōhau Stream water flows to its own uses, Kapalua Resort (2 mgd), and formerly other uses by Pioneer Mill (5.5 mgd).[89]

Wesley Nohara (of MLP) responded to Honokōhau farmer concerns about MLP diversions by asking CWRM to provide a list of declarations for water use by others in Honokōhau Valley. MLP's concern anticipated complaints from kalo farmers in Honokōhau Valley.

By letter dated October 29, 1991, the WMMTFA filed a Citizen's Complaint with CWRM. CWRM rules provide for any person to file a complaint: if "any other person is wasting or polluting water, or is making a diversion, withdrawal, impoundment, consumptive use of waters or any other activity occurring within or outside of a water management area, not expressly exempted under this code, without a permit where one is required, the commission shall cause an investigation to be made, take appropriate action, and notify the complainant thereof."[90]

Aimoku Pali helped establish WMMFTA, composed of seventy-two farmers from rural areas on Maui and Molokaʻi, and which later received a three-year federal grant towards bolstering the agricultural industry. Pali explained, "Our goal is to be self-sufficient. The organization was formed out of the desire to maintain and revive the traditional rural lifestyle and at the same time generate income."[91] Pali also aligned WMMFTA with a contemporaneous Native Hawaiian cultural revival, commenting, "It's as if we're learning our culture all over again."[92]

WMMTFA included seven Honokōhau taro farmers, including Pali, who had moved back to his kuleana lands in 1972. These farmers could farm no more than three to four acres of loʻi along Honokōhau Stream, because MLP constructed a dam on the upper part of the valley that reduced streamflow to the farmers. WMMFTA wrote:

> No one is diverting water above us and we would like more water to flow down stream. Our ʻauwaiʻs [*sic*] are cleaned and our diversions are repaired. We need more water. Our crops are being damaged because of the lack of water and it is frustrating for us.

WMMFTA was represented by the Native Hawaiian Advisory Council, Inc.'s (NHAC) Elizabeth Ann Hoʻoipo Pa Martin, now Elizabeth Pa Nakea. Nakea, who was raised in Kāneʻohe, founded NHAC in 1987 to support native Hawaiian interests including water rights, sovereignty, self-determination, educational initiatives, and repatriation of Native Hawaiian iwi kūpuna.

David Martin, also with NHAC, described how Williamson B. Chang, who was on the first board of directors, pointed out a passage in the Water Code that had the requirement that people had to register their water uses.[93] NHAC started out with five or six attorneys who went out into communities to let them know that they had to register their water uses.

In January 1992, William W. Paty, Chair of the Department of Land and Natural Resources (DLNR), under which CWRM is housed, indicated that it did not want to be caught in the middle. Responding to MLP's Nohara, Paty said that WMMTFA had identified that their shortage of water was caused by MLP's ditch intake, although they had not contacted MLP. Paty wrote, "The first step towards accomplishing the goal of . . . a positive working relationship between Maui Pineapple and the water users of Honokōhau Valley" was for the two groups to talk to each other. NHAC's Elizabeth Pa Martin strongly rejected this analysis.

> The problem is not a lack of communication between the taro farmers and Maui Pineapple. The problem is Maui Pineapple has been controlling the water flow of the Honokōhau Stream for decades. It diverts water to land outside the watershed and deprives taro farmers of their appurtenant water rights. Taro farmers do not have enough water and Maui Pineapples appears unwilling to change the status quo. The status quo is totally unacceptable to the farmers. We believe it should also be unacceptable to the Water Commission.[94]

On March 26, 1992, CWRM conducted a preliminary field inspection "to explore the nature and status of problems being experienced by taro farmers along Honokōhau Stream, West Maui" under Bill Rozeboom.[95] Also present at the preliminary field inspection were MLP's Wesley Nohara; David Martin and David Penn from NHAC; Oliver Dukelow, a "diverter" from WMMTFA; and approximately fifteen other valley residents and farmers. Photos from the field inspection disclosed that the stream above the taro gate was completely dry, and a slow stream began at the gate.

WMMFTA farmers were only able to farm approximately 3.13 acres at the time of the inspection, but planned to open another eight acres soon and as much additional land for loʻi kalo as possible in the long term. Some of the planned loʻi were located above the taro gate, and accordingly, their plans hinged on the return of flows both above and below the taro gate. Pre-1930 private survey maps detailed loʻi extending for miles along Honokōhau Stream. The maps, however, did not extend all the way up to the MLP diversion, which CWRM surmised made it difficult to establish the location of parcels for which appurtenant water rights were claimed.

On April 29, 1992, CWRM conducted a second, official field inspection of the MLP dam and taro gate.[96] While the March inspection focused on non-MLP diversions of Honokōhau streams, the April investigation focused on the MLP diversion and taro gate. MLP's Wes Nohara, David Martin of NHAC, and ʻAimoku Pali of the Honokōhau Valley Residents Association also attended the site visit. Their hike began at MLP's second intake for the Honolua Ditch system located on Kaluanui Stream, and they moved up towards MLP's first intake from Honokōhau Stream. Kaluanui was not a perennial stream; it flowed only during rainy periods.

Adits along the Honolua Ditch system are numbered sequentially beginning from Honokōhau Stream (Adit No. 1) and go up to Adit No. 16, where one four-inch and two eight-inch pipes take from the stream. The four-inch pipe supplies the county water system for Honokōhau Valley. One of the two eight-inch pipes provides irrigation for MLP fields above Honokōhau Valley, and the other pipe provides water to the hydroelectric plant in Honokōhau Valley.

At Adit No. 15 is the taro gate, which returns approximately 0.75 mgd flow to Honokōhau Stream, with an additional 0.3 mgd returned from the hydroelectric facility.

On November 2, 1993, MLP's Wesley Nohara wrote to Rae Loui, the deputy director of CWRM, regarding a September 24, 1993 public meeting on Maui concerning stream protection and management.[97] Honokōhau

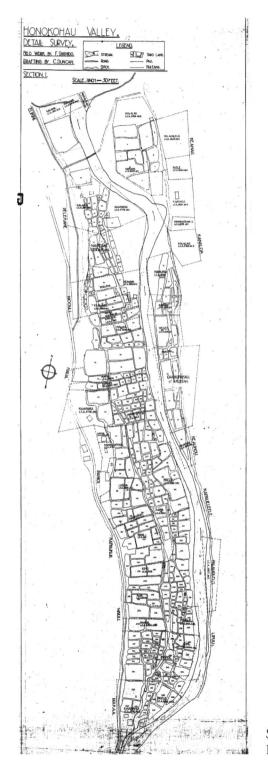

Shishido and Duncan,
Honokōhau Valley Map Section 1

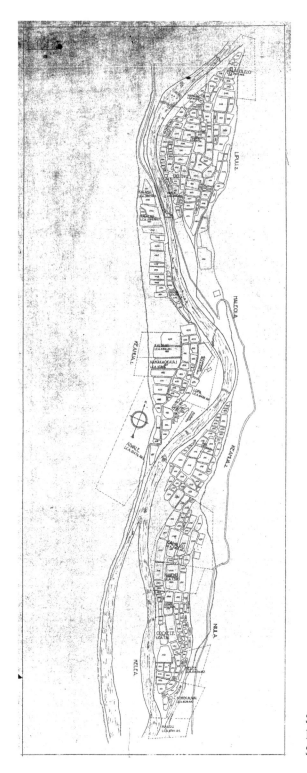

Shishido and Duncan,
Honokōhau Valley Map
Section 2

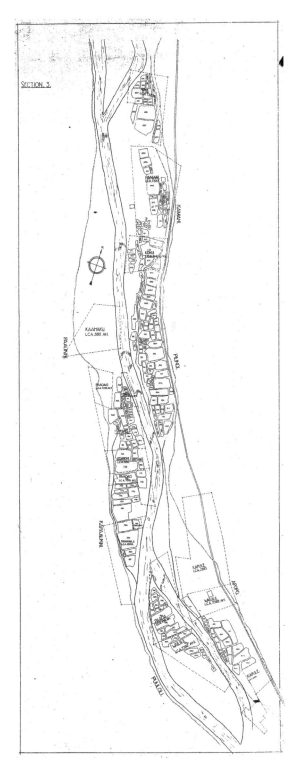

Shishido and Duncan,
Honokōhau Valley Map
Section 3

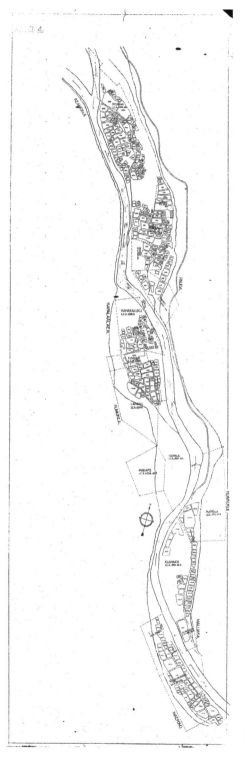

Shishido and Duncan, Honokōhau
Valley Map Section 4

community member Aimoku Pali stated at the meeting, "The State Water Commission required Maui Land and Pineapple Company, Ltd., to release an additional one (1) million gallons of water per day, but there was no response from Maui Land and Pineapple." Nohara refuted this in a reply, claiming MLP was releasing 650,000 gpd from the taro gate and another 350,000 gpd from the hydroelectric plant, and that no further water was required to be released into the stream.

On November 10, 1993, CWRM's Keith Ahue wrote to MLP's Joseph Hartley, Jr., carbon-copying Nohara, to summarize the agency's findings regarding the WMMTFA complaint.[98] Although CWRM noted MLP made fewer than 1.0 mgd generally available to taro farmers below the MLP diversions, CWRM also pointed to the insufficiencies of the WMMFTA diversion dam. WMMFTA's diversion dam, CWRM wrote, "consisted of loose rocks and plastic sheeting, which appeared vulnerable to flood damage and . . . require[d] constant maintenance." Most crucially, CWRM stated:

> Our overall impression of the dam and auwai system supported MPC's assertion that the farmers' immediate problems with insufficient water for their existing (1992) taro cultivation was due to an inefficient water delivery system rather than the quantity of water available from the stream.[99]

WMMFTA, however, was "acting in good faith in making improvements to its water delivery system" and "some initial inefficiency in its operations is unavoidable, given the task for restoring 'auwai systems which have been unused for decades."[100] In order to give WMMFTA farmers "a fair opportunity to grow," CWRM asked MPC to "consider increasing the return flow to Honokōhau Stream from 1.0 to 2.0 mgd."[101]

MPC responded to CWRM by disagreeing with the request for an additional 1 mgd.[102] MPC's records from the 1960s allegedly showed that far greater amounts of taro were sustained by 1.0 mgd released by the MPC taro gate. Further, MPC sought to count 2 mgd of water from a spring mauka of the taro gate and "[c]onsequently, there is an excess of 3.0 mgd of water right now flowing downstream to the taro farmers."[103] MPC believed the farmers' diversions and 'auwai needed work, and suggested that a USGS study be commissioned to quantify the actual flows available to the taro downstream from the MLP diversions. Finally, MPC argued that the end users of the MLP system were Pioneer Mill Company and the Maui Department of Water Supply—"[w]hich of these users should have their allocation reduced?"

In 1993, an appurtenant rights advisory group assembled by the Commission published a "manual" for appurtenant rights researchers.[104] Preparers specifically examined Honokōhau appurtenant rights as a case study, which included estimating the historical acreage of loʻi in the valley. Their analysis of maps dated circa 1900, prepared from surveys performed by Duncan and Shishido, show approximately 51.75 acres of loʻi.[105] The estimate did not include all historic loʻi and did not document changes in ownership up to 1993. Researchers noted approximately 21.67 acres of the kuleana were claimed by MLP and its predecessors (MLP was formerly part of Alexander & Baldwin, Co.).[106] Although the 1993 study did not find active loʻi cultivation of the upper reaches of Honokōhau Valley, it noted extensive archaeological evidence of loʻi terraces and "confirm[ed] that the morphology of the existing structures as well as their distribution had not been altered or modified, at the least, since the pre-Māhele period, and most likely since the prehistoric construction of many of these features." (Appurtenant Rights Manual at 6-3.)

On February 9, 1994, Alan Murakami, an attorney from the Native Hawaiian Legal Corporation (NHLC), wrote to CWRM's Rae Loui seeking dispute resolution on behalf of Aimoku Pali. Pali sought to restore his kuleana land as loʻi kalo, "but cannot withdraw water from the nearby stream because of the massive diversion dam constructed and maintained by Maui Land and Pine."[107] On March 4, 1994, Loui wrote back to Murakami requesting more information.

Each loʻi was marked with numbered stone. These stones numbered into the thousands. This stone marks an active loʻi at Wili Wood's parcel in Honokōhau.

In late June 1994, USGS and CWRM staff conducted field measurements of Honokōhau Stream. Phil Jones, a Honokōhau farmer, asked to attend the June 21, 1994 site visit and to show CWRM representatives where the various outlets and runoff areas were located.[108] On the morning of the site visit, it had been raining for a week and up to an hour prior to the site visit. "[T]he river was high. I asked if they could come back another time, maybe later in the week, because the height of the river would give a reading not representative of normal conditions. They said that only if it was raining they would then cancel this visit and return."[109] Jones said the "so-called spring" above the taro gate was "really a place of runoff from the higher watershed areas" and on the day of the visit, had much more water than usual. However, by the time the site visit was concluding, the streams had markedly declined in volume, so the last measurement was lower than the first. How, Jones asked, can these measurements be "representative of normal conditions?"[110]

In regard to the taro farmers' 'auwai, CWRM's Yoshi Shiroma questioned Jones about their intakes and diversions. Jones wrote, "In a subsequent conversation he said we were in violation of instream flow standards because we have opened up the three auwai's [sic], he warned me not to improve the efficiency of the intakes and that doing so [sic] I would open myself up to the possibility of fines."[111] Further, Shiroma informed Jones that he would need a Stream Channelization Alteration Permit (SCAP), although no further surface water diversions were going to be allowed. Jones countered with the understanding that CWRM and MLP were objecting to releasing further water to the farmers unless more taro lands were opened and that their dam leaks showed the farmers were not using water efficiently.[112] Jones closed by stating that he was confused, concerned, and upset about the situation, requesting advice about how the farmers should be communicating with the Water Commission, and for clarifications about Shiroma's statements, if any.[113] No response to Jones was on file with CWRM. In its summary of Jones' letter, CWRM staff noted only that Jones requested remeasurement of the streams during more normal conditions.[114]

Around the same time, the Review Commission on the State Water Code was holding public hearings on proposed changes to the water code. The Review Commission was created by Act 45 §5, Sess. L. Hawai'i (1987).

The Review Commission's eighth public meeting was held at the Maui County Council Chambers in Wailuku at 7pm.[115] Public testimony was led off by MLP's Douglas McCluer, but was dominated by Honokōhau Valley community spokespeople. McCluer argued against a statewide water management system, against expansion of government management of water resources, and in favor of vesting private rights in exploratory wells.[116] Jackie Lee of Honokōhau Valley Association informed the Review Commission that Maui County had told them to develop their own private water system and that MLP had dewatered Honokōhau Stream.[117] Jerry Watlund (we believe the Commission minutes are in error and this is a Jory Watland), Laura Sakamoto, Lehua Pali, and Aimoku Pali also testified as members of the Honokōhau Valley Association. They pointed out that MLP was diverting over 90 percent of the stream, which is supposed to be perennial but was not as a consequence of the diversions. Pali pointed out that Honokōhau Stream was, at the time, the only mauka-to-makai stream in the Lahaina district.[118] Pali further testified that MLP had bulldozed all diversions from the stream except their own, but he planned to restore his dam in order to grow taro.[119] Although he wanted to assert his water rights, he understood that he was required to have his land surveyed first, which would cost him $40,000.[120] This system was not feasible for him or people like him. "It is strange," he wryly noted, "that there is $120 million for the Hawai'i Visitor Bureau and $64 million for rapid transit, but not enough money to manage the state's water resources."[121] Many others from Honokōhau Valley also attended, but were not listed as testifiers. These include Tim Harder, Robert Wilson, and Kainoa Wilson.

Kimo Lindsey, a kalo farmer and plaintiff in the existing NHLC complaint, testified that half of last year's crop had been lost to root rot because of high water temperatures and the stream 'ōpae, hīhīwai, and 'o'opu were likewise affected by the reduced streamflow.[122] Today, members of the younger generation struggling to return water for lo'i speak with admiration for Lindsey's efforts to spearhead water issues for Honokōhau.[123]

Phil Jones, a Honokōhau Valley taro farmer, testified that he had very little success getting MLP to cooperate with taro farmers and further reported on the ongoing disputes within CWRM. CWRM had asked MLP to release more water into Honokōhau Stream to allow planting of additional lo'i and also told the taro farmers not to plant more lo'i until they were allowed to increase their own stream diversions.[124]

CWRM Response

By letter dated August 26, 1994, David Martin of NHAC wrote to Rae Loui, also informing CWRM that streamflow had been greater than normal on the date of the field measurements and there was a need to re-measure the flows.[125] Martin further reiterated that continuous data sets were needed to obtain adequate information and long-term hydrological monitoring in Honokōhau should be sought as part of CWRM's cooperative agreement with the USGS. Martin connected Honokōhau Stream issues with those facing Waiāhole Stream on Oʻahu. Both streams supported extensive kalo farming historically and presently, and further, reports surfaced concerning dumping water from both streams.

On November 3, 1994, CWRM's Loui replied to Martin, requesting more information from NHAC, stating CWRM could not afford additional gauging stations at Honokōhau streams, and denying awareness "of any practice of releasing water from Honolua Ditch."[126] More promisingly, Loui noted USGS would be preparing a groundwater model of West Maui and would be meeting with them to ascertain information needed to act on Pali's complaint. Also at that time, Loui contacted William Meyer of the USGS in regard to Honokōhau Stream.

WATER COMMISSION AND HAWAIIAN WATER RIGHTS

WMMFTA's Honokōhau surface water struggles were taking place against a backdrop of larger questions about how CWRM was obligated to enforce constitutional provisions for native Hawaiian traditional and customary rights.[127] In 1993, CWRM formed the Hawaiian Water Rights Task force, which was charged with developing draft administrative rules for Part IX of the State Water Code to address the protection of Hawaiian water rights.[128] The task force was chaired by Dr. Michael Chun, president of Kamehameha Schools and former water commissioner. Other members include Jackie Mahi Erickson, David Martin of NHAC, William Makaimoku, Walter Ragsdale, Raynard Soon, and David Sproat, another kalo farmer from Waipā, Kauaʻi. Task force discussions addressed water reservations for DHHL and other Hawaiian lands, water for kuleana lands specifically, appurtenant water rights, historical fishponds, and traditional and customary gathering rights.

The Hawaiian Water Rights Task Force met with the Review Commission, which was tasked with assessing the State Water Code. In its Final Report to the Legislature in 1994, the Review Commission reported its conclusions and recommendations. The Review Commission was headed by Fred Trotter, a descendant of James Campbell and an administrator of the Campbell estate. First, they concluded that more important than expanding Hawaiian water rights is establishing the means to implement existing Hawaiian water rights; and second, the adoption of administrative rules for Part IX will provide needed clarification of existing Hawaiian water rights.[129] Accordingly, the Review Commission recommended: (1) Hawaiian water rights, as set forth in the State Constitution, the Hawaiian Homes Commission Act of 1920, the State Water Code, and Act 325 of 1991 be recognized in a proposed Hierarchy of Water Uses for reserved uses of water; (2) DHHL should be required to prepare a water plan that quantifies the department's water needs for the foreseeable future; (3) the Office of Hawaiian Affairs should also prepare a water plan quantifying all Hawaiian water rights, including amounts needed to ensure the propagation of native species in streams and for growing kalo and other traditional crops on lands historically used for those purposes; (4) CWRM should adopt by rule procedures to validate claims to appurtenant rights; and, (5) a Special Assistant, at the level of branch chief, should be added to the staff of the CWRM to ensure that issues relating to Hawaiian water rights are adequately addressed.[130]

Many of the Review Commission's recommendations were not implemented. No hierarchy of water uses was enacted as Part III of the State Water Code, perhaps because water use permitting procedures already recognize heightened protections for public trust uses. Those permitting procedures, however, are only implemented in WMAs. In May 2017, DHHL submitted a Final Report of its Update to the State Water Projects Plan, which quantified DHHL water needs through 2031. The highly ambitious recommendation that OHA quantify water needs for all Hawaiian traditional and customary practices was not implemented, although OHA funded a USGS study that quantified water needs for loʻi kalo.[131] Appurtenant rights remain an issue in CWRM processes and no Special Assistant was added to CWRM staff.

In 1995, CWRM proposed new administrative rules (HAR Title 13, Chapter 172) relating to "Hawaiian Water Rights," based on the draft and recommendations produced by the task force.[132] However, these proposed rules were first vetted by CWRM staff prior to being presented statewide at public hearings. NHAC strongly objected to the proposed rules targeting "sweeping changes proposed by staff" because they "eliminated a number of critical elements required to adequately implement protections of Hawaiian water rights."[133] Specifically, NHAC criticized recommendations to limited reservation requests to the Water Commission and DHHL, elimination of reference to traditional and customary agriculture, and deletion of a chapter addressing fishpond water needs because these "totally subvert the good faith efforts of the Hawaiian Water Rights Task Force."[134] NHAC asked that the Hawaiian Water Rights Task Force be consulted, if not reconvened, prior to sending the rules out for public hearing and comment. Ultimately, CWRM did not promulgate HAR Title 13, Chapter 172.

Honokōhau Water Struggles Continue

In an odd turn of events, in an article dated September 13, 1995, *Maui News* staff writer Harry Eager reported that a five-point agreement had been reached between Honokōhau Valley residents and MLP.[135] In response, the Honokōhau Valley Association (HVA) wrote an open letter decrying the article and alleged five-point agreement.[136] "Not one resident of Honokōhau Valley nor a Hono-kōhau Valley Association member was ever contacted or informed of these 'agreements,'" HVA wrote. "As for the five points, none really addresses our main concern, which is restoration of Honokōhau Stream."[137] HVA raised practical concerns that would delay restoration of even the one mgd that CWRM indicated MLP should restore. "But, one mgd is nothing more than a token offer. If this laborious process is to be pursued, let us at least work with a meaningful amount of water. Perhaps half the stream flow would be a good starting point."[138] The third part of the agreement specified that valley farmers should clean out the 'auwai to improve efficiency. HVA said that this 'auwai cleaning day was already a regular monthly practice. "Everyone who can, helps to walk the centuries-old ditch and clears shrubs that grow on moist banks. Afterwards, we have a potluck and talk story. It's a great community get-together."[139]

Galling to HVA was MLP's suggestion that the 'auwai be lined with PVC pipes and implement other recommendations. MLP did not understand "how much it irks native farmers to be told that the water delivery system laid out by their ancestors and used for hundreds of years needs to be improved so that MLP can continue to steal the stream."[140] The questionable situation MLP's announced five point settlement created put HVA "in a position of mistrust." Nevertheless, HVA concluded its open letter by affirming, "Trying to restore our stream has helped us to learn much about the way policies are made. We will continue to learn, even if it is the hard way."[141]

In 1997, environmental groups sought a county council resolution through which MLP "could make good on alleged violations of wastewater disposal laws by restoring a minimum of five million gallons a day of Honokōhau Stream water to taro farmers and residents below."[142] Earthjustice attorney Paul Achitoff told members of the County Council's Committee of the Whole that state records show MLP had repeatedly violated the Federal Clean Water Act and other national and state environmental laws in its discharge of wastewater in Central Maui.[143] Although MLP had rerouted their wastewater, the state was considering penalties against MLP and, in connection with those discussions, the Native Hawaiian Advisory Council and Native Hawaiian Legal Corporation asked the state to impose a "Supplemental Environmental Review" requirement on MLP. As part of that project, NHAC and NHLC asked that MLP return five mgd to the Honokōhau Stream, which was currently diverted by MLP primarily, and to a lesser extent, the county and Pioneer Mill. "There is no constitutional right to divert all water from a stream," said Achitoff. "Streams can be restored, whether Maui Land & Pine likes it or not."[144] Honokōhau Valley landowner Kimo Lindsey reportedly stated that he believed that MLP's full diversion of the stream, seven miles up the river, is illegal and that a release of at least four mgd would help farmers located below the taro gate. The County Council, led by Councilman Sol Kahoʻohalahala, refused to take action on the issue one way or the other because MLP was not present. He said the resolution revolves around serious issues, such as the long-standing disputes concerning the diversion of Honokōhau Stream water, so the best route would be to invite representatives from the state and MLP, "bring all the players in," and discuss solutions.

At its June 25, 1999 meeting, BLNR considered a staff proposal to use part of a $3 million legislative appropriation for agricultural purchases to acquire Honokōhau Ditch to ensure it stays in working order and to protect the 1,600 acres of DLNR land irrigated with Honokōhau Ditch water.[145] Honokōhau Ditch was irrigating approximately 6,200 acres of state and private lands in West Maui. Amfac, however, vehemently opposed the state acquisition.[146] DLNR voted to authorize negotiations for the acquisition of Honokōhau ditch.

In June 2000, at a West Maui Water Advisory Committee meeting, Charley Ice of the Water Commission noted, "Generally, out of a dozen users on the west side, only three report reliably and regularly." Ice, the meeting minutes continue, "also points out that there is much less reporting (either required or submitted) for surface water use than for groundwater use, so that there are large gaps in our knowledge of the source. Nor does CWRM have much luck with follow-through."[147]

In 2003, USGS published its report on the continuing impact of the Honokōhau Ditch on the stream:

Eighty-six percent of the total flow upstream from the ditch is diverted from the stream. Immediately downstream from the diversion dam there is no flow in the stream 91.2 percent of the time, except for minor leakage through the dam. Flow releases at the Taro Gate, from Honokōhau Ditch back into the stream, are inconsistent and were found to be less than the target release of 1.55 cubic feet per second on 9 of the 10 days on which measurements were made. Previous estimates of base-flow availability downstream from the Taro Gate release range from 2.32 to 4.6 cubic feet per second (1.5 to 3.0 million gallons per day). At the two principal sites where water is currently being diverted for agricultural use in the valley (MacDonald's and Chun's Dams), base flows of 2.32 cubic feet per second (1.5 million gallons per day) are available more than 95 percent of the time at MacDonald's Dam and 80 percent of the time at Chun's Dam. Base flows of 4.6 cubic feet per second (3.0 million gallons per day) are available 65 and 56 percent of the time, respectively.[148]

On December 7, 2005, the Maui County Council Land Use Committee held a hearing on an amendment to the West Maui Community Plan and Land Use Map to move approximately 475 acres from Agricultural to Open Space, respectively, to West Maui Project District 2 (Kapalua Mauka) to facilitate a request from MLP to develop a 690-unit resort development and amenities at Honokahua, Napili, Lahaina, Maui.[149] Kimokeo Kapahulehua, who identified himself as a resident in Honokōhau, called the council's attention to the impacts MLP's Kapalua Mauka project would have on Honokōhau. Kapahulehua noted about eight families were living in the valley restoring loʻi: "I wanted to tell you that we do have our water that flows through the kaha and that we have sufficient water for the amount of farming that we do down there." He further noted that they have formed a nonprofit Ka Honokōhau Restoration Association in

Loʻi on the property of Wili Wood, Honokōhau valley.

Wili Wood, March 3, 2017.

partnership with MLP to conduct the restoration work. Kapahulehua, however, was equivocal on whether he would oppose the project so long as enough water was being provided to the farmers. This position was markedly different from his earlier statements that water should be kept available for future farming.

In 2006, the community was rehabilitating loʻi kalo in Honokōhau Valley. They included Kimokeo Kapahulehua and Wili Wood, a kalo farmer in Honokōhau Valley. Wood has 33 out of what used to be over 4,000 taro patches a hundred years ago running through his property. Their loʻi restoration work continues today with the help of friends, family and the community. In 2018, CWRM amended the IIFSs for the southernmost four streams in West Maui, with plans to move up the coast to complete other amendments. Proceedings on Honokōhau Stream IIFS amendments have been initiated, but not completed, as of this writing.

2019 Honokōhau, Honolua, and Honokōwai IIFS Proceedings

Today, a renewed community in Honokōhau is organizing for their rights to stream water to the valley so that families, long estranged from the area, can return to restore the loʻi kalo and the stream itself. Dozens of community members turned out for an evening CWRM public fact-gathering session on September 9, 2019. The session was meant to give the community an opportunity to submit information on three Instream Flow Standard Assessment Reports (IFSARs) for Honokōhau, Honolua, and Honokōwai Streams respectively. Though many had just put in a day's work and were juggling childcare responsibilities, the crowd grew and submitted oral testimony on the proposed IFSARs, and affirmed the interim instream flow standard process overall in West Maui.

More than a few community members pointed with frustration to the situation whereby their domestic water needs were dependent on a rickety seven-mile-long pipe, maintained by the Maui Department of Water Supply, to route water from MLP's Kapalua residential development. The Honokōhau MDWS system repeatedly broke down. In 2014, the Honokōhau system had thirteen connections providing an average daily flow of 2,378 gallons (0.002 mgd) as a consecutive system to the Kapalua Water Company system. Currently, Kapalua Wells Nos. 1 and 2, owned by the Kapalua Water Company, serve both the Kapalua and Honokōhau water systems. Storage is provided by 8,000- and 30,000-gallon storage tanks. MDWS is exploring the potential to source water for this system from a Honokōhau tunnel on MLP land, which currently flows at about one mgd, but will need to address source development, transmission and maintenance, and power needs, in addition to other regulatory requirements.[150]

In September 2019, the community had been going weeks without running water and instead had to collect water from a water truck parked at the mouth of the valley. Although not directly related to the IFSAR process, Honokōhau residents pointed out that it would be much simpler to have a water filtration device installed in Honokōhau Valley and allow residents to treat surface water for domestic needs. For this, as Honokōhau resident Karyn Kanekoa pointed out, CWRM should properly include in the IIFS an amount of surface water for domestic uses.

At the same time as the Honokōhau community was engaging with the CWRM IIFSs process, they pressed their rights with the county. In a letter to Maui Department of Water Supply Director Jeffrey Pearson, Honokōhau Valley residents noted their reliance on regular potable water service to maintain their unique, rural lifestyles, which includes the traditional and customary practice of growing kalo, and sought help with funding and implementing a new water system in Honokōhau.

County obligations to water consumers are particularly emphasized in regard to Honokōhau communities. The domestic and agricultural activities of Honokōhau Valley communities are specifically recognized and protected by the West Maui Community Plan. (See West Maui Community Plan [1996] at 12 [preserve and protect the region's cultural resources and traditional life-styles, including the agricultural pursuits of Native Hawaiians in Honokōhau Valley"] and 26 ["Protect and preserve Honokōhau Valley's historic and traditional use for domestic and agricultural activities, ensuring the availability of sufficient quantities and quality of water for these activities by recognizing Native Hawaiian water rights and traditional access protected by Article XII, Section 7, of the State Constitution, and Section 1.1, Hawaii Revised Statutes."]). The Maui County Charter requires the Department of Water Supply to implement these "plans in the administration of its affairs." (County Charter §8-11.2 [amended 2002, 1988].)

Sy Feliciano, a community member who formerly worked for Hoaʻāina Farm Service, which maintained the Honokōhau Ditch, stepped forward to testify. He noted that the response time for ditch maintenance from MLP was about four days, but in that time he had seen fish stressing in the stream. He understood that they would die within that four-day period, and responses should happen within 24 hours. Since he left Hoaʻāina Farm Services, Feliciano noted that no one had been maintaining Aotaki gate and no one had been taking care of the ditch for years. "Community taro farmers shouldn't have to wait for workers to go up and protect their rights," he said, "I want to see more farms go in the place—not golf courses and gated communities."

Darryl Aiwohi, who has an extensive family in Honokōhau, is also a kalo farmer and testified at the September 9, 2019 meeting. "When I was growing up," he said, "the whole valley was in taro." He asked, "When will we have enough water for young people to grow taro?" Many other community members raised the correlation between the diversion of Honokōhau water and the estrangement of Honokōhau family members from the valley. After Hurricane Olivia, the stream was "trashed," and many still have not been able to restore loʻi kalo. Darryl Aiwohi sought help from the Water Commission and clarification on how the stream could be operationally restored. Commission staff, who do not normally respond to testimony, felt moved to at least offer to "try to answer questions after."

Darryl's grandson, Kaʻapuni Aiwohi, a Hui o Nā Wai ʻEhā board member, testified, "We don't have enough water to farm in Honokōhau Valley. The right thing to do is to restore 100 percent of the water." Kaʻapuni Aiwohi was also concerned about the injustice caused by the offstream demand for water, "Everyone wants water from the valley—but no one is there to get in there and do the work. All these people want water but where are they when it is time to clean it? It's the people in the valley."

Councilmember and longtime community advocate Tamara Paltin pointed to the need to look forward to the place that West Maui could become through restored streams. "Last month, we opened a loʻi in Honokōhau in three hours. It's a mistake to look at the three acres or whatever is currently there because that is based on current circumstances. We need to plan for exponential growth of more loʻi." Paltin also commented on the diversions in Honolua, demanding that although MLP represents that there is "only a small little pipe," they could remove the broken diversion structures and those that are really taking water." Paltin has been an active voice in the Save Honolua Coalition.

Honokōhau farmer Wili Wood also emphasized the need to look at the potential for kalo restoration and not only the existing acreage. "There may be only three acres of kalo now, but that is due to insufficient water flow," he said, "Plenty of families want to get back on their land. We need you guys to help us, especially with the irrigator." Wood is amongst those who have lost loʻi. Since 2005, he has worked with canoe clubs and schools to produce hundreds of pounds of kalo for fundraisers. "It's heartbreaking to see the community come to do all the work and then the patch is spoiled because the water was running too warm," said Wood. He described harvesting spoiled kalo, so rotten that his fingers went right through the corm.

Kaipo Kekona, a Kāʻanapali Aha Moku representative, testified that 5,000 loʻi used to be in Honokōhau. "Before, we resourced the water to the 5,000 loʻi and then put it back into the source.... Understand how the source existed before our interruption. That is how we can begin to move forward and coexist with this source."

While MLP sent no representatives to the meeting, residents in the MLP developed Kapalua area took a much more cooperative tone than MLP ever had historically. A representative from the Kapalua Plantation Estates, Jon Kindred, stepped forward to describe landscaping needs for Honokōhau Ditch water. "We are part of this community and depend on these water systems, and we are deeply interested in these proceedings." he said. "...we recognize that water in Hawaiʻi is held as a Public Trust, there are four protected "Public Trust" uses of water that courts have recognized, and our community's irrigation uses are not one of those protected uses... as we live below one of the wettest areas on earth, with abundant ground and surface water sources, in an era after expansive plantation agriculture has ended, we believe there is enough water to fully provide for Public Trust uses, existing uses, and future uses anticipated in state and county plans. This will be possible if the CWRM and other stakeholders move forward together in a thoughtful, respectful, and practical way.

Kanoe Steward, a Hawaiian immersion school teacher and West Maui community member, related that she had worked with Skippy Hau, an aquatics biologist who was previously with the Nature Conservancy. Stewart pointed to specific stream biota missing from the Honokōhau IFSAR. " 'Ōpae kuahiwi is also seen and not listed, but it is in your table. But the table missed 'o'opu napili." Steward suggested that CWRM partner with community members to train them to collect data and hand it over to CWRM. "You guys don't have capacity to monitor all year round. We can get the kids and schools involved. Let's get more creative."

Conclusion

Kuleana owners have a practical, personal relationship with Hawai'i waters and lands that are only disjointedly accommodated by current laws and policies. This chapter reviewed some of the many efforts by kuleana owners to preserve water rights and the world that those rights attempt to secure. Many questions remaining have less to do with whether those rights should be asserted than with the whereabouts of actual water resources. Many reservoirs have been decommissioned throughout West Maui. Fewer are farming, and Pioneer Mill has ceased to operate as a plantation. The streams, however, have not been restored and these efforts are requiring highly engaged state and community intervention.

CHAPTER 8

MANAGING HAWAIʻI PUBLIC TRUST RESOURCES IN A CONTESTED HAWAIʻI

Itʼs our destiny to set the water free.

—Kapali Keahi, 2005.[1]

Much like the distance between *Horner v. Kumuliʻiliʻi* and the pirate-ship-themed kids pool of contemporary Kāʻanapali, todayʼs efforts to protect water resources can seem far from the historic violence of Native dispossession.[2] This sense of distance can be mobilized as an aggressive belief in the virtuous-ness of all conservation—a presumption that a purely selfless love of Hawaiʻiʼs streams and aquifers or academic desire to learn about them is sufficient to guide conservation efforts. On another level it can be expressed in a practical view that it does not matter why someone kills invasive species or builds bulwarks against erosion, so long as the work gets done. These approaches to conservation in Hawaiʻi have often met resistance from Kānaka Maoli and other local populations, sometimes with the result that conservation is thwarted.[3] Another problem with these approaches is that they make Hawaiian self-determination a mere adjunct to the main task of conservation.[4]

Our concern is related, but not identical, to efforts to make environmental conservation more "Hawaiian." The Hawaiʻi Conservation Alliance adopted the position that integration of Native Hawaiian culture is essential to conserva-tion.[5] Hawaiian conservationists had offered cogent, practical recommendations for aligning conservation work with Hawaiian community needs: recruiting Hawaiians into conservation work, applying traditional resource management, and using Hawaiian language, values, and knowledges. However, decolonizing water resource protection requires also addressing conservation as a colonial practice that maintains Native resources in settler-state hands.[6] Amongst other things, this means recognizing agendas that the state brings with their protections of Hawai'i's natural resources.

Rather, our concern is to understand these conflicts on the ground, so that work to conserve water be pursued in a manner similar to how Noelani Goodyear-Ka'ōpua called for ways that "settlers can develop close relationships with land but without eliding the ongoing issue of Hawaiian sovereignty."[7] This approach can avoid what K. Wayne Wang targeted as "settler environmentalism"—an "effort to redeem the settler as ecological."[8] Such natural resource management efforts are "settler moves to innocence—diversions, distractions, which relieve the settler of feelings of guilt or responsibility, and conceal the need to give up land or power or privilege." (Tuck and Yang 2012:21.)

Settler-state stewardship can be an attempt to institutionalize non-native relationships to Native lands that bypass decolonization. One can think of the US military's claim to being the biggest conservation institution in Hawai'i while incidentally failing to mention that it has to spend a lot on conservation to make up for its environmental destruction elsewhere—and often with the result that Native lands are cordoned off for, unironically, Native species propagation projects. We have sought to attend to the ways settler institutions deform the highly specific, grounded plans of West Maui communities.

Kapali Keahi is one of West Maui's most talented singers and songwriters, and cousin to Kekai Keahi, whose community advocacy efforts are discussed elsewhere in this book. Setting "water free" means restoring streams and protecting aquifers from overexploitation and pollution. In practice, this effort overlaps substantially with environmentalist campaigns premised on legal protections for clean water. Keahi's invocation of "destiny" does not merely describe a poetic description of a commitment to restoring streams; it invokes an identity as a kia'i (protector, guardian) of the resource in an alternate cosmology to the state's technocratic resource management. In this view, water is not only "ka waiwai"—a kind of wealth—but a medium of intimate relationship with the land itself.[9]

Nearly ten years after Kapali Keahi uttered those words, Kahoma Stream began flowing mauka to makai for the first time in a century. Many, including community leaders who pushed for the restoration, were taken aback by the speed with which the stream and its ecosystems recovered. 'O'opu in varieties they had not seen in Kahoma in memory appeared with a few years.

Restoration of stream flows to Kahoma and other streams, however, only point to the larger retransformation of West Maui land and waterscapes sought by community members. One next effort will be to address the Army Corps of Engineers' Kahoma flood control project, which was built to channelize flood water away from nearshore development. The channels, however, also prevent the historic floodplain from re-emerging. Before the resorts, residences, and stores of this area, the coastal plain harbored the Alamihi fishpond; its precise dimensions at different points in time are unclear.

The streams restored are awakening ancient landscapes immanent in West Maui. How we receive these insistent reminders of what West Maui has been naturally engineered to be will reflect the values we place on the kinds of people collectively who can thrive in Hawai'i. As streams are restored, floodplains can flood, stream channelization structures can be replaced, and communities can return to live in valleys. One key to whether and how official decisionmakers across Hawai'i will enable or thwart this destiny is their approach to the concept of "compromise."

Compromise, reasonableness, and "tough decisions" are often the language of state agencies whose implicit task is to work over (and sometimes consciously within) the contradictions of settler colonialism, most often by quelling or befuddling conflict. Such decisionmaking is consistently evacuated of historical context—specifically histories of prior compromise and inequity. In August 2019, testifying on the desire of Mahi Pono to continue to dewater the Nā Wai 'Ehā area of West Maui for their central valley plantation succeeding on the operations of Hawai'i Commercial and Sugar Company (HC&S), kalo farmer and Hawaiian scholar Hōkūao Pellegrino specifically called out this ahistoric approach: "Mahi Pono seems to be asking to share the water," he said. "Yet for over 120-plus years, Native Hawaiians have suffered at the hand of plantations. And I often wonder if Mahi Pono is HC&S 2.0, because tonight they showed their cards, and they don't seem to be serious about really engaging with the Native Hawaiian community and traditional farmers within the Na Wai 'Ehā area, as well as protecting water resources."[10]

Even as we complete the final words in *Water and Power in West Maui*, of course, the end of West Maui water struggles are nowhere in sight. Nothing on the terrain of water resource management and development in Hawai'i, much less West Maui, is settled. Disputes over surface water from Launiupoko and Kaua'ula continue despite the Water Commission's restorations of significant amounts to the latter stream. The Water Commission decision on interim instream flow standards for Honokōwai, Honolua, and Honokōhau are set to occur in the next twelve months (before November 2020). Communities hope for a decision fully and finally restoring surface water resources to a level that would at least not be a barrier to functioning ecosystems and the return of Hawaiian traditional and customary practitioners to their kuleana parcels. Newer residents and businesses seek to protect their current uses, and developers also have desires for these waters. Faced with this impending conflict, many agencies, including the Water Commission, pursue an idea of compromise. However, in the context of West Maui and Hawaiʻi, this idea of compromise seems to not allow for an approach to water protection as kuleana and destiny, and thus may perpetuate the fights costly to all sides, to communities, and the resource itself.

Water resource protection is, for many Kānaka Maoli, a self-determination issue. As Kanaka Maoli scholar Jonathan Osorio has said, these lands "will be ours one day." Osorio here points to the horizon of Hawaiʻi's public trust while also recognizing that he, and all of us, do not live there yet.

As documented in this book and as lived over the last four decades in Hawaiʻi, the concept of the public trust in water has been foundational to the reemergence of a water management scheme that acknowledges noncommercial uses of water. Our concerns with public trust protections for water are located with a seeming silence on exactly what is dicey and limited about water resource management work in West Maui. This work typically involves state agencies, namely the Commission on Water Resource Management, tasked with maintaining public trust resources; and when it does a bad job of protecting those resources, the agency gets sued for violations of environmental laws and Hawaiʻi's public trust.

In this legal landscape, the State Constitution mandates protections for natural resources under public trust provisions and traditional and customary Hawaiian practices.[11] Hawaiʻi regulations define Hawaiian cultural resources inclusively as "natural resources."[12] This is appropriate, as many cultural practices utilize plants, winds, living creatures, and waters.[13] Hawaiʻi's public *land* trust further obligates the state to administer certain lands for public interests, and for Hawaiians in particular. What is particular to Hawaiians are entitlements to land revenues, resources, and access rights.[14] These legal protections for Hawaiian interests are historical formations marked by ongoing Native negotiations with and within settler legal institutions.[15]

Too quickly, however, names like "partnership" and "collaboration" get placed on all actions on these rights. These names gloss over the ongoing labor of keeping the state accountable to its trust obligations. It is further complicit with efforts to whittle these obligations down to their leanest existence.

At the Water Commission staff's September 9, 2019 public fact-gathering meeting, community members met calls for "compromise" from diverters with a history of that compromise. "The kahawai has suffered for hundreds years," said Karyn Kanekoa, a Kānaka Maoli Honokōhau resident. Referring to others' claim that Honokōhau stream water is needed for landscaping irrigation, Kanekoa continued: "Palm trees are not more important. Water is a public trust and these keiki, these families, have priority." Kanekoa pointed to the inequities of applying a vacuous, progressive rule of compromise to the very communities that are supposed to be protected by water resource laws. Our point is that water resource administrators too often adopt not a standard seeking thriving communities, but only what may minimally allow resources and Hawaiian culture to *survive* as a permissible standard.

Instituting compromise as a rule, absent any firm fallback, is also a means of progressively eroding the resource. "Balancing" cannot be the answer to the problem of resource exploitation where that resource has already been 90 percent depleted. A "balance" between diversion and conservation uses of the last 10 percent would not only leave the diverter with 95 percent of the resource. It would leave us with a rule that permits future balances between the remaining five percent, 2.5 percent, where a Zeno's paradox would always leave room for some so called reasonable compromise. Compromise cannot be the rule. "The ability to define the content and scope of 'law' and 'politics,' remains vested in the settler's legal architecture, which also never fails to appear competent, singular, and ahistorical."[16]

Public trust claims have been and are useful for protecting water resources. Public trust litigation has helped restore water rights to kalo farmers and near-shore ecosystems,[17] prevented private landowners from usurping shoreline access,[18] stopped the taking of Kaua'i freshwater for commercial sale,[19] and stymied the desecration of sacred summits by industrial astronomy development.[20] But public trust claims do not, at least currently, articulate the fundamental disrepair of settler-state control over Native resources and settler access to them. And, as we have described, these claims are double-edged tools for creating relationships between decolonization and conservation.

Disrepairs of the public trust devolve from its use of the term "public." An undifferentiated settler-citizen "public" disarticulates that public from the colonial legacies that fracture Hawai'i's polity.[21] The "public" beneficiary of trust resources creates something like a settler "commons," with the attendant, presumptive appropriation of Native resources.[22] This disjuncture shows up in full relief whenever claims to water resources for traditional and customary rights or the Department of Hawaiian Home Lands are made to face off with the "needs of the general public," and where that public is never seen as coextensive with the same Hawaiian cultural practitioners and beneficiaries seeking to enforce rights to water.

Drawing on an antipodal context, legal scholars Timothy Neale and Stephen Turner observe: "Where the focus of concern about water access, rights and control remains the purview of settler government agencies, laws and processes, then the very fact of government control is occluded."[23] Where Keahi talks about destiny and Kanekoa invokes the suffering of the stream itself, the Water Commission's discusses the legal, reasonable, and beneficial allocation of water rights and not, importantly, how its authority was installed in the first place. One cause for that omission of discussion of authority may relate to regular attempts to erode or eliminate the power of the Commission entirely, as was attempted in 2005 when the Water Commission's own chair, Peter Young, advocated for its elimination.[24]

Yet, attempts to resolve the question over different priorities for stream water—how to distribute water for ecosystem regeneration, loʻi kalo, or off stream irrigation—"cannot but raise other issues regarding the nature of the thing recognized, the form of its recognition and the space in which recognition takes place."[25] These other issues are rife in the field of water resources management and conservation.

Just as the word "public" in Public Trust can be problematic, so can the idea of Trust. "Trusting" the state risks "reif[ying] the legitimacy of the US government"[26] and fosters a stultifying politics of demand that reinvests political futurity in a paternalistic state.[27] Fiduciary principles riddle trust resource management with real property conventions that can enable frameworks of settler colonial control.[28] In turn, property concepts tend to assess cultural values of land "parcels"[29] in ways that fail to recognize indigenous relationships between land, epistemology, and ontology.[30]

The problem is not only that the state needs to be a better protector—or that the public trust is premised on disrepaired structures. Premise is not identity, particularly where we are using legal instruments. *The problem is when the public trust becomes a method of producing state control as something that protects Hawaiian culture.*

For the state, the work entails producing Hawaiian culture as a resource that can be managed in the first place.[31] Culture-as-resource works in tandem with public trust jurisprudence to make feasible the settler state's governance of the differences of Indigenous communities and the pasts that produce it.[32]

George Yúdice discusses a neoliberal "expediency of culture," wherein culture becomes something "called on to resolve a range of problems *for* community, which seems only to be able to recognize itself in culture, which in turn has lost its specificity."[33] What is expedient about this rendering of Hawaiian culture is that the state can protect it, usually under a management plan, thereby safeguarding the resource-glue that presumably coheres Hawaiian community; and thus allows the settler state to conclude that it protects Hawaiian culture without having to address Hawaiian claims and self-determination.

Importantly, the state's role under the public trust harbors a desire for reconciliation, which Tuck and Yang decry as being "about rescuing settler normalcy, about rescuing a settler future."[34] Decolonization, by contrast, means the repatriation of land and resources. Period. It does not harbor promises for settler-state futurity. A decolonized future is not worked out until it is. As Frantz Fanon put it, "Every action is an answer or a question. Perhaps both[.]"[35] We will find answers as we act to get to Osorio's horizon.

We've attempted to locate efforts to realize public trust protections within this open-ended decolonization program. Here, Osorio's point that environmental protections are bound to Hawai'i natural resources that will one day be restored to Hawaiians cogently articulates the gap between state control of public trust resources and decolonization as a function of time. The decolonial temporality the public trust makes possible is also a "colonial entanglement."[36] Conservation can be here a stopgap measure—an instrument picked up in the messy middle of settler colonialism.[37] In this meantime, Hawaii's public trust offers a malleable form that fits many kinds of conservation actors without becoming mired in political identity questions, many of which remain unanswerable absent the restoration of Hawaiian independence and land base. Here, distinguishing what will have been, for or against settler colonialism, is complicated by the unevenness of the settler state's organization of claims that can be visible as political as opposed to cultural.[38]

The holding pattern established by the public trust, as we discuss more fully in earlier chapters, marks the implicit excision of forms of Native selfhood that may occur prior and simultaneous with the production of its settler public. Here, state environmentalism operates through an administrative apparatus—"a mechanism for constituting and securing a public, establishing the boundaries of inclusion, and producing an abject body against which the proper, public body of the citizen can stand."[39] This apparatus "work[s] from the secular humanist canon to reconcile Indigenous people to the sovereignty of the settler-colonial nation, and not from an undeterminable alterity towards an undetermined autonomy."[40] These are problems Glen Coulthard identified for Native sovereignties premised on state recognition.[41]

The take-home message, and alongside our other caveats against wholesale reliance on settler-state water management, is that we should see the state's overtures and recalcitrance towards Hawaiian culture as happening on grounds given by colonialism, because we may otherwise miss enunciations of Indigenous sovereignty that fall outside of conventional political forms of participation.[42] In missing these enunciations, progress towards meaningful and just management of resources can be thwarted. This does not render state water resource management toxic to decolonization or ineffective at conservation, but marks another way "management" can bypass what would be meaningful about Hawaiian self-determination.

"WE'RE NOT GOING ANYWHERE."

In May 2019, Water Commission staff met with community members from Honokōwai, Wahikuli, Honolua, and Honokōhau to discuss a water-wasting complaint and the Water Commission's overall approach to West Maui water resource management more generally. The idea of designating West Maui as a ground and surface water management area arose as a solution to uncertainties about water use and problems with enforcement against over-exploitation. Water Commission staff cautioned that the process is complicated and "could take YEARS, maybe DECADES!" The dozen or so community members were unphased by the caution, with several saying, "OK, whatever, we'll figure it out. Let's do it!" The agency staff looked confused and repeated their caution. They were used to dealing with hurried developer timelines keyed to construction schedules and financing deadlines. Finally, one uncle explained, "You don't understand. We're not going anywhere." And this is a historical fact that marks the cusp between Kānaka Maoli, aloha 'āina, and the state's efforts to manage them as subjects.

This book sought to recognize the more difficult space that longtime West Maui communities occupy in both their cultural practices and community organizing, and the public processes structured by state regulation. These claims to water rights are not simply claims to a resource. Rather, they are claims to a West Maui embodied in tactile geologies and the immanent life that its lands and waters hold within it. Water set into its natural courses, "freed" from the uses that the plantations set for it, abets the restoration of an entire landscape that depended on it. Whether this sleeping, intransient power will be awakened or stifled under channels and concrete for another decade or century will pivot on the changing course decided by climate change, state governance, and diverse West Maui communities themselves.

Here, in a landscape that has been transformed by forced mobility of labor and capital, communities have this advantage of a generations-long vision for the future of West Maui. They aren't going anywhere.

Notes

1. Magoon, J. A. Defendents' Brief, Pioneer Mill vs. Kumuliilii et al, First Circuit Court (1895).
2. Web page for the Pools at the Westin Ka'anapali, 2017. Available at www .westinkaanapali.com/beach-pool. Retrieved August 21, 2017.
3. Giambelluca, T. W., Q. Chen, A. G. Frazier, J. P. Price, Y.-L. Chen, P.-S. Chu, J. K. Eischeid, and D. M. Delparte, 2013: Online Rainfall Atlas of Hawai'i. *Bull. Amer. Meteor. Soc.* 94, 313–316, doi: 10.1175/BAMS-D-11-00228.1.
4. "Hawaiian" and "native Hawaiian" are English words with state and federal legal definitions, respectively. "Native Hawaiian" references "an individual who is a descendant of the aboriginal peoples who, prior to 1778, occupied and exercised sovereignty in the Hawaiian islands, the area that now constitutes the State of Hawai'i[.]" Haw. Rev. Stat. § 10H-3. By contrast with "Native Hawaiians," lower-case-n "native Hawaiians" are those persons with fifty percent or more blood quantum as identified by the Hawaiian Homes Commission Act (Act 42 of Jul. 9, 1921), Pub. L. No. 34, 42 Stat. 108 (1920).

   This genealogical definition of "Native Hawaiian" does not reflect state negotiations with Hawaiians only, but also Hawaiian political theorists' recommendations based on their analyses of the Kingdom's historical experiences with multiracial citizenship. Hawaiian national sovereignty advocates such as Ka Lāhui Hawai'i and the Council of Regency also consider genealogy to be a defining aspect of Native Hawaiian citizenship. They note, "[a]llowing haole citizenship did not make haole loyal to the Kingdom in the same way that Natives were loyal, and for the maka'ainana of the 1840s, that loyalty was important, not just politically but also socially and culturally." Jonathan Kamakawiwo'ole Osorio, *Kū'ē and Kū'oko'a (Resistance and Independence): History, Law and Other Faiths,* 1 Haw. J.L. & Pol. 92, 109 (2004). Such a genealogical definition also makes sense as a safeguard against fraudulent claims to Native Hawaiian rights by non-Hawaiians. See Lisa Kahaleole Hall, '*Hawaiian at Heart' and other Fictions,* 17 The Contemporary Pacific 404 (2005).

   Alternately, indigenous scholars have used the term "kanaka Maoli," described by McGregor and MacKenzie: "Maoli means native, indigenous, genuine, true, and real according to the Hawaiian dictionary. Kanaka maoli has been popularized as the appropriate indigenous term for Native Hawaiian by advocates of Native Hawaiian sovereignty and independence...." (McGregor,

Davianna and Melody K. MacKenzie. 2014. *Mo'olelo Ea O Nā Hawai'i: History of Native Hawaiian Governance in Hawai'i.* Honolulu: Office of Hawaiian Affairs. Available at www.doi.gov/sites/doi.opengov.ibmcloud.com/files/uploads /Mo'olelo%20Ea%20O%20Nā%20Hawai'i(8-23-15).pdf.

5. Cooper, George, and Gavan Daws. *Land and Power in Hawaii: The Democratic Years* at 14. Benchmark Books, Inc., 1995.

6. For Maui, "Full build-out under County Zoning and DHHL land use plans would result in a hypothetical maximum demand of 931 million gallons per day (mgd). The full build-out scenario would exceed the island's sustainable yield and assessed available surface water if demand were supplied entirely by conventional water resources." P. 166 in Maui Island Water Use and Development Plan Draft March 2019.

7. "Aloha 'āina" can refer to those who have aloha for Hawaii's land and people, as those are inextricable from each other. It also references patriots of the Kingdom of Hawai'i. The term has deep meaning that is perhaps best historically contextualized by Noenoe Silva's *Aloha Betrayed: Native Hawaiian Resistance to American Colonialism* (Durham and London: Duke University Press, 2004).

8. The individuals sued were named as follows; K indicates Kane (male) and W, Wahine (female): Kumuliilii (K), Kalua Kanawaliwali (K), Kukue (K), Kukaia (K), Ilaika (W), Kauahikaua (K), Wahinepio (W), Kahai (K), Kalua (K), Charles Liilh (K), Henry Hairama (K), U. Kahaulelio (K), Noa Kahaulelio (K), Keao (K), Kawahamana (W), Kaaeae (K), Kapili (K), Kahooneeaina (W), Piimoku (W), Kealo (K), Maikeike Ihihi (K), Kaleihoomio (K), Kahulikaa (K), Elia (K), Kulu (K), Kukue (K), Punihele (K), Kaminamina (W), A. Pali (K), Wili Aholo (Boy), Mrs. Iiattie Ayers (W), Wm. White (K), Henry Smith (K), Kualau (W), Waihoioahu (K), Kanelawahine (K), Liliuokalani (W), Likua (K), Opunui (K), Palakiko (K), D. Kahaulelio (K), Kahoino (W), Hoohilahila (W), Joe Paniole (K), Rev. J. Waiamau (K), Uilama Hinau (K), Kahalepuna (W), Moku (K), Mrs. Sylva, Mrs. Espinda, J. Espinda (K), Mrs. Pratt Of Honolulu, Kaloiele (K), Mrs. J. F. Brown Of Honolulu, G. K. Halemano (K), S. Koko (K), J. F. Brown, M. Makalua, Kanekoa (K), and C. Aiiwai.

9. Maly, Magoon, and Onaona Maly, *He Wahi Mo'olelo No Kaua'ula a Me Kekāhi 'Āina o Lahaina i Maui: A Collection of Traditions and Historical Accounts of Kaua'ula and Other Lands of Lahaina, Maui,* prepared for Makila Land Co. & Kamehameha Schools, Vol. 1, at 925 (Jun. 1, 2007) ("Maly V.1").

10. Ladd, William, 1838. "Remarks upon the Natural Resources of the Sandwich Islands: read before the Sandwich Island Institute, January 30, 1838." *The Hawaiian Spectator* 1:68–79.

11. Translation (unaccredited, from State Archives) of the Complaint of the Plaintiffs in *Horner v. Kumuli'ili'i.*

12. *Horner v. Kumuli'ili'i,* 10 Haw. 174 (1895).

Chapter 2: Regulatory Overview

1. Maui Department of Water Supply, Maui Island Water Use & Development Plan, Public Meeting—West Maui, Meeting Summary (Mar. 17, 2016) available at www.co.maui.hi.us/DocumentCenter/View/102799.

2. Maui Department of Water Supply, Maui Island Water Use & Development Plan, Public Meeting—West Maui, Meeting Summary (Mar. 17, 2016) available at www.co.maui.hi.us/DocumentCenter/View/102799.

3. Stearns, Harold T., and Gordon A. MacDonald. *Geology and Ground-Water Resources of the Island of Maui, Hawaii*, 7 Bulletins of the Division of Hydrography, Territory of Hawai'i, at 7 (Oct. 1942) available at https://pubs.usgs.gov/misc/stearns/Maui.pdf.

4. Ibid. at 8.

5. Neale, Timothy, and Stephen Turner. "Other people's country: law, water, entitlement," 5(4) *Settler Colonial Studies* 277, 277 (2015).

6. *The Hawaiian Gazette*. (Honolulu), 05 Nov. 1915, page 3. "Chronicling America: Historic American Newspapers." Lib. of Congress. Available at http://chroniclingamerica.loc.gov/lccn/sn83025121/1915-11-05/ed-1/seq-3/

7. *The Hawaiian Gazette*. (Honolulu), 05 Nov. 1915, page 3. "Chronicling America: Historic American Newspapers." Lib. of Congress. Available at http://chroniclingamerica.loc.gov/lccn/sn83025121/1915-11-05/ed-1/seq-3/

8. Gingerich, S. B., and D. S. Oki, Ground Water in Hawaii: U.S. Geological Survey, Fact Sheet 126-00 (2000).

9. HRS §174C-7(b).

10. For instance, while the Code was amended in 2003 to add the requirement that "one member shall have substantial experience or expertise in traditional Hawaiian water resource management techniques", it was eight years before a Kanaka Maoli was appointed into that seat. This is notable even though the two individuals who served in that role both aggressively advocated for implementation of the code.

11. HRS §174C-45.

12. HRS §174C-44.

13. HRS §174C-44.

14. AWUDP at xi.

15. Akana, Akoni, "The History of Moku'ula," by Guy Gaumont, Maui Filmworks, at 16:10 min. (1999) available at https://www.youtube.com/watch?v=Gm4I4VggmOg.

16. Cheng, Chui Ling, *Low-Flow Characteristics of Streams in the Lahaina District, West Maui, Hawai'i*, Scientific Investigation Report 2014–5087, 5 (2014) available at https://pubs.er.usgs.gov/publication/sir20145087.

17. Cheng, Chui Ling, *Low-Flow Characteristics of Streams in the Lahaina District,*

West Maui, Hawai'i, Scientific Investigation Report 2014–5087, 5 (2014). Available at https://pubs.er.usgs.gov/publication/sir20145087.

18. USGS Lahaina Groundwater at iii (2012).

19. Maly, Kepā, and Onaona Maly, "He Wahi Moʻolelo No Kauaʻula a Me Kekāhi ʻĀina o Lahaina i Maui: A Collection of Traditions and Historical Accounts of Kauaʻula and Other Lands of Lahaina, Maui, prepared for Makila Land Co. & Kamehameha Schools," Vol. 1, at ii (Jun. 1, 2007) ("Maly V.1").

20. HRS §174C-44.

21. HRS §174C-31.

22. Maui DWS, WUDP Presentation, West Maui Meeting Presentation at 14 (Mar. 17, 2016) available at http://www.co.maui.hi.us/DocumentCenter/View/102802.

23. Draft Maui WUDP, 78–79.

24. Draft Maui WUDP, 101 citing CWRM Well Index (May 29, 2015).

25. Draft Maui WUDP at 118–19.

26. Draft Maui WUDP at 119.

27. See Application, *In the Matter of Application of Olowalu Water Company, Inc.,* Public Utilities Comm'n Docket No. 2008-0165, filed Aug. 21, 2008.

28. "Application." *In the matter of the application of Launiupoko Irrigation Co., LLC,* Public Utilities Comm'n Dkt. No. 02-0203 (Aug. 1, 2012).

29. "Application." *In the matter of the application of Launiupoko Irrigation Co., LLC,* Public Utilities Comm'n Dkt. No. 02-0203 (Aug. 1, 2012).

30. "Application." *In the matter of the application of Launiupoko Irrigation Co., LLC,* Public Utilities Comm'n Dkt. No. 02-0203 (Aug. 1, 2012).

31. HRS § 174C-2; Hawaii Administrative Rules (HAR) § 13-171-2.

32. In its 2002 findings in regard to ʻĪao aquifer designation, CWRM found "total projected demand" was 29.2 mgd, which included water demands from projects with pending permits and/or lacked water commitments. CWRM, Iao and Waihee Aquifer Systems State Aquifer Codes 60102 and 60103 Ground-Water Management Area Designation Findings of Fact, at 69–70 (Nov. 14, 2002) (on file with author).

33. CWRM, State of Hawaiʻi, Findings of Fact, Petition to Designate the Island of Molokai as a Water Management Area, at 15 (Feb. 1992).

34. Rae Loui, Deputy Director, CWRM, Resubmittal: Petition to Designate Windward Oahu as a Water Management Area, at 2 (May 5, 1992) (on file with author).

35. CWRM, DRAFT: Findings of Fact Report for the Petition on Designating the Island of Lanai as a Water Management Area for the Commission on Water Resource Management, at 18–20 [PDF 26–28] (Jan. 1990) (on file with author).

36. CWRM's considered the following in calculating APU for Lānaʻi: proposed developments consisting in resort hotels, golf courses, parks, open areas, roadways, and multi- and single-family subdivisions, commercial development and new sewage treatment plants; projected residential and visitor population increases through 2010; variability between environmental assessments and development

plans; and the pace of total projected development. CWRM noted that 70% of total projected development and population growth through 2010 would occur by 1995. CWRM, DRAFT: Findings of Fact Report for the Petition on Designating the Island of Lanai as a Water Management Area for the Commission on Water Resource Management, at 18–20 [PDF 26–28] (on file with author). (Draft FOFs for Lānaʻi WMA petition).

37. CWRM, Draft FOFs for Lānaʻi WMA petition, at 19–20 (Jan. 1990).
38. CWRM, Draft FOFs for Lānaʻi WMA petition, at 19 (Jan. 1990).
39. CWRM, Draft FOFs for Lānaʻi WMA petition, at 25 (Jan. 1990).
40. CWRM, Draft FOFs for Lānaʻi WMA petition, at 22 (Jan. 1990).
41. CWRM, Draft FOFs for Lānaʻi WMA petition, at 25 (Jan. 1990).
42. CWRM, Draft FOFs for Lānaʻi WMA petition, at 18–20 [PDF 26–28] (Jan. 1990).
43. State of Hawaiʻi Land Use Commission, "Findings of Fact, Conclusions of Law, and Decision and Order In the Matter of the Petition of Lanai Resort Partners," Dkt. No. A92-674, FOF #57 at 16 (Oct. 24, 1994). Available at http://files.hawaii .gov/luc/comaui/a92674_lanai_resort_10241994.pdf.
44. In 1989, Lanai Resort Partners filed a petition to change 110.243 acres from rural to urban land use and 28.334 acres from agricultural to urban land use in order to develop the Manele Bay resort golf course, which required 0.8 mgd for irrigation purposes. State of Hawaiʻi Land Use Commission, "Findings of Fact, Conclusions of Law, and Decision and Order In the Matter of the Petition of Lanai Resort Partners," Dkt. No. A89-649 (Apr. 16, 1991) available at http://luc.state .hi.us/comaui/a89649_dando_04161991.pdf. LUC did not grant the Manele Bay resort land use amendment petition until April 16, 1991. On April 30, 1992, Lanai Resort Partners filed another LUC petition to reclassify another 319.447 acres from agricultural and rural districts to urban designation in order to permit the construction of the residential component of the Manele bay resort, which would require another 0.4 mgd. State of Hawaiʻi Land Use Commission, "Findings of Fact, Conclusions of Law, and Decision and Order In the Matter of the Petition of Lanai Resort Partners," Dkt. No. A92-674 (Oct. 24, 1994) available at http:// files.hawaii.gov/luc/comaui/a92674_lanai_resort_10241994.pdf. LUC did not grant this petition until October 24, 1994.
45. In its decisionmaking on the 1988 petition to designate Windward Oʻahu WMA, CWRM first found that criterion one "could not be used as a firm argument for ground water designation since neither present use nor total possible future uses reach 90 percent of the sustainable yield of the proposed water management area." This finding was based on uses proposed in a Board of Water Supply Final Environmental Impact Statement, which would require another 82 mgd or 74 percent of Oʻahu Windward WMA's 111.5 mgd SY. CWRM, "Findings of Fact: Petition to Designate Windward Oahu as a Water Management Area," ref. CWRM-WMA-OA-1, at 13–14 (Mar. 1990) (on file with author).

46. Rae Loui, Deputy Director, CWRM, Resubmittal: Petition to Designate Windward Oahu as a Water Management Area, at 2–3 (May 5, 1992) (on file with author).

47. Rae Loui, Deputy Director, CWRM, Resubmittal: Petition to Designate Windward Oahu as a Water Management Area, at 2 (May 5, 1992) (on file with author).

48. Rae Loui, Deputy Director, CWRM, Resubmittal: Petition to Designate Windward Oahu as a Water Management Area, at 2–3 (May 5, 1992) (on file with author).

49. See *Koʻolau Agricultural Co., Ltd. v. Commʻn on Water Res. Mgmt*, 83 Hawaiʻi 484, 489, 927 P.2d 1367, 1372 (1994). The Koʻolau Agricultural Company later filed suit, seeking invalidation of WMA designation on the basis of CWRM's interpretation of "APUs" and application of "developable yield." The Hawaiʻi Supreme court concluded it lacked jurisdiction to review WMA designation, which was final and not-appealable. Ibid., 83 Hawaiʻi at 494, 927 P.2d at 1377.

50. See Dept. of General Planning, City & County of Honolulu, Oʻahu Water Management Plan, prepared by Wilson Okamoto and Associates, Inc., at 5–1 [PDF 150] (Mar. 1990). Available at http://files.hawaii.gov/dlnr/cwrm/planning/wudpoa1990.pdf. (Oʻahu WUDP).

51. CWRM relied on water demand figures in the 1990 Oʻahu WUDP, which were projected out to 2010 (twenty years out from 1990). See Oʻahu WUDP at 4–5 through 4–10 [PDF 128–132].

52. CWRM, State of Hawaiʻi, Findings of Fact, Petition to Designate the Island of Molokai as a Water Management Area, at 15–16 (Feb. 1992).

53. CWRM, Molokaʻi WMA FOFs at 14 (1992).

54. A copy of the Hastings, Martin, Chew & Associates, Ltd. (Jul. 1981) report has been requested, but not obtained, at the time of this writing. Email from Bianca Isaki to Jacky Takakura, Administrator, Maui DWS (Nov. 28, 2014).

55. Maui County Planning Depʻt, "Molokai Community Plan Technical Report," prepared by EDAW Inc. at 37 (Oct. 1981) (on file with the University of Hawaiʻi at Mānoa, Hawaiian Collection).

56. Maui County Planning Depʻt, "Molokai Community Plan Technical Report," prepared by EDAW, Inc. (Oct. 1981).

57. Maui County Planning Depʻt, "Molokai Community Plan Technical Report," prepared by EDAW Inc. at 37 (Oct. 1981) (on file with University of Hawaiʻi at Mānoa, Hawaiian Collection).

58. CWRM, Iao and Waihee Aquifer Systems State Aquifer Codes 60102 and 60103 Ground-Water Management Area Designation Findings of Fact, at 77 (Nov. 14, 2002) (on file with author).

59. CWRM, Iao and Waihee Aquifer Systems State Aquifer Codes 60102 and 60103 Ground-Water Management Area Designation Findings of Fact, at x–xi (Nov. 14, 2002) (on file with author).

60. 2002 'Īao FOFs at 71.
61. 2002 'Īao FOFs at 71.
62. Although it did not need to look further than existing uses under criterion 1, CWRM examined three other estimates of future water demand: (1) the Maui WUDP (1990) predicted Maui BWS water demand for the Central Maui system would be 30.5 mgd by 2010; (2) Maui BWS' "most probable" estimate of a 2 or 2.5 mgd increase by the end of 1998; and (3) Maui BWS commitments under an unspecified timeframe. CWRM, 1996 'Īao FOFs at 34, 36 [PDF 42, 44].
63. CWRM, 1996 'Īao FOFs at 34 [PDF 42].
64. CWRM, 2002 'Īao FOFs at 69–70.
65. CWRM, 2002 'Īao FOFs at 70.
66. CWRM, 2002 'Īao FOFs at 70 n. 2.
67. CWRM derived its 31.1 mgd figure for 'Īao aquifer projected uses from the Maui WUDP, which predicted total groundwater withdrawals and transfers from the "Iao system" to be 18.5 mgd by the year 2010. CWRM, 2002 'Īao FOFs at 69, 108.
68. 'Īao aquifer serves Wailuku, Waiheʻe, Kahului, Kihei, Maalaea, and Paia-Kuau water systems. See CWRM, 2002 'Īao FOFs at 71.
69. CWRM, Meeting Minutes, Item 5: Maui Meadows Homeowners Association, c/o James Williamson, Vice President, Petition to Designate Ground Water Management Areas Action Iao & Waihee Aquifer Systems (60102 & 60103) Wailuku, Maui, at 8 (Nov. 20, 2002) available at http://files.hawaii.gov/dlnr/cwrm/minute/2002/mn20021120.pdf.
70. David Craddick, director of Maui's Department of Water Supply (Dec. 1999); quoted by Mansel Blackford, *Fragile Paradise: The Impact of Tourism on Maui 1950–2000*, 114 (Univ. Press of Arkansas, 2001).
71. "Clean Water for Napili in One Year," *Lahaina Sun*, Vol.1, No. 13, at 4 (Feb. 3, 1971).
72. "Clean Water for Napili in One Year," *Lahaina Sun*, Vol.1, No. 13, at 4 (Feb. 3, 1971).
73. See CWRM, 2019 Water Resources Protection Plan Update *Draft* (Oct. 2018) available at http://files.hawaii.gov/dlnr/cwrm/planning/wrpp2019update/WRPP_DRAFT_ONLY_201810.pdf
74. Department of Water Supply, County of Maui, Maui Water Use Development Plan Update, at 7 (Nov. 2018) available at https://www.mauicounty.gov/2051/Maui-Island-Water-Use-Development-Plan/ (2018 Maui WUDP Update).
75. CWRM is required to consider the following in determining whether to designate a groundwater management area:

    1) Whether an increase in water use or authorized planned use may cause the maximum rate of withdrawal from the groundwater source to reach 90 percent of the sustainable yield of the proposed groundwater management area;

2) There is an actual or threatened water quality degradation as determined by the Department of Health;

3) Whether regulation is necessary to preserve the diminishing groundwater supply for future needs, as evidenced by excessively declining groundwater levels;

4) Whether the rates, times, spatial patterns, or depths of existing withdrawals of groundwater are endangering the stability or optimum development of the groundwater body due to upconing or encroachment of saltwater;

5) Whether the chloride contents of existing wells are increasing to levels that materially reduce the value of their existing uses;

6) Whether excessive preventable waste of groundwater is occurring;

7) Serious disputes respecting the use of groundwater resources are occurring; or

8) Whether water development projects that have received any federal, state, or county approval may result, in the opinion of the commission, in one of the above conditions.

HRS §174C-44.

76. The CWRM Water Bulletin reported the following:

Dec. 2018: Launiupoko (2) 4-7-012:004 6-5139-003, Strombeck Steve & Tina Strombeck applicants for irrigation. Proposed Use: 0.072 mgd at a rate of 50gpm.

Launiupoko (2) 4-7-009:016 6-5138-003, Duvall Craig A. Duvall Trust, applicants. Proposed both a pump and well installation for domestic uses of 0.036 mgd and a rate 25gpm.

Sep. 2018: Launiupoko (2) 4-7-001:049 6-5137-002, Maria Lynn Moyer Memorial Timothy & Harline Moyer Trust, applicants, for both a pump and well installation for domestic uses of 0.005 mgd and a capacity of 40gpm.

Launiupoko (2) 4-7-003:005 6-5139-002, McDonald well and pump installation for agricultural purposes, using 0.2 mgd, 250 gpm, 0.360 mgd capacity.

Honokowai (4) 4-4-004:002 6-5639-004, DHHL Honokowai and Maui Department of Water Pump, for municipal uses of 0.680 mgd, at a rate of 700gpm 1.008mgd capacity

Nov. 2016: Launiupoko (2) 4-7-003:004 6-5139-001 LIC 1 Launiupoko Irrigation Co., Inc., applicant sought well and pump installation for agricultural uses of 0.700mgd, 500gpm, with a 0.720 capacity.

Aug. 2015: Launiupoko (2) 4-6-032:001 6-5140-001 Puamana Community Association Well 1 proposed, (no information on proposed use or capacity). Approved 09/18/2015

May 2015: Honokōwai (2) 4-4-014:005 6-5641-004 KOR Lot 3 saltwater backup Starwood Vacation Ownership Inc., sought a well and pump installation permit for industrial uses, for a well pumping at a rate of 3000 gpm with a 4.32 mpg capacity, but with zero proposed use.

Mar. 2015: Launiupoko (3) 4-7-001:049 6-5137-002 Maria Lynn Moyer Memorial, Timothy Moyer sought a well and pump installation permit for domestic uses, for 0.005 mgd uses and a capacity of 0.058 mgd.

Dec 2014: Honolua (2) 4-3-001:017 6-5738-002, the Kahana Department of Water Supply Well

Jan. 2014: Honokowai (2) 4-4-004:018 6-5539-003, the Kaanapali P-3 well, Hawaii Water Service sought a well and pump installation permit for municipal uses, for a well using 0.720 mgd and a capacity of 0.720.

Industrial uses are reported as "zero" for all of Lahaina. Maui WUDP at 22.

77. See Maui County Council Affordable Housing Committee, Agenda Item Nos. AH-1, AH-27, June 19, 2019 available at www.mauicounty.gov/ArchiveCenter /ViewFile/Item/26124.

78. Further research is needed to determine whether wells approved after 2014 were given after-the-fact permits, which may mean that the wells were installed and their usage included in the 2014 Maui DWS figure.

79. Maui County Draft WUDP (Nov. 3, 2017) at 8.

80. Draft WRPP 2018 at 32.

81. Draft WRPP 2018 at 32.

82. Draft WRPP 2018 at 32.

83. HRS §174C-44(4).

84. HRS §174C-3.

85. HRS §174C-3.

86. HRS §174C-3.

87. Draft Maui WUDP at 149–150.

88. Commission on Water Resource Management, Dep't. Land & Natural Resources, Identification of Rivers and Streams Worthy of Protection, Report to the Twenty-Sixth Legislature, 2012 Legislative Session, 7–8 (Nov. 2011) available at http:// files.hawaii.gov/dlnr/cwrm/legislature/CW2012_IDofRivers.pdf.

89. Cheng, Chui Ling, *Low-Flow Characteristics of Streams in the Lahaina District, West Maui, Hawai'i*, Scientific Investigation Report 2014–5087 (2014) available at https://pubs.er.usgs.gov/publication/sir20145087.

90. Commission on Water Resource Management, Dep't Land & Natural Resources, Identification of Rivers and Streams Worthy of Protection, Report to the Twenty-Sixth Legislature, 2012 Legislative Session, 7–8 (Nov. 2011) available at http://files.hawaii.gov/dlnr/cwrm/legislature/CW2012_IDofRivers.pdf.

91. Blackford, Mansel, *Fragile Paradise: The Impact of Tourism on Maui 1950–2000*, 137–138 (Univ. Press of Arkansas, 2001).

92. Interview with Chris Brosius, Operations Manager, West Maui Watershed Partnership, Lahaina, Maui (Mar. 28, 2017).

93. Interview with Chris Brosius, Operations Manager, West Maui Watershed Partnership, Lahaina, Maui (Mar. 28, 2017).

94. Interview with Chris Brosius, Operations Manager, West Maui Watershed Partnership, Lahaina, Maui (Mar. 28, 2017).

95. Interview with Chris Brosius, Operations Manager, West Maui Watershed Partnership, Lahaina, Maui (Mar. 28, 2017).

96. Coral Reef Conservation Program, NOAA, West Maui Ridge 2 Reef Initiative, *Wahikuli-Honokōwai Watershed Management Plan, V.1: Watershed Characterization*, at 17 (Dec. 2012). Available at health.hawaii.gov/cwb/files/2013/05/WHWMP_Vol1_WatershedCharacterization_Dec2012small.pdf.

97. West Maui Land, Co. "Rules and Regulations for Olowalu Potable Water" (2015) available at http://water.westmauiland.com/docs/2015/OWC/Rules_Regs_Olowalu_Potable_Final.pdf.

98. West Maui Land Co., Inc. "Mahanalua Nui Water System report to the Consumer for Calendar Year 2014" (2015) available at http://water.westmauiland.com/wp-content/uploads/2015/05/LWC-CCR-2014-revised.pdf.

99. See West Maui Land Co., Launiupoko Water Company, Inc. Rules and Regulations (2015) available at http://water.westmauiland.com/docs/2015/LWC/LWC_rules-regulations_rev_2-08_to_INC.pdf.

100. See West Maui Land Co., Launiupoko Irrigation Company, Inc. Rules and Regulations (2015). Available at http://water.westmauiland.com/docs/2015/LIC/LIC_Rules_Regs_2-08_to_INC_copy.pdf.

101. See Application of Kāʻanapali Water Corp., 678 P.2d 584 (1984).

102. Sugidono, Chris, "Resort customers challenge private water company to 'do better,'" *The Maui News* (online) (Mar. 6, 2016).

103. Perry, Brian, "'Reasonable' rate increase OK'd for Kaanapali water users," *The Maui News* (online) (Sep. 19, 2016).

104. Sugidono, Chris, "Resort customers challenge private water company to 'do better,'" *The Maui News* (online) (Mar. 6, 2016).

105. Sugidono, Chris, "Private provider seeks to increase rates up to 30% with hotels footing higher share of costs," *The Maui News* (online) (Mar. 24, 2016).

106. Sugidono, Chris, "Private provider seeks to increase rates up to 30% with hotels footing higher share of costs," *The Maui News* (online) (Mar. 24, 2016).

107. Perry, Brian, "'Reasonable' rate increase OK'd for Kaanapali water users," *The Maui News* (online) (Sep. 19, 2016).

108. *Ka Paʻakai*, 94 Hawaiʻi at 31, 7 P.3d at 1068 (footnote omitted).

109. LUC's order granting the developer's boundary amendment provided that the developer "*will develop*" a resource management plan (RMP); "*would coordinate* development with native Hawaiian rights to coastal access[;]" "concept[ualize] the RMP," which was an approximately 235 acre resource management area; and would make their RMP consistent with an ahupuaʻa plan that "*will involve* native Hawaiians[.]" *Ka Paʻakai*, 94 Hawaiʻi at 37–38, 7 P.3d at 1074–1075 (emphases in original). LUC further conditioned the permit: 18. *[The developer] shall preserve*

and protect any gathering and access rights of native Hawaiians who have customarily and traditionally exercised subsistence, cultural and religious practices on the subject property.

110. *Waiāhole I*, 94 Hawaiʻi at 142, 9 P.3d at 454 (emphasis added).

111. *Kauaʻi Springs*, 133 Hawaiʻi at 175, 324 P.3d at 985.

CHAPTER 3: DITCH SYSTEM HISTORY

1. Maly, Kepā, and Onaona Maly, Kumu Pono Associates, LLC, He Wahi Moʻolelo No Kauaʻula a Me Kekāhi ʻĀina O Lahaina i Maui (A Collection of Traditions and Historical Accounts of Kauaʻula and Other Lands of Lahaina, Maui), V. 1 at 18 (2007).

2. "Additional Water Supplies for Maui," *Maui News*, February 1903.

3. *Maui News*, Sep. 8, 1900, page 3.

4. *Maui News*, Saturday Nov. 17, 1900, page 2.

5. *Maui News*, Saturday Nov. 3, 1900, page 1.

6. Maly V.1 at 10 (cited material omitted).

7. Maly V.1 at 10–11.

8. Maly V.1 at 16 (quoting Pualewa, trans. Maly.)

9. Maly V.1 at 17.

10. Maly V.1 at 922.

11. Maly V.1 at 922.

12. On August 1, 1865, A. Makekau and Meri, his wife, deeded to Campbell and Turton land at Panaʻewa and ʻŌpaeʻula in exchange for cash payment and a parcel of land "on the Kula (Breadfruit Zone)." Maly, Kepā, and Onaona Maly, *He Wahi Moʻoelo no Kauaʻula a me Lahaina i Maui: A Collection fo Traditions and Historical Accounts of Kauaʻula and Other Lands of Lahaina, Maui*, Kumu Pono Associates, LLC, Vol. 2, at 922, 977 (Jun. 1, 2007).

13. Abel Keliionuuanu Makekau was born to Naohulelu and Kumiaiakea of Kailua Kona on October 16, 1820 in Kailua, Hawaiʻi. Abel later relocated to Lahaina, Maui where he married Mele Kahiwa.

14. Perkins, Leialoha Apo. 2009–2010. *On the missing moʻolelo of ʻohana genealogies: the Makekau clan*. 8 vols. Vol. 4, at 188 (Makaha: Kamaluʻuluolele, Ka Hale Paʻi).

15. Perkins, Leialoha Apo. 2012. *On the missing moolelo of ʻohana genealogies the Makekau clan: Vol. 3: Lahaina, Sketches—Growing Up*, 1930s. 8 vols. Vol. 3., at 152 (Makaha: Ka Hale Paʻi).

16. For a more complete discussion of the relationship between the Makekau ʻohana and Pioneer Mill, see Bianca Isaki, "Post Plantation Worker Memories and Tourism Futures in West Maui," in *Tourism Impacts West Maui* (eds. L. Collins & B. Isaki) (NBWMBF 2016).

17. Wilcox, Carol, *Sugar Water: Hawaiʻi's Plantation Ditches*, 134 (UH Press, 1998).

18. Wilcox, Carol, *Sugar Water: Hawaiʻi's Plantation Ditches*, 134 (UH Press, 1998).
19. Thrum, Thomas, *Hawaiian Annual*, "Irrigation in Hawaii" p. 156–61 (1905) quoted by Maly V.1 at 943–44.
20. Maly V.1 at 6.
21. Maly V.1 at 6.
22. Blackford, Mansel G., *Fragile Paradise: The Impact of Tourism on Maui, 1959–2000*. Lawrence, KS (Blackford 2001).
23. Hibbard, Don J., prepared for Nat'l Park Srvc, Dep't of Interior, Historic American Engineer Record (HAER) No. HI-88, Lahaina Pump Ditch Number 1, Pioneer Mill Company, Lahaina, Maui, Hawaiʻi (Aug. 2009) available at https:// cdn.loc.gov/master/pnp/habshaer/hi/hi0800/hi0895/data/hi0895data.pdf ("HAER Rpt."). HAER Rpt. at 4.
24. HAER Rpt. at 4.
25. Maly V.2 at 942, quoting "Pioneer Mill of Lahaina." *The Friend*, p. 48 (Jun. 1899).
26. Ibid.
27. HAER Rpt.
28. Maly V.1 at 47.
29. Maly V.1 at 47.
30. HAER Rpt. at 2.
31. Interview with James Higuchi, Lahaina, Maui, *Pioneer Mill Company: A Maui Sugar Plantation Legacy* (ed. Warren Nishimoto), Honolulu: Univ. of Hawaiʻi, Ctr for Oral History, Social Sci. Res. Inst., chap. 10, at 21 (2003) ("Higuchi Interview").
32. Higuchi Interview at 21.
33. Interview with Anthony Vierra, Lahaina, Maui by Warren Nishimoto, *Pioneer Mill Company: A Maui Sugar Plantation Legacy* (ed. Warren Nishimoto), Honolulu: Univ. of Hawaiʻi, Ctr for Oral History, Social Sci. Res. Inst., Chap. 8, at 5 (2003) ("Vierra Interview").
34. HAER Rpt. at 2.
35. HAER Rpt. at 3.
36. Blackford, Mansel G., *Fragile Paradise: The Impact of Tourism on Maui, 1959–2000*. Lawrence, KS: (Blackford 2001).
37. Cooper, George, and Gavan Daws, *Land and Power in Hawaii: The Democratic Years* (Benchmark Books, Honolulu 1985), 179.
38. Cooper, George, and Gavan Daws, *Land and Power in Hawaii: The Democratic Years* (Benchmark Books, Honolulu 1985), 184.
39. Commission on Water Resource Management, State of Hawaiʻi, *Agricultural Water Use Development Plan*, 63 (2004) available at http://files.hawaii.gov/dlnr /cwrm/planning/awudp2004.pdf.
40. Cheng, USGS Lahaina Low-flow study, at 7.
41. Cheng, USGS Lahaina Low-flow study, at 7.
42. Cheng, USGS Lahaina Low-flow study, at 7.

43. Commission on Water Resource Management, State of Hawaiʻi, *Agricultural Water Use Development Plan*, 63 (2004) available at http://files.hawaii.gov/dlnr /cwrm/planning/awudp2004.pdf.

44. Interview with Frederick Higuchi, Lahaina, Maui, *Pioneer Mill Company: A Maui Sugar Plantation Legacy* (ed. Warren Nishimoto), Honolulu: Univ. of Hawaiʻi, Ctr for Oral History, Social Sci. Res. Inst., at 14 (2003).

45. Thrum, Thomas, *Hawaiian Annual*, "Irrigation in Hawaii" p. 160–62 (1905) quoted by Maly V.1 at 944.

46. *The Pacific Commercial Advertiser*, at 13 (Jan. 1, 1905).

47. *The Pacific Commercial Advertiser*, at 3 (Feb. 15, 1904).

48. *The Maui News*. (Wailuku, Maui), 19 Dec. 1903. *Chronicling America: Historic American Newspapers*. Lib. of Congress. Available at http://chroniclingamerica .loc.gov/lccn/sn82014689/1903-12-19/ed-1/seq-4/.

49. "Great Engineering Work on Maui" *The Hawaiian Gazette* on June 7, 1904 p. 3.

50. "Big Ditch Completed," *Pacific Commercial Advertiser*, p. 8 (Jun. 6, 1904).

51. *Evening Bulletin*. (Honolulu, Oahu), 17 Oct. 1904. *Chronicling America: Historic American Newspapers*. Lib. of Congress. Available at http://chroniclingamerica .loc.gov/lccn/sn82016413/1904-10-17/ed-1/seq-4/.

52. "Big Ditch Completed," *Pacific Commercial Advertiser*, p. 8 (Jun. 6, 1904).

53. *Evening Bulletin Industrial Edition*, March 25, 1909, page 4.

54. *Evening bulletin*. (Honolulu [Oahu, Hawaii], 09 Aug. 1911. *Chronicling America: Historic American Newspapers*. Lib. of Congress. Available at http:// chroniclingamerica.loc.gov/lccn/sn82016413/1911-08-09/ed-1/seq-1/.

55. *Honolulu Star Bulletin*, May 8, 1915, page 21.

56. Interview with Kazukiyo "Jiggs" Kuboyama (b. 1929), Lahaina, Maui by Warren Nishimoto, *Pioneer Mill Company: A Maui Sugar Plantation Legacy* (ed. Warren Nishimoto), Honolulu: Univ. of Hawaiʻi, Ctr for Oral History, Social Sci. Res. Inst., chap. 3, at 4 (2003) ("Kuboyama Interview").

57. Kuboyama Interview at 16.

58. Kuboyama Interview at 17.

59. Interview with Minoru Hinahara, Lahaina, Maui by Warren Nishimoto, *Pioneer Mill Company: A Maui Sugar Plantation Legacy* (ed. Warren Nishimoto), Honolulu: Univ. of Hawaiʻi, Ctr for Oral History, Social Sci. Res. Inst., chap. 13, at 10 (2003) ("Hinahara Interview").

60. Hinahara Interview at 10.

61. "Action Postponed on Mill Request," *Lahaina Sun*, Vol. 1, No. 44, p. 5 (Sept. 8, 1971).

62. "Harbor Pollution, Cane Burning, Junk Cars Cited in Report," Vol. 1, No. 13, p. 5 *Lahaina Sun* (Feb. 3, 1971).

63. "That Rotten Egg Smell," *Lahaina Sun*, Vol. 1, No. 33, p. 9 (Jun. 23, 1971).

64. Telephone interview with Keoki Freeland, by Bianca Isaki (Jan. 8, 2018).

65. Advertisement in *Lahaina Sun*, Vol. 1, No. 21, p. 6 (Mar. 31, 1971).
66. "Sewage Plant Proposed," *Lahaina Sun*, Vol. 1, No. 21, p. 1, 8 (Mar. 31, 1971).
67. "Sewage Plant Proposed," *Lahaina Sun*, Vol. 1, No. 21, p. 1, 8 (Mar. 31, 1971).
68. "Sewage Plant Proposed," *Lahaina Sun*, Vol. 1, No. 21, p. 1, 8 (Mar. 31, 1971).
69. "Sewage Plant Proposed," *Lahaina Sun*, Vol. 1, No. 21, p. 1, 8 (Mar. 31, 1971).
70. "New Water Tester," *Lahaina Sun*, Vol. 1, No. 29, p. 2 (May 26, 1971).
71. Hussey, Ikaika, "A Modern History of West Maui's Wastewater," in *Social Change in West Maui* at 91–92, eds. Bianca Isaki and Lance D. Collins (2019).
72. Maly, Kepā and Onaona Maly, *He Wahi Mo'olelo No Kaua'ula a Me Kekāhi 'Āina o Lahaina i Maui: A Collection of Traditions and Historical Accounts of Kaua'ula and Other Lands of Lahaina, Maui*, prepared for Makila Land Co. & Kamehameha Schools, Vol. 1, at 4 (Jun. 1, 2007) ("Maly V.1").
73. Maly V.1 at 5 quoting Honokohau Water Co. "Water cost report" (1919–1928).
74. *The Polynesian*, p. 34, July 18, 1846 (quoted by Maly V.1 at 46).
75. Maly V.1 at 5 quoting Honokohau Water Co. "Water cost report" (1919–1928). These customary rules were central to the *Horner v. Kumuliilii* decision of the Hawaiian Supreme Court, discussed in chapter 1.
76. Maly V.1 at 105.
77. *The Pacific commercial advertiser.* (Honolulu, Hawaiian Islands), 27 Sept. 1901. *Chronicling America: Historic American Newspapers.* Lib. of Congress. Available at http://chroniclingamerica.loc.gov/lccn/sn85047084/1901-09-27/ed-1/seq-10/.
78. Dukelow, Robbie, *Hawaiian Soul: A Documentary*, produced by VKP (1987) available at https://www.youtube.com/watch?v=YT7NEG_ikYA&feature=youtu.be.
79. Telephone Interview by Jennifer Frey (Dec. 21, 2009), in the Draft Environmental Assessment for the West Maui Community Federal Credit Union (Aug. 8, 2010) available at http://oeqc.doh.hawaii.gov/Shared%20Documents/EA_and_EIS_Online_Library/Maui/2010s/2010-08-08-MA-DEA-West-Maui-Comm-Fed-Credit-Union.pdf.
80. Telephone interview with Keoki Freeland, by Bianca Isaki (Jan. 8, 2018).
81. Telephone interview with Keoki Freeland, by Bianca Isaki (Jan. 8, 2018).
82. Telephone interview with Keoki Freeland, by Bianca Isaki (Jan. 8, 2018).
83. Telephone interview with Keoki Freeland, by Bianca Isaki (Jan. 8, 2018).
84. Zalburg, Sanford, *A Spark is Struck! Jack Hall & the ILWU in Hawaii*, 160–61 (U. Hawai'i Press, 1979).
85. Interview with Susumu "Peanut" Sodetani, Lahaina, Maui by Warren Nishimoto, *Pioneer Mill Company: A Maui Sugar Plantation Legacy* (ed. Warren Nishimoto), Honolulu: Univ. of Hawai'i, Ctr for Oral History, Social Sci. Res. Inst., at 83 (2003).
86. Zalburg, Sanford, *A Spark is Struck! Jack Hall & the ILWU in Hawaii*, 162 (U. Hawai'i Press, 1979).
87. Telephone interview with Keoki Freeland, by Bianca Isaki (Jan. 8, 2018).

88. Maly V.1 at 4 quoting Honokohau Water Co. "Water cost report" (1919–1928).
89. Maly V.1 at 4 quoting Honokohau Water Co. "Water cost report" (1919–1928).
90. Maly V.1 at 6.
91. Maly V.1 at 13.
92. Maly V.1 at 13.
93. Handy, E. S. Craighill, *The Hawaiian Planter*, no. 161, 103 (1940).
94. Maly V.1 at 103 quoting E. S. Craighill Handy, *The Hawaiian Planter*, no. 161 (1940).
95. Maly V.1 at 103 quoting E. S. Craighill Handy, *The Hawaiian Planter*, no. 161 (1940).
96. Maly V.1 at 107.
97. Maly V.1 at 40.
98. Maly V.1 at 354.
99. Maly V.1 at 47 quoting *The Friend*, February 1915 (page 41); *Reminiscences of Rev. Joseph Emerson (by J. S. Emerson) Development of the Lahainaluna Ditch* (1842–1846).
100. Maly V.1 at 47.
101. Maly V.1 at 103 quoting E. S. Craighill Handy, *The Hawaiian Planter*, no. 161 (1940).
102. Maly V.1 at 9.
103. Interview with Susumu "Peanut" Sodetani, Lahaina, Maui by Warren Nishimoto, *Pioneer Mill Company: A Maui Sugar Plantation Legacy* (ed. Warren Nishimoto), Honolulu: Univ. of Hawai'i, Ctr for Oral History, Social Sci. Res. Inst., at 84 (2003).
104. Interview with Susumu "Peanut" Sodetani, Lahaina, Maui by Warren Nishimoto, *Pioneer Mill Company: A Maui Sugar Plantation Legacy* (ed. Warren Nishimoto), Honolulu: Univ. of Hawai'i, Ctr for Oral History, Social Sci. Res. Inst., at 83 (2003).
105. *The Hawaiian Star* (Honolulu), 10 March 1902, page 7. *Chronicling America: Historic American Newspapers*. Lib. of Congress. Available at http://chroniclingamerica .loc.gov/lccn/sn82015415/1902-03-10/ed-1/seq-7/.
106. "Lahaina Notes," *Maui News*, Mar. 8 , 1902, page 3.
107. *The Maui News*. (Wailuku, Maui), 21 June 1902, page 3. *Chronicling America: Historic American Newspapers*. Lib. of Congress. Available at http:// chroniclingamerica.loc.gov/lccn/sn82014689/1902-06-21/ed-1/seq-3/.
108. *The Maui News* (Wailuku, Maui), 12 May 1916, page 1. *Chronicling America: Historic American Newspapers*. Lib. of Congress. Available at http://chroniclingamerica .loc.gov/lccn/sn82014689/1916-05-12/ed-1/seq-1/.
109. "Locomotive Turns Over Into Stream", *The Maui News*. (Wailuku, Maui), 12 May 1916. *Chronicling America: Historic American Newspapers*. Lib. of Congress. Available at http://chroniclingamerica.loc.gov/lccn/sn82014689/1916-05-12/ed-1/seq-1/.

110. *The Maui News* (Wailuku, Maui), 11 Aug. 1916. *Chronicling America: Historic American Newspapers.* Lib. of Congress. Available at http://chroniclingamerica .loc.gov/lccn/sn82014689/1916-08-11/ed-1/seq-1/.

111. Maly V.1 at 103 quoting E.S. Craighill Handy, *The Hawaiian Planter*, no. 161 (1940).

112. Maly V.1 at 103 quoting E.S. Craighill Handy, *The Hawaiian Planter*, no. 161 (1940).

113. "Proposal Protested," *Lahaina Sun*, Vol.1, No. 23, p. 2 (Apr. 14, 1971).

114. "Proposal Protested," *Lahaina Sun*, Vol.1, No. 23, p. 2 (Apr. 14, 1971).

115. Maly V.1 at 106.

116. "Lahaina Notes," *Maui News*, Sat., Mar. 23, 1912, page 5.

117. *The Maui News.* (Wailuku, Maui), 20 Aug. 1920, page 7. *Chronicling America: Historic American Newspapers.* Lib. of Congress. Available at http://chroniclingamerica .loc.gov/lccn/sn82014689/1920-08-20/ed-1/seq-7/.

118. Maly V.1 at 106.

119. Hoʻoipo, Elizabeth Ann, et al., "Cultures in Conflict in Hawaiʻi: The Law and Politics of Native Hawaiian Water Rights," 18 U. Haw. L. Rev. 71, 134 n.176 (1996).

120. "Trout Fry Planted and Game Birds are Secured for Maui," *The Maui News.* (Wailuku, Maui), 20 June 1922. *Chronicling America: Historic American Newspapers.* Lib. of Congress. Available at http://chroniclingamerica.loc.gov/lccn /sn82014689/1922-06-20/ed-1/seq-1/.

121. "Clean Water for Napili in One Year," *Lahaina Sun*, Vol.1, No. 13, p. 4 (Feb. 3, 1971).

122. "Clean Water for Napili in One Year," *Lahaina Sun*, Vol.1, No. 13, p. 4 (Feb. 3, 1971).

123. Telephone interview with Kapali Keahi (Mar. 15, 2017).

124. Telephone interview with Kapali Keahi (Mar. 15, 2017).

125. TMK No. 4-4-07:009 was not included in the 1989 Yamamura appraisal report.

126. The "Reasons for Recommendation" in the appraisal report indicate 4.898 acres in accord with the June 22, 1984 submittal.

127. Lease of Non-Exclusive Easement S-5262 between BLNR and Pioneer Mill Co., Ltd, dated Aug. 5, 1997 and approved by the BLNR at its meeting held on June 22, 1984 (on file with DLNR Land Division).

128. Dawson, Teresa, "As Sugar Winds Down, DLNR Moves to Save Ditches on Kauaʻi, Maui." *Environment Hawaiʻi* Vol. 10, No. 2 (Aug. 1999).

129. Letter from Sonia Faust, Supervising Deputy Attorney General to Dean Uchida, Administrator, Land Division, Re: Lease of Non-Exclusive Easement, Honokōhau Ditch, Lahaina, Maui AG No. 99-20206 (in regard to inquiry to condemn AMFAC lands).

130. See June 11, 2002, Second Amended Joint Plan of Reorganization of AMFAC Hawaiʻi, LLC, and Certain of its Subsidiaries (authorizing reassume unexpired leases) (on file with DLNR Land Division).

131. See Letter from Jason Koga, DLNR Maui Land Agent, to David "Buddy" Nobriga,

Chair, West Maui Soil and Water Conservation District, Subject: Maintenance and Repair of the Honokōhau Ditch, GL S-5262 (Jul. 17, 2002) (on file with DLNR Land Division).

132. The Honokowai Tunnel is a transmission tunnel and not a water development tunnel. Approximately five mgd of water diverted from two branches of the Honokowai Stream passes through the tunnel to irrigate some 500 acres of agricultural lands.

133. Letter from Karen Seddon, Exec. Dir. DBEDT, HHFDC, to DLNR Land Division, Subject: Decommissioning of Wahikuli Reservoir and Dam Extension of Easement S-5262 to Honokōhau Ditch, Villages of Leialiʻi, Lahaina, TMK (2) 4-5-21:22 (por) (Apr. 5, 2010) (on file with DLNR Land Division).

CHAPTER 4: A CYCLE OF HYDROLOGIC FAILURE

1. Land Use Commission meeting held On December 7, 2015 commencing at 3:51 P.M; Docket A10-786 Olowalu Town LLC and Olowalu Ekolu LLC. Action to consider acceptance of the FEIS Volume 3 (at Page 42).

2. Staff Submittal for the meeting of the Commission On Water Resource Management, March 20, 2018, Kahului, Maui; Amended Interim Instream Flow Standards For the Surface Water Hydrologic Units of Ukumehame (6004), Olowalu (6005), Launiupoko, (6006), and Kauaʻula (6007), Maui. (at Page 17).

3. For comparison, the University of Hawaiʻi fired its football coach, Norm Chow, in 2015, when his team was 2-7 and 10-36 over four seasons—a 72% loss record. Trahan, Kevin, 2015. "Hawaii fires coach Norm Chow." www.sbnation.com /college-football/2015/11/1/9655554/hawaii-warriors-fire-norm-chow.

4. Sproat, D. Kapuaʻala. 2015. "From Wai to Kanawai: Water Law in Hawaiʻi," in *Native Hawaiian Law: A Treatise*. Honolulu: Kamehameha Publishing.

5. P. 65 in Handy, E. S. Craighill, Elizabeth Green Handy and Mary Kawena Pukui. 1972 (2d ed). *Native Planters in Old Hawaii: Their Life, Lore, and Environment*. Honolulu: Bishop Museum Press.

6. P. 65 in Handy, E.S Craighill, Elizabeth Green Handy and Mary Kawena Pukui. 1972 (2nd ed.), *Native Planters in Old Hawaii: Their Life, Lore, and Environment*. Honolulu: Bishop Museum Press.

7. Peck is held to be the oldest water rights case that came before the Supreme Court; however, it appears in *Hawaii Reports* after some other cases that have later dates for decision making. While the reports claims it was decided in 1867, Peck was only published in the mid-1890s, at a time when the court was deciding other water cases and needed precedent to rely on. The phrasing on the decision states that it was settled but not previously reported.

8. Nakuina, Emma Metcalf. 1893. *Ancient Hawaiian Water Rights And Some Of The Customs Pertaining To Them*. In Thrum's *Hawaiian Annual*.

9. Nakuina, Emma Metcalf. 1893. *Ancient Hawaiian Water Rights And Some Of The Customs Pertaining To Them.* In Thrum's Hawaiian Annual.

10. Section 221(c), Hawaiian Homes Commission Act.

11. This language is not meant to imply that the Territorial or state claims of title are necessarily valid.

12. Plantiff Reppun is the same as in the Waiāhole Water Case, which is illustrative of the long-standing commitment of the windward parties to protecting the rights of kalo farmers to water.

13. Martin, Elizabeth Pa, et. al, "Cultures in Conflict of Hawai'i: The Law and Politics of Native Hawaiian Water Rights," 18 U. Haw. L. Rev. 71, 109 (1996).

14. Martin et al. 1996.

15. Hawaiian Home Lands enjoy senior water rights somewhat akin to "Winters" rights and other federally reserved water rights, though the Hawai'i Supreme Court specifically declined to extend the *Winters* doctrine to Hawai'i. "Winters" rights are the rights to water that Indian reservations have, so called because of the US Supreme Court case that recognized them, *Winters v. United States* (207 U.S. 564).

    Winters and other cases found that when the federal government set aside land for Indian reservations and other federal purposes, it was a clear, if unstated, intent that the lands have water available to them in sufficient quantity to fulfill the purpose for which the land was set aside. For a general discussion of *Winters* rights, see Canby (1988), and regarding their relationship to Hawai'i, see Vandermoer (1993).

16. Review Commission on the State Water Code State of Hawaii, "Final Report to the State Legislature," Honolulu: Legislative Reference Bureau (1994).

17. Review Commission 1994, at 24.

18. Martin et al. 1996.

19. September 26, 2006 letter from CWRM to the Kaua'i Planning Commission, quoted in *Kaua'i Springs* (page 10 of slip opinion).

20. Hawai'i State Constitution Article XVI, Section 4 requires that all officers of the state (which includes CWRM members) take an oath as follows: "I do solemnly swear (or affirm) that I will support and defend the Constitution of the United States, and the Constitution of the State of Hawaii, and that I will faithfully discharge my duties as .... to best of my ability."

21. CWRM agendas and minutes, as well as some staff submittals, for the years 1999–2019 can be found at https://dlnr.hawaii.gov/cwrm/newsevents/meetings/.

22. Mr. Pearson subsequently became head of the Maui County Department of Water Supply.

23. Staff submittal for item A2, Item A2: Find that Landowner, Hooululahui LLC, Allegedly Violated Section 174C-93, Hawaii Revised Statutes (HRS) by Installing a Stream Diversion Works Without a Permit; Request the Issuance of Admin-

istrative and Civil Penalties of $4,500 Per HRS §174C-15; Approve a Stream Diversion Works Permit (SDWP.4175.6) Application for Existing Uses; A Petition to Amend the Instream Flow Standard is Not Required Under HRS §174C-71; Wailuku River, Wailuku, Maui, TMK: (2) 3-5-003:018, Nā Wai 'Ehā Water Management Area. Available at http://files.hawaii.gov/dlnr/cwrm/submittal/2016/sb20160816A2.pdf

24. "The decision came after more than three hours of oral testimony and an estimated 500 submissions of written testimony in support of the Duey 'ohana, expressing concern over a $4,500 fine that was proposed for alleged violations involving an incomplete permit." https://mauinow.com/2016/08/17/water-commission-drops-proposed-fine-against-resident-taro-farmers/

25. Staff submittal, ibid.

26. Minutes for the Meeting of the Commission On Water Resource Management, Item C-1, May, 16, 2012, available at https://files.hawaii.gov/dlnr/cwrm/minute/2012/mn20120516.pdf]

27. Minutes for the Meeting of the Commission On Water Resource Management, August 16, 2016, available at http://files.hawaii.gov/dlnr/cwrm/minute/2016/mn20160816.pdf

28. Minutes for the Meeting of the Commission On Water Resource Management, May 15, 2018, available at http://files.hawaii.gov/dlnr/cwrm/minute/2018/mn20180515.pdf

CHAPTER 5: ONGOING ISSUES WITH INTERIM
INSTREAM FLOW STANDARDS

1. A significant disconnect in Hawai'i water law and management is not addressed in this book as it has not actively arisen in West Maui, though it may in the future. As addressed in chapter 4, from approximately 1852 to 1973 water jurisprudence in the islands transformed the legal understandings of water. While water always was held by the sovereign in trust for the people, court rulings and later laws were passed that treated water increasingly like private property. During the Kingdom, the government began to lease water coming off it its lands to sugar companies, and that practice has continued to this day, enshrined in HRS 171-58. The staff of the DLNR has interpreted this to mean that only water emanating from state-controlled lands also requires a water lease, even though the law is clear that all water is held by the state in trust and there is no private property in water. The state has continued these uses for decades in a year to year "revocable permit" process, and thereby so far avoiding the issuance of long term water leases. Thus the water leasing process described for Kaua'i here has not been employed in West Maui, despite the fact that all water diverted or pumped by private companies is water held by the state in Trust.

2. Testimony of Kekai Keahi at the Public Hearing on West Maui IIFS, Lahaina, Maui, Hawaiʻi (March 20, 2018).

3. CWRM, Declarations of Water Use Volume No. I, Circular C-123 (Sep. 1992) available at http://files.hawaii.gov/dlnr/cwrm/circulars/C-123_Vol1.pdf.

4. Lahaina WUDP Update at 16.

5. CWRM AWUDP at 17.

6. HRS §174C-71(1)(C).

7. HAR §13-169-48.

8. Complaint/Dispute Resolution Form from Hui o Na Wai Eha & Maui Tomorrow Foundation, Inc. dated October 19, 2004, in Contested Case Hearing Case No. CCH-MA06-01, on file with CWRM.

9. Moncur, James, Jim Roumasset, Rodney Smith, "Optimal Allocation of Ground and Surface Water in Oahu: Water Wars in Paradise," in Richard E. Just and Sinaia Netanyahu, eds., *Conflict and Cooperation on Trans-Boundary Water Resources*, Springer Science & Business Media (2012), 340; also James Moncur, Jim Roumasset, Rodney Smith, "Optimal Allocation of Ground and Surface Water in Oahu: Water Wars in Paradise," Working Paper No. 97-7, at 9 (May 1997) available at www.economics.hawaii.edu/research/workingpapers/88-98/wp_97-7.pdf.

10. CWRM Staff Submittal, Item C-1 Request to Authorize the Chairperson to Enter into Joint Funding Agreements with U.S. Geological Survey to Conduct a Study on Low-Flow Characteristics for Streams in the Lahaina District, West Maui, Hawaiʻi (Mar. 16, 2011) available at http://files.hawaii.gov/dlnr/cwrm/submittal /2011/sb201103C1.pdf.

11. Maui Land and Pineapple Co., Petition for Establishment of Instream Flow Standard or, in the alternative, for Amendment of Interim Instream Flow Standard, for Honokohau Stream, West Maui, Hawaii, submitted to CWRM (rec'd Aug. 23, 2006) (on file with CWRM) ("MLP Petition").

12. MLP IFS Petition at 3.

13. CWRM Staff Submittal, "Request to Authorize the Chairperson to Enter in Joint Funding Agreements with U.S. Geological Survey to Conduct a Study on Low-Flow Characteristics for Streams in the Lahaina District, West Maui, Hawaiʻi," Honolulu, Oʻahu (Mar. 16, 2011).

14. Cheng, Chui Ling, *Low-flow characteristics of streams in the Lahaina District, West Maui, Hawaiʻi*, U.S. Geological Survey Scientific Investigations Report 2014–5087 (2014).

15. Cheng, USGS Lahaina Low-flow study, at iv.

16. Cheng, USGS Lahaina Low-flow study, at iv.

17. Chaston, Katherine and Tomas Oberding, *Honolua Bay Review: A review and analysis of available marine, terrestrial and land-use information in the Honolua Ahupuaa Maui 1970–2007*, at 51 (Dec. 2007), available at www.savehonolua.org /images2/chasten_reports/Honolua%20Bay%20Review%20%20&%20Analysis %20Final%20Dec%202007%20compressed.pdf, citing SWCA Environmen-

tal Consultants, Supporting Biological Documentation, Petition to Establish Instream Flow Standards in Honolua Stream, West Maui, Hawaiʻi, prepared for Maui Land & Pineapple Company, Inc. (2006).

18. *Waiāhole I*, 94 Hawaiʻi 97, 148, 9 P.3d 409, 9 P.2d 409, 460 (2000).

19. CWRM, Compilation of Public Testimony, Hydrologic Units: Ukumehame (6004), Olowalu (6005), Launiupoko (6006), Kauaʻula (6007), Island of Maui, Doc. No. PR-2018-05 (March 2018).

20. Quoted by Lahaina WUDP Update at 16.

21. Maui DWS, Lahaina Aquifer Sector Update, at 15–16 (Nov. 2017) available at www .mauicounty.gov/DocumentCenter/View/110685/Sector-Area-Reports-Lahaina -110317 (Lahaina WUDP Update) quoting E.S.C. Handy, *Hawaiian Planter*, 103 Sterling, Elspeth P., *Sites of Maui*. Bishop Museum Press, at 24 (1997).

22. CWRM Staff Submittal, Item B-1, at 26 (Mar. 20, 2018).

23. CWRM Staff Submittal, Item B-1, at 26 (Mar. 20, 2018).

24. CWRM Staff Submittal, Item B-1, at 6 (Mar. 20, 2018).

25. CWRM, Launiupoko Instream Flow Standard Assessment Report, Draft PR 2017-03 at 59 (Aug. 2017) (Launiupoko IFSAR).

26. CWRM, Compilation of Public Testimony, at 5.

27. CWRM, Compilation of Public Testimony, at 8–9.

28. CWRM, Compilation of Public Testimony, at 10–11.

29. Telephone interview with Kapali Keahi (Mar. 15, 2017).

30. CWRM, Compilation of Public Testimony, at 9.

31. CWRM, Compilation of Public Testimony, at 11.

32. CWRM, Compilation of Public Testimony, at 12.

33. CWRM Staff Submittal, Item B-1, at 25 (Mar. 20, 2018).

34. LIC would later seek approval from the Public Utilities Commission to levy a water rate increase on its customers, primarily comprised of these subdivision groups. LIC's request for rate increases were premised on its alleged need to install more capital improvements to develop water sources to replace diversion from Kauaʻula stream. Yet, U.S. Geological Survey gages installed at the diversion show LIC is not restoring enough to meet the IIFS. Further troubling is the approval of at least two further subdivisions requested by Peter Martin's companies for this area.

35. Clute, Eve, "Work on long-awaited Lahaina flood control system to begin," *Lahaina News* (Sep. 24, 2009).

36. US Dep't of Agriculture, Soil Conservation Service, Findings of No Significant Impact for Lahaina Watershed Flood Control Project, County of Maui (Feb. 20, 1991) available at http://oeqc2.doh.hawaii.gov/EA_EIS_Archive/1991-01-08-MA -FEA-Lahaina-Watershed-Flood-Control.pdf.

37. Clute, Eve, "Work on long-awaited Lahaina flood control system to begin," *Lahaina News* (Sep. 24, 2009).

38. US Dep't of Agriculture, Natural Resources and Conservation Service, Final Environmental Impact Statement for Lahaina Watershed Flood Control Project,

County of Maui (Dec. 2003) available at www.nrcs.usda.gov/Internet/FSE _DOCUMENTS/nrcs142p2_037262.pdf.

39. Lahaina Flood Control Project FEIS at 33.

40. Joerger, Pauline King, and Michael W. Kaschiko, Hawaii Marine Research, A Cultural History Overview of the Kahoma Stream Flood Control Project, Lahaina, Maui and Maʻalaea Small Boat Harbor Project, prepared for the U.S. Dep't of the Army Corps of Engineers, at 6 (May 17, 1983) available at www.dtic.mil/dtic /tr/fulltext/u2/a128221.pdf.

41. Joerger, Pauline King and Michael W. Kaschiko, Hawaii Marine Research, A Cultural History Overview of the Kahoma Stream Flood Control Project, Lahaina, Maui and Maʻalaea Small Boat Harbor Project, prepared for the U.S. Dep't of the Army Corps of Engineers, at 6 (May 17, 1983) available at www.dtic.mil/dtic /tr/fulltext/u2/a128221.pdf.

42. Ibid. at 10.

43. Telephone interview with Keoki Freeland, by Bianca Isaki (Jan. 8, 2018).

44. 1975 Kahakuloa Water Project EISPN, at 29.

45. Ibid. at 38.

46. Ibid. at 39.

47. Ibid.

48. CWRM staff submittal, Item C-1 "Request to Authorize the Chairperson to Enter into Joint Funding Agreements with U.S. Geological Survey To Conduct a Study on Low-Flow Characteristics for Streams In the Lahaina District, West Maui, Hawaiʻi" (Mar. 16, 2011), Available at http://files.hawaii.gov/dlnr/cwrm /submittal/2011/sb201103C1.pdf.

49. Cheng, USGS Lahaina Low-flow study, at 5.

50. Cheng, USGS Lahaina Low-flow study, at 5 quoting Pomaikaʻi D. Kaniaupio-Crozier, Maui Land and Pineapple Company, Inc., oral commun., 2013.

51. Cheng, USGS Lahaina Low-flow study, at 5 quoting Robert Vorfeld, Kāʻanapali Land Management Corp., oral commun., 2013.

52. Kāʻanapali Land Management Corp., Kāʻanapali Coffee Farms Website (2017) available at www.kaanapalicoffeefarms.com/.

53. Dep't of Water Supply, County of Maui, Final Environmental Assessment for the Lahaina Water Treatment Plant, at 1 (Dec. 23, 1991) available at http://oeqc.doh .hawaii.gov/Shared%20Documents/EA_and_EIS_Online_Library/Maui/1990s /1991-12-23-MA-FEA-LAHAINA-WATER-TREATMENT-PLANT.pdf.

Chapter 6: Protecting Water While It Is Below Ground

1. Draft Environmental Assessment and Anticipated Finding of No Significant Impact for the Proposed West Maui Source Development Project, 2019, p 52.

2. P. 70 in Gingerich, S. B. and J. A. Engott, 2012, Groundwater availability in the

Lahaina District, West Maui, Hawaiʻi: U.S. Geological Survey Scientific Investigations Report 2012–5010, 90 p.

3. At the hearing where staff recommended and CWRM agreed to deny a petition to designate the Keauhou Aquifer on Hawaiʻi Island, Groundwater Hydrologic Program Manager Roy Hardy reviewed the SY for that aquifer. He noted recent higher estimated recharge numbers, and stated, "So, it extended the range from 104 to 183 on the recharge. Sustainable yield is a percentage of that. And from the—the point I'm trying to make here is that from these ranges, to apply the precautionary principle, what we do is we take the minimum number in that range."

4. HRS §174C-44 "Ground water criteria for designation. In designating an area for water use regulation, the commission shall consider the following: (1) Whether an increase in water use or authorized planned use may cause the maximum rate of withdrawal from the ground water source to reach ninety percent of the sustainable yield of the proposed ground water management area."

5. For example, US Representative Tulsi Gabbard wrote to CWRM Chair William Ailā in 2014, opposing the designation of the Keauhou Aquifer: "Most scientists and engineers who monitor the water on Hawaiʻi Island believe that the Aquifer is nowhere near using the 90 percent of sustainable yield that would trigger the need for a designation; it is believed to be closer to 30 percent." September 24, 2014.

6. For example, the creator of the Robust Analytical Model used to calculate SY, John Mink, noted, "The aquifers of all of Southern Oahu from Manoa Valley to the Waianae Mountains are hydraulically connected." (P. 1 in Mink, J.F., 1980, State of the groundwater resources of Southern Oahu, Honolulu: Board of Water Supply, Honolulu, Hawaii.). The CWRM cites this study in its Water Resources Protection Plan, yet separates that same area into more than ten hydrologic units.

7. For example, "In 2008, the Commission's Water Resources Protection Plan (WRPP, 2008) set the sustainable yield for the *Keauhou Aquifer System Area* (KASA) at 38 million gallons per day (mgd), which covers all aquifers within the area (basal, high-level, and deep confined freshwater)." P. 3 in US Department of Interior, National Park Service, Kaloko-Honokōhau National Historical Park, Chairperson Recommendation on Petition for Ground Water Management Area Designation, Keauhou Aquifer System Area, North Kona, Hawaii, February 14, 2017.

8. As explained further below, another assumption is that aquifers are isotropic (having uniform properties in any direction). This assumption is necessary to simplify the math used later, but then becomes problematic when combined with other key assumptions, including one that assumes withdrawals are uniformly distributed.

9. As the Hawaiʻi Supreme Court noted in *Waiāhole I*, the CWRM itself adopted a definition of the precautionary principle as follows: "That is, where there are present or potential threats of serious damage, lack of full scientific certainty should not be a basis for postponing effective measures to prevent environmental degradation.... In addition, where uncertainty exists, a trustee's duty to protect the resource

mitigates in favor of choosing presumptions that also protect the resource." *In re Water Use Permit Applications*, 94 Hawai'i 97, 115, 9 P.3d 409, 427 (2000).

10. HRS §174C-44(1).

11. At the hearing where staff recommended and CWRM agreed to deny a petition to designate the Keauhou Aquifer on Hawai'i Island, Groundwater Hydrologic Program Manager Roy Hardy summarized the first criterion for the Commission: "So, that's the first criteria. Hasn't reached 90. It's at 74 percent." Transcript, page 66, lines 13–16.

12. P. 22, Appendix H, table H-7. Water Resource Protection Plan 2019 Update Public Review Draft October 2018.

13. P. 21, Appendix H, table H-6. Water Resource Protection Plan 2019 Update Public Review Draft October 2018.

14. State of Hawaii, Commission on Water Resource Management, Department of Land and Natural Resources. 2003. "Public Notice: Iao ground-water management area designation island of Maui." *Honolulu Star-Bulletin*. July 21, 2003.

15. At the time of the designation of the 'Īao Aquifer, the official name for the main surface water body was the 'Īao Stream. However, one of the key community members who led efforts to restore stream flow to Nā Wai 'Ehā, John Duey, later successfully had the name restored to its original name, the Wailuku River. See: www.mauinews.com/news/local-news/2015/12/name-of-lower-section-of-waterway-officially-returns-to-wailuku-river/

16. In 2004, former CWRM Deputy Director Ernest Lau stated that "[t]he designation of the Iao Aquifer was for ground water only. Therefore, the use of surface water is not regulated by the Commission through water use permits." Letter from Ernest Lau to John Duey (dated Mar. 25, 2004).

17. Sevilla, Duke. 2016. Written testimony of Duke Sevilla in CWRM CCH-MA15-01, Surface Water Use Permit Applications, Integration of Appurtenant Rights and Amendments to the Interim Instream Flow Standards, Nā Wai 'Ehā Surface Water Management Areas of Waihe'e, Waiehu, 'Iao, & Waikapū Streams, Maui.

18. CWRM 2018. Amended Interim Instream Flow Standards For the Surface Water Hydrologic Units of Ukumehame (6004), Olowalu (6005), Launiupoko, (6006), and Kaua'ula (6007), Maui. Staff Submittal B 1, March 20, 2018, p. 9.

19. Water Resource Protection Plan 2019 Update Public Review Draft October 2018. Appendix F, page 41.

20. HRS 174C-71(1)(C): "Each instream flow standard shall describe the flows necessary to protect the public interest in the particular stream."

21. This is evocative of how the late science fiction writer Douglas Adams described the galaxy's dominant Sirius Cybernetics Corporation and its products: "It is very easy to be blinded to the essential uselessness of [their products] by the sense of achievement you get from getting them to work at all. In other words—and this is the rock-solid principle on which the whole of the Corporation's galaxywide

success is founded—their fundamental design flaws are completely hidden by their superficial design flaws." In *So Long and Thanks for all the Fish.*

22. The code here refers to dividing counties into units, rather than islands, despite the fact that Kauaʻi and Maui are multi-island counties, the island of Molokaʻi is overseen by two counties, and there are no hydraulic connections between islands. This is likely because elements of the Hawaiʻi Water Plan include the County Water Use and Development Plans.

23. Engott, J. A., 2011, A water-budget model and assessment of groundwater recharge for the Island of Hawaiʻi: US Geological Survey Scientific Investigations Report 2011–5078, 53 p.

24. Johnson, A. G., J. A. Engott, Maoya Bassiouni, and Kolja Rotzoll, 2018, Spatially distributed groundwater recharge estimated using a water-budget model for the Island of Maui, Hawaiʻi, 1978–2007 (ver. 2.0, February 2018): US Geological Survey Scientific Investigations Report 2014–5168, 53 p., https://doi.org/10.3133 /sir20145168.

25. Helweg, D. A., V. Keener, and J. M. Burgett, 2016, Report from the workshop on climate downscaling and its application in high Hawaiian Islands, September 16–17, 2015: US Geological Survey Open-File Report 2016–1102, 25 p., http://dx .doi.org/10.3133/ofr20161102.

26. WRPP Appendix F, p. 68.

27. P. 7, Draft Environmental Assessment for Proposed West Maui Source Development Project (Mahinahina Well [Well No. 6-5638-004] and Kahana Well [Well No. 6-5738-002)]). Lahaina, Maui.

28. Mair, Alan. Estimating Climate-Change Impacts on Groundwater Recharge for the Island of Maui, Hawaiʻi. Meeting of the State of Hawaiʻi Commission on Water Resource Management. Honolulu, July 20, 2016. Available at http://files .hawaii.gov/dlnr/cwrm/submittal/2016/sb20160720C2.pdf.

29. Izuka, S.K., Engott, J.A., Rotzoll, Kolja, Bassiouni, Maoya, Johnson, A.G., Miller, L.D., and Mair, Alan, 2018, Volcanic aquifers of Hawaiʻi—Hydrogeology, water budgets, and conceptual models (ver. 2.0, March 2018): US Geological Survey Scientific Investigations Report 2015–5164, 158 p., https://doi.org/10.3133/sir20155164.

30. Water Resources Protection Plan (2008) p. V-2.

31. WRPP Appendix F p.63, Table F-8.

32. P. 3 in Gingerich, S.B., and Engott, J.A., 2012, Groundwater availability in the Lahaina District, West Maui, Hawaiʻi: US Geological Survey Scientific Investigations Report 2012–5010, 90 p.

Chapter 7: Carrying Kuleana

1. Osorio, Jonathan Kamakawiwoʻole, *Conservation District Use Application HA -3568 for the Thirty Meter Telescope at the Mauna Kea Science Reserve, Kaʻohe Mauka,*

Hāmākua, Hawai'i TMK (3) 4-4-015:009, Board of Land and Natural Resources, State of Hawai'i, BLNR-CC-16-002, at Tr. 1/12/17 at 1:10:00.

2. Garovoy, Jocelyn B., "Ua Koe Ke Kuleana O Na Kanaka" (Reserving The Rights Of Native Tenants): Integrating Kuleana Rights And Land Trust Priorities in Hawai'i" 29 *Harvard Env. L. R.* 524, 527 (2004).

3. Garovoy, Jocelyn B., "Ua Koe Ke Kuleana O Na Kanaka" (Reserving The Rights Of Native Tenants): Integrating Kuleana Rights And Land Trust Priorities in Hawai'i" 29 *Harvard Env. L. R.* 524, 527 (2004).

4. Preza, Donovan C., The empirical writes back: Reexamining Hawaiian dispossession resulting from the Māhele of 1848 (Master's thesis). University of Hawai'i at Mānoa, Honolulu, (2010).

5. For a cogent overview of Hawaiian law, see D. Kapu'ala Sproat, "Avoiding Trouble in Paradise: Understanding Hawaii's Law and Indigenous Culture," 18(2) *Business Law Today* (Nov/ Dec. 2008) available at https://apps.americanbar.org /buslaw/blt/2008-11-12/sproat.shtml.

6. Castle, John, and Alan Murakami, "Water Rights" *Native Hawaiian Rights Handbook*, ed. Melody Mackenzie, at 152–53 (Honolulu: Native Hawaiian Legal Corp. 1991).

7. Maly, Kepā, and Onaona Maly, *He Wahi Mo'Olelo No Kaua'ula a Me Kekāhi 'Āina o Lahaina i Maui: A Collection of Traditions and Historical Accounts of Kaua'ula and Other Lands of Lahaina, Maui* at 101 (2007).

8. Kamins, Robert R., *Ownership of Geothermal Resources in Hawaii*, 1 U. Haw. L. Rev. 69, 71 fn 5 (1979), quoting *Terr. Of Hawai'i v. Lili'uokalani*, 49 Haw. 88, 104 (1902).

9. Kamins, 71 fn.15 quoting *Thurston v. Bishop*, 7 Haw 421, 429 (1888).

10. *Lili'uokalani v. United States*, 45 Ct. Cl. 418 (1910).

11. Article 95 of the constitution of July 3, 1894, Fundamental Laws of Hawaii at 237.

12. Resolution No. 55 of July 7, 1898 (Newlands Resolution), 30 Stat. 750 (emphasis added).

13. Hong, Tany S., State of Hawai'i Attorney General Opinion to Hon. Susumu Ono, Chairman DLNR, 6 (June 24, 1982).

14. Hong, Tany S., State of Hawai'i Attorney General Opinion to Hon. Susumu Ono, Chairman DLNR, 9 (June 24, 1982).

15. *In re: Robinson*, 49 Haw. 429, 431 (1966) citing "An Act to Organize the Executive Departments of the Hawaiian Islands," pt. I, ch. VII, art. IV, S.L. 1845-6, p. 107, effective February 7, 1846. This Act prescribed the form of Royal Patents.

16. *State v. Zimring*, 58 Haw. 106 (1977).

17. Act of March 18, 1959, Pub. L. 86-3, 73 Stat. 4 (Admission Act).

18. Act of March 18, 1959, Pub. L. 86-3, 73 Stat. 4.

19. Resolution No. 55 of July 7, 1898 [Newlands Resolution], 30 Stat. 750.

20. 03-03 Op. Haw. Att'y Gen 6-7 (2003).

21. 03-03 Op. Haw. Att'y Gen 6-7 (2003).

22. *Zimring*, 58 Haw. at 120.

23. *Zimring*, 58 Haw. at 21–25.

24. Ibid. at 123 citing Admission Act § 5(g).

25. Hong, Tany S., State of Hawai'i Attorney General Opinion to Hon. Susumu Ono, Chairman DLNR, 9 (June 24, 1982) *Interpreting State v. Zimring*, 58 Haw. 106 (1977).

26. Maly V.1 at 5.

27. Maly V.1 at 5.

28. Maly V.1 at 6.

29. "Pioneer Mill Plans New Ditch," *Evening Bulletin*, Aug. 9, 1911, page 1 available at http://chroniclingamerica.loc.gov/lccn/sn82016413/1911-08-09/ed-1/seq-1/.

30. "Realty Transactions," *The Hawaiian star.* (Honolulu [Oahu]), 21 Sept. 1906, page 2. *Chronicling America: Historic American Newspapers*. Lib. of Congress available at http://chroniclingamerica.loc.gov/lccn/sn82015415/1906-09-21/ed-1/seq-2/.

31. "Realty Transactions" *The Hawaiian star.* (Honolulu [Oahu]), 02 Dec. 1907, page 7 *Chronicling America: Historic American Newspapers*. Lib. of Congress available at http://chroniclingamerica.loc.gov/lccn/sn82015415/1907-12-02/ed-1/seq-7/.

32. Interview with James Higuchi, Lahaina, Maui, *Pioneer Mill Company: A Maui Sugar Plantation Legacy* (ed. Warren Nishimoto), Honolulu: Univ. of Hawai'i, Ctr for Oral History, Social Sci. Res. Inst., at 268 (2003).

33. Telephone interview with Keoki Freeland, by Bianca Isaki (Jan. 8, 2018).

34. Trask, H.-K. "The Birth of the Modern Hawaiian Movement: Kalama Valley, O'ahu." 21 *The Hawaiian Journal of History* 126–153 (1987).

35. Panel Discussion on Kānaka Maoli Self Governance, Honolulu, Hawai'i, William S. Richardson School of Law, 'Ahahui o Hawai'i (Oct. 22, 2015).

36. Telephone interview with Kapali Keahi (Mar. 15, 2017)

37. Lahaina WUDP Update at 17 quoting Sterling, Elspeth P. Sites of Maui. Bishop Museum Press, at 30 (1997).

38. *Maui News*, page 6 (Jan. 1, 1903).

39. *Maui News*, page 6 (Jan. 1, 1903).

40. *Maui News*, page 6 (Jan. 1, 1903).

41. *Maui News*, page 6 (Jan. 1, 1903).

42. "Aheong vs Haiku Sugar Co." *Maui News* Sat. June 30, 1906 page 1.

43. "Aheong vs Haiku Sugar Co." *Maui News* Sat. June 30, 1906 page 1.

44. "A Hot Time in the Old Town: The Haiku Water Case" *Maui News* Saturday July 7, 1906.

45. "A Poi Dealers' Trust," *Maui News*, page 5 (Sat. Aug. 30, 1910) available at https://chroniclingamerica.loc.gov/lccn/sn82014689/1910-08-20/ed-1/seq-5.pdf.

46. "Maui Took Most of the Prizes at Big Fair," *Maui News*, page 3 (Fri. Jun. 21, 1918).

47. "Taro" *The Hawaiian Gazette*, at 3 (Aug. 17, 1894).

48. *The Daily Bulletin* (Honolulu) at 5 (Tues. Apr. 27, 1886).

49. *The Daily Bulletin* (Honolulu) at 5 (Tues. Apr. 27, 1886).

50. *The Daily Bulletin* (Honolulu) at 5 (Tues. Apr. 27, 1886).

51. "Rush of Requests for Free Water in Wailuku Raises Serious Problems," *Maui News*, page 1 (Tue. Jul. 18, 1922).

52. "Rush of Requests for Free Water in Wailuku Raises Serious Problems," *Maui News*, page 1 (Tue. Jul. 18, 1922).

53. "Requests for Free Water in Wailuku Raise New Problem," *Maui News*, page 6 (Tue. Jul. 18, 1922).

54. Quoted in the Lahaina WUDP Update at 16.

55. "Order Denying Plaintiffs' Motion For Partial Summary Judgment On Counts II, IV And V of the Complaint (ECF No. 29)" in *Shayefar v. Kaleleiki*, Civ. No. 14-00322 HG-KSC; (D. Hawai'i Jul. 10, 2015).

56. *Shayefar v. Kaleleiki*, Civ. No. 14-00322 HG-KSC, (D. Hawaii 2016) ("Based on the foregoing chain of title, there is a good and complete chain for the Subject Property as a portion of Land Commission Award Number 7779 issued to Kaleleiki from 1853 to Plaintiffs and title to the Subject Property is vested in Plaintiffs.")

57. CREXi, "Ukumehame, Lahaina" (accessed Aug. 9, 2018) available at www.crexi .com/properties/26508/ukumehame.

58. CREXi, "Ukumehame, Lahaina" (accessed Aug. 9, 2018) available at www.crexi .com/properties/26508/ukumehame.

59. CREXi, "Ukumehame, Lahaina" (accessed Aug. 9, 2018) available at https://www .crexi.com/properties/26508/ukumehame.

60. CWRM, Compilation of Public Testimony, Hydrologic Units: Ukumehame (6004), Olowalu (6005), Launiupoko (6006), Kaua'ula (6007), Island of Maui, Doc. No. PR-2018-05, at 11 (March 2018).

61. CWRM, Staff Submittal Item B-1 (Nov. 21, 2017).

62. CWRM Staff Submittal, Item B-1, at 15 (Mar. 20, 2018).

63. CWRM Staff Submittal, Item B-1, at 15 (Mar. 20, 2018).

64. DLNR Engineer Division Staff Submittal, Item L-3x "Approve issuance of a DLNR Dam Safety Permit and Authorize Removal of Dam from DLNR Regulatory Oversight Permit No. 77 - Ukumehame Reservoirs (MA-0140) Dam Removal, Maui," (Oct. 27, 2017) available at https://dlnr.hawaii.gov/wp-content /uploads/2017/10/L-3x.pdf.

65. Act 252, 2016 Haw. Sess. Laws (H.B. No. 2198 S.D.1).

66. DLNR Engineer Division Staff Submittal, Item L-3x "Approve issuance of a DLNR Dam Safety Permit and Authorize Removal of Dam from DLNR Regulatory Oversight Permit No. 77 - Ukumehame Reservoirs (MA-0140) Dam Removal, Maui," (Oct. 27, 2017) available at https://dlnr.hawaii.gov/wp-content /uploads/2017/10/L-3x.pdf.

67. CWRM Staff Submittal, Item B-1, at 6 (Table No. 4) (Mar. 20, 2018).

68. CWRM Staff Submittal, Item B-1, at 25 (Mar. 20, 2018).

69. H.B. 2198, 2016 House Journal available at www.capitol.hawaii.gov/Archives /measure_indiv_Archives.aspx?billtype=HB&billnumber=2198&year=2016.

70. CWRM, Item C-1, Application for Stream Channel Alteration Permit (SCAP.1989.6) to stabilize existing retaining wall on Kanaha Stream, Lahaina, Maui TMK (2): 4-6-017:012 (Oct. 28, 2008) available at http://files.hawaii.gov /dlnr/cwrm/submittal/2008/sb200810C1.pdf.

71. CWRM, Item C-1, Application for Stream Channel Alteration Permit (SCAP.1989.6) to stabilize existing retaining wall on Kanaha Stream, Lahaina, Maui TMK (2): 4-6-017:012 (Oct. 28, 2008) available at http://files.hawaii.gov /dlnr/cwrm/submittal/2008/sb200810C1.pdf.

72. County of Maui, Department of Water Supply, Water Use Development Plan, at 42 (2017).

73. The Land Court Application No. 403 is available at www.westmauilandcourtarchive .org/403.html.

74. *In the Matter of the Application of the Territory of Hawai'i, to register and confirm its title to land situate at Lahaina, Maui, Territory of Hawai'i*, Application No. 403, 73 (Land Ct. Hawai'i).

75. County of Maui, Water Resources Committee, at 3 (Oct. 12, 2010) available at www.mauicounty.gov/Archive/ViewFile/Item/13900.

76. County of Maui, Water Resources Committee, at 4 (Oct. 12, 2010) available at www.mauicounty.gov/Archive/ViewFile/Item/13900.

77. County of Maui, Water Resources Committee, at 4 (Oct. 12, 2010) available at www.mauicounty.gov/Archive/ViewFile/Item/13900.

78. County of Maui, Water Resources Committee, at 7 (Oct. 12, 2010) available at www.mauicounty.gov/Archive/ViewFile/Item/13900.

79. County of Maui, Water Resources Committee, at 7–8 (Oct. 12, 2010) available at www.mauicounty.gov/Archive/ViewFile/Item/13900.

80. County of Maui, Water Resources Committee, at 6 (Oct. 12, 2010 available at www.mauicounty.gov/Archive/ViewFile/Item/13900.

81. County of Maui, Water Resources Committee, at 6, 10–11 (Oct. 12, 2010).

82. Lahaina Water Treatment Plant Final Environmental Impact Statement, at 11 (Dec. 23, 1991).

83. Lahaina Water Treatment Plant FEIS at 11.

84. Richardson, Mahealani, "Kalo is back in West Maui's Kahoma Valley—after a 130-year absence," *Hawai'i News Now* (online) (Jul. 31, 2017) available at www .hawaiinewsnow.com/story/36016947/kalo-is-back-in-west-mauis-kahoma-valley -after-a-130-year-absence.

85. Maly V.1 at 13.

86. Conrad "Mac" Goodwin, Lands of the Pioneer Mill, Lahaina, Hawai'i, paper presented at the Association of American Geographers 95th Annual Meeting, Honolulu (Mar. 23–27, 1999).

87. See "Reviving a Culture," (Aug. 28, 2017) available at www.ksbe.edu/imua/article /reviving-kahoma-reviving-a-culture/.

88. Louise Rockett, "Planting of kalo in Kahoma expands cultural restoration for community," *Lahaina News* (Aug. 10, 2017) available at www.lahainanews.com /page/content.detail/id/564050/Planting-of-kalo-in-Kahoma-expands--cultural -restoration-for-community.html?nav=19.

89. Hoʻoipo, Elizabeth Ann, et al, "Cultures in Conflict in Hawaiʻi: The Law and Politics of Native Hawaiian Water Rights," 18 U. Haw. L. Rev. 71, 134 n.176 (1996).

90. HAR §13-167-82 (eff. May 1988).

91. Quoted in Jocelyn K. Fujii, *Stories of Aloha: Homegrown Treasures of Hawaiʻi*, 166 (Hawaiʻi: Hula Moon Press, 2009).

92. Quoted in Jocelyn K. Fujii, *Stories of Aloha: Homegrown Treasures of Hawaiʻi*, 166 (Hawaiʻi: Hula Moon Press, 2009).

93. Martin, David, Panel: "Balance at Risk," Transcripts of the 1993 Hawaiian Water Law Symposium, Univ. Hawaiʻi William S. Richardson School of Law, at 32 13:16-14:18 (Apr. 9–10, 1993).

94. Letter from Elizabeth Pa Martin, NHAC, to William W. Paty, Chairperson, CWRM, Re: West Maui-Molokaʻi Taro Farmers Association Citizen Complaint (Jan. 23, 1992) (on file with CWRM, accessed Jun. 15, 2017).

95. Rozeboom, Bill, Inspection Report, Subject: West Maui-Molokai Taro Farmers Association Complaint Re: Water Availability in Honokohau Stream Preliminary Field Inspection, March 26, 1992 (Mar. 27, 1992) (on file with CWRM).

96. Rozeboom, Bill, Inspection Report, Subject: West Maui-Molokai Taro Farmers Association Complaint Re: Water Availability in Honokohau Stream Preliminary Field Inspection, April 29, 1992 (Apr. 30, 1992) (on file with CWRM).

97. Letter from Wesley Nohara, Maui Land and Pine, to Rae Loui, Deputy Director, CWRM, re: Comment on the Public Meeting on Maui, September 24, 1993 on Stream Protection and Management (Nov. 2, 1993) (on file with CWRM).

98. Letter from Keith W. Ahue, CWRM, to Joseph Hartley, Jr., President, Maui Pineapple Company, Ltd., Re: Honokōhau Valley Taro Water Requirements (Nov. 10, 1993) (on file with CWRM).

99. Letter from Keith W. Ahue, CWRM, to Joseph Hartley, Jr., President, Maui Pineapple Company, Ltd., Re: Honokōhau Valley Taro Water Requirements, at 2 (Nov. 10, 1993) (on file with CWRM).

100. Letter from Keith W. Ahue, CWRM, to Joseph Hartley, Jr., President, Maui Pineapple Company, Ltd., Re: Honokōhau Valley Taro Water Requirements, at 2 (Nov. 10, 1993) (on file with CWRM).

101. Letter from Keith W. Ahue, CWRM, to Joseph Hartley, Jr., President, Maui Pineapple Company, Ltd., Re: Honokōhau Valley Taro Water Requirements, at 2 (Nov. 10, 1993) (on file with CWRM).

102. Letter from Wes Nohara, Plantation Superintendent, Maui Land & Pineapple, Ltd., to Rae Loui, Deputy Director, CWRM, RE: Honokōhau Valley Taro Water Requirements (Nov. 19, 1993) (on file with CWRM).

103. Letter from Wes Nohara, Plantation Superintendent, Maui Land & Pineapple, Ltd., to Rae Loui, Deputy Director, CWRM, RE: Honokōhau Valley Taro Water Requirements (Nov. 19, 1993) (on file with CWRM).

104. See Draft Appurtenant Water Rights Survey Phase 1, prepared by Eugene P. Dashiell Planning Srvcs., George Cooper, Lehman Henry, Royce Jones, Malia Ka'ai, Marion Kelly, Jon Olsen, Barry Nakamura, Doris Rowland, and Aki Sinoto (Feb. 14, 1993) (Appurtenant Rights Manual).

105. See Appurtenant Rights Manual at 6–11.

106. Most, if not all, of the MLP-claimed kuleana have been largely abandoned and many Honokōhau community members have been using those lands to cultivate crops and lo'i. It was not until the *Mcbryde Sugar Co. v. Robinson*, 54 Haw. 174, 504 P.2d 1330 (1973) decision that the Hawai'i Supreme Court interrupted plantations' practice of diverting water based on appurtenant rights under a theory that waters appurtenant to one parcel could be transported to another watershed. This may offer some explanation as to why MLP/ A&B historically sought Honokōhau kuleana land during the Territorial period.

107. Letter from Alan Murakami, Attorney, Native Hawaiian Legal Corporation of Hawai'i, to Rae Loui, Deputy Director, CWRM, Re: Request for Dispute Resolution and Citizen Complaint - Aimoku Pali,

108. Letter from Phil Jones to CWRM, Re: Honokōhau Stream Investigation (Aug. 26, 1994) (on file with CWRM).

109. Letter from Phil Jones to CWRM, Re: Honokōhau Stream Investigation (Aug. 26, 1994) (on file with CWRM).

110. Letter from Phil Jones to CWRM, Re: Honokōhau Stream Investigation (Aug. 26, 1994) (on file with CWRM).

111. Letter from Phil Jones to CWRM, Re: Honokōhau Stream Investigation (Aug. 26, 1994) (on file with CWRM).

112. Letter from Phil Jones to CWRM, Re: Honokōhau Stream Investigation (Aug. 26, 1994) (on file with CWRM).

113. Letter from Phil Jones to CWRM, Re: Honokōhau Stream Investigation (Aug. 26, 1994) (on file with CWRM).

114. Memorandum from Ed Sakoda, Staff, CWRM, Subject: September 11, 1995 Meeting on the Honokōhau Valley Water Issue (on file with CWRM).

115. See Minutes of the Eighth Public Hearing on Proposed Changes to Improve the State Water Code of the Review Commission on the State Water Code, Wailuku, Maui, Hawai'i (Wed. Jul. 20, 1994) (William S. Richardson School of Law Library holdings) ("8th Public Hearing").

116. 8th Public Hearing at 2.

117. 8th Public Hearing at 2.

118. 8th Public Hearing at 2.

119. 8th Public Hearing at 2.

120. 8th Public Hearing at 2.

121. 8th Public Hearing at 2.

122. 8th Public Hearing at 2.

123. Telephone interview with Kapali Keahi (Mar. 15, 2017).

124. 8th Public Hearing at 3.

125. Letter from David L. Martin, Water Claims Manager, Native Hawaiian Advisory Council, to Rae Loui, Deputy Director, CWRM Re: Honokōhau streamflow measurements (Aug. 26, 1994) (on file with CWRM).

126. Letter from Rae Loui, Deputy Director, CWRM, to David Martin, NHAC (Nov. 3, 1994) (on file with CWRM).

127. Memorandum from Ed Sakoda, Staff, CWRM, Subject: September 11, 1995 Meeting on the Honokōhau Valley Water Issue (on file with CWRM).

128. Review Commission on the State Water Code, State of Hawai'i, Final Report to the Hawai'i State Legislature, 15 (Dec. 28, 1994) available at https://evols .library.manoa.hawaii.edu/bitstream/10524/12108/1/1994-Hawaii-Final-Report -Legislature.pdf.

129. Review Commission on the State Water Code, State of Hawai'i, Final Report to the Hawai'i State Legislature, 15 (Dec. 28, 1994) available at https://evols .library.manoa.hawaii.edu/bitstream/10524/12108/1/1994-Hawaii-Final-Report -Legislature.pdf.

130. Review Commission on the State Water Code, State of Hawai'i, Final Report to the Hawai'i State Legislature, 15 (Dec. 28, 1994) available at https://evols .library.manoa.hawaii.edu/bitstream/10524/12108/1/1994-Hawaii-Final-Report -Legislature.pdf.

131. Gingerich, Stephen B., Chiu W. Yeung, Tracy-Joy N. Ibarra, and John A. Engott, "Water use in wetland kalo cultivation in Hawai'i," USGS Open File Rpt. No. 2007-1157 (2007). Available at http://pubs.usgs.gov/of/2007/1157/.

132. Review Commission on the State Water Code, State of Hawai'i, Final Report to the Hawai'i State Legislature (Dec. 28, 1994) available at https://evols.library.manoa .hawaii.edu/bitstream/10524/12108/1/1994-Hawaii-Final-Report-Legislature.pdf.

133. Testimony of Native Hawaiian Advisory Council to CWRM, Regular Meeting, submitted by Kalani Haia, Honolulu, at 4 (Dec. 6, 1995).

134. Testimony of Native Hawaiian Advisory Council to CWRM, Regular Meeting, submitted by Kalani Haia, Honolulu, at 4 (Dec. 6, 1995).

135. Eager, Harry, "West Maui hotels remain in plans," Maui News (Sep. 13, 1995).

136. Monette, Fredric S., Secretary, Honokōhau Valley Association, "Open Letter to the People of Maui, Maui County Council, Editor," (Oct. 4, 1995) (on file with CWRM).

137. Monette, Fredric S., Secretary, Honokōhau Valley Association, "Open Letter to the People of Maui, Maui County Council, Editor," (Oct. 4, 1995) (on file with CWRM).

138. Monette, Fredric S., Secretary, Honokōhau Valley Association, "Open Letter to the People of Maui, Maui County Council, Editor," (Oct. 4, 1995) (on file with CWRM).

139. Monette, Fredric S., Secretary, Honokōhau Valley Association, "Open Letter to the People of Maui, Maui County Council, Editor," (Oct. 4, 1995) (on file with CWRM).

140. Monette, Fredric S., Secretary, Honokōhau Valley Association, "Open Letter to the People of Maui, Maui County Council, Editor," (Oct. 4, 1995) (on file with CWRM).

141. Monette, Fredric S., Secretary, Honokōhau Valley Association, "Open Letter to the People of Maui, Maui County Council, Editor," (Oct. 4, 1995) (on file with CWRM).

142. Vieth, Mark, "Environmental group seeks to free more water for Honokohau Valley" *Lahaina News* (online) (Oct. 6, 1997) available at http://www.users .miamioh.edu/shermarc/p412/lhn/taro106.shtml.

143. Ibid.

144. Ibid.

145. Dawson, Teresa, "As Sugar Winds Down, DLNR Moves to Save Ditches on Kauaʻi, Maui," *Environment Hawaiʻi* V. 10, No. 2 (Aug. 1999).

146. Dawson, Teresa, "As Sugar Winds Down, DLNR Moves to Save Ditches on Kauaʻi, Maui," *Environment Hawaiʻi* V. 10, No. 2 (Aug. 1999).

147. 2004 West Maui Water Development, Environment Hawaiʻi Volume 14, Number 12 June 2004. Available at www.environment-Hawaiʻi.org/?p=2976.

148. U.S. Geological Survey, Availability and Distribution of Base Flow in Lower Honokohau Stream, Island of Maui, Water Resources Investigations Rpt. No. 03-4060 (2003).

149. Land Use Committee, Maui County Council, Item No. 69 West Maui Project District 2 (Kapalua Mauka) (Lahaina), at 7–9 (Dec. 7, 2005) available at www.co .maui.hi.us/ArchiveCenter/ViewFile/Item/9910.

150. MDWS, WUDP, Lahaina Sector Dec. 2016.

Chapter 8: Managing Hawaiʻi Public Trust Resources in a Contested Hawaiʻi

1. Goodyear-Kaʻōpua, Noelani, "Rebuilding the ʻauwai: Connecting ecology, economy and education in Hawaiian schools," 5(2) *AlterNative: An International Journal of Indigenous Scholarship* 46, 50 (2009).

2. See Lilikalā Kameʻeleihiwa, *Native Land and Foreign Desires: Pehea Lā e Pono Ai?*

(1992); David Stannard, *Before the Horror: The Population of Hawai'i on the Eve of Western Contact* (1989) (quantifying the decimation of the Hawaiian population upon and after Western colonization).

3. Derr, Patrick G., and Edward MacNamara. *Case Studies in Environmental Ethics (2003) (Chapter 25: Hawaiian Feral Pigs).*

4. A more usual concept used to discuss beliefs in state rationality is "hegemony," as first elaborated by Antonio Gramsci. See Antonio Gramsci, *Selections from the Prison Notebooks* (Quintin Hoare and G. Nowell Smith, trans. 1971).

5. Chang, Kevin et al, Position Paper: Hawaiian culture and conservation in Hawai'i," Hawai'i Conservation Alliance (Dec. 9, 2010).

6. The concept of decolonization used here and throughout these chapters is conversant with that of Haunani-Kay Trask in *From a Native Daughter: Colonialism and Sovereignty in Hawai'i* (Common Courage Press, 1993), who discussed the term as used by Ngũgĩ wa Thiong'o in his *Decolonising the Mind: The Politics of Language in African Literature* (Heinemann Press 1986).

7. Goodyear-Ka'ōpua, Noelani. "Sovereign Pedagogies: Two Talks and Spoken Word from Hawai'i to Palestine." In *Indigenous Politics*, edited by J. Kēhaulani Kauanui. New York, 2013.

8. Paperson, L. (2014). "A ghetto land pedagogy: an antidote for settler environmentalism." *Environmental Education Research* 20(1): 115–130, 121.

9. In testimony to the State Land Use Commission, Hawaiian cultural practitioner and Papahulihonua (earth science) researcher Ku'ulei Higashi Kanahele contrasted a very "Western view" of "gods" as unearthly beings with Hawaiian ontologies of godliness. "Pele means lava. It does not mean the 'god' of lava. Lava is a god," she explained. "Hawaiians have a very personal personal relationships with 'gods.'" Ku'ulei H. Kanahele, Oral Testimony to the Land Use Commission of the State of Hawai'i, Hilo, Hawai'i (Oct. 25, 2019).

10. Uechi, Colleen. Mahi Pono unclear on needs from Na Wai 'Eha streams; Company seeks to take place of HC&S on water use permit. *The Maui News*. August 30, 2019. Available at www.mauinews.com/news/local-news/2019/08/mahi-pono -unclear-on-needs-from-na-wai-eha-streams/.

11. Reservations of Hawai'i's public trust revenues for Native Hawaiians under Article XII, Section 4 of the Hawai'i State Constitution were created through the 1978 Hawai'i State Constitutional Convention, which "marked a watershed for the Kanaka 'Oiwi movement." Davianna Pomaika'i McGregor, "Statehood: Catalyst of the Twentieth-Century Kanaka 'Ōiwi Cultural Renaissance and Sovereignty Movement," *Journal of Asian American Studies* 13, no. 1 (2010): 316.

12. HAR § 13-5-2.

13. "[W]ithout the resources provided to us by the land and sea, our lawai'a [fishing] traditions would not exist" (Lawai'a Action Network). Lawai'a Action Network, Mālama Ka'ena, a mālama Ka'ena ia 'oe: A Community Plan for Culturally-based

Resource Management at Kaʻena, Oʻahu, 5 (2010) (unpublished manuscript) (on file with the Office of Hawaiian Affairs, Compliance Division).

14. Hawaiʻi's public trust is a constitutional mandate that "[a]ll public natural resources are held in trust by the State for the benefit of the people." (Haw. Const. art. XI, § 1.) Hawaiʻi's public land trust requires the state to allocate 20% of revenues from specific "ceded lands" to native Hawaiian beneficiaries.

15. See Beamer, K. (2009). "Aliʻi Selective Appropriation of Modernity: Examining Colonial Assumptions in Hawaiʻi Prior to 1893." AlterNative: An International Journal of Indigenous Peoples 5(2): 138–155. In adding what is now Article XII, Section 7 to the State Constitution, the state's Committee on Hawaiian Affairs also recognized that "[s]ustenance, religious and cultural practices of native Hawaiians are an integral part of their culture, tradition and heritage, with such practices forming the basis of Hawaiian identity and value systems." *Ka Paʻakai O Ka ʻĀina v. Land Use Comm'n*, 94 Hawaiʻi 31, 45, 7 P.3d 1068, 1082 (2000) (holding that the state failed its constitutional obligation to protect Hawaiian cultural resources against private land developers) citing Comm. Whole Rep. No. 12, in 1 Proceedings of the Constitutional Convention of 1978, at 1016. While the 1978 State Constitutional Convention helped codify these protections, the impetus proceeded from a longer and ongoing history of Hawaiian involvement in the crafting of Hawaiʻi state jurisprudence. See *Ka lama kū o kanoʻeau = The Standing Torch of Wisdom: Selected Opinions of William S. Richardson, Chief Justice, Hawaiʻi Supreme Court, 1966–1982*. Honolulu: University of Hawaiʻi William S. Richardson School of Law, 2009.

16. Turner, Stephen, and Timothy Neale, "First law and the force of water: law, water, entitlement," 5(4) *Settler Colonial Studies* 387 (2015), quoting Mark Rifkin, "Indigenizing Agamben: rethinking sovereignty in light of the 'peculiar' status of native peoples," *Cultural Critique* 73, Fall (2009): 90–1.

17. See *In re Water Use Permit Applications*, 105 Hawaiʻi 1, 93 P.3d 643 (2004) and *In re Water Use Permit Applications*, 105 Hawaiʻi 1, 11, 93 P.3d 643, 653 (2004).

18. See *Diamond v. Dobbin*, 319 P.3d 1017 (Hawaiʻi 2014).

19. See *Kauai Springs, Inc. v. Planning Comm'n of Cnty. of Kauaʻi*, 133 Hawaiʻi 141, 324 P.3d 951 (2014).

20. See *Pub. Access Shoreline Hawaii by Rothstein v. Hawaiʻi Cnty. Planning Comm'n by Fujimoto*, 79 Hawaiʻi 425, 903 P.2d 1246 (1995) and *Pele Def. Fund v. Puna Geothermal Venture*, 77 Hawaiʻi 64, 881 P.2d 1210 (1994).

21. Relevant in this regard, Byrd points out that in Hawaiʻi, the "playing field is *not* only not level between Indigenous peoples and all others who have arrived from all over the world, it is, first and foremost, comprised of indigenous lands that remain indigenous regardless of the colonizing state's superseding assertions of control over them" (Byrd 2014: 177). (Emphasis in original).

22. See Wolfe, P. (2013). "Recuperating Binarism: a heretical introduction." *Settler*

Colonial Studies Journal 3(3–4): 257–279, 265. Its call to protect those lands and resources does not render the public trust other than a settler state device of control over those Native territories. "Even the progressive concept of land as Commons to be occupied, collectively shared and stewarded, may require the negation of Indigenous sovereignty. 'The people still speak of the sacredness of places now claimed by the park services for instance[.]'" (Paperson 2014: 121) citing Goeman, M., "From Place to Territories and Back Again: Centering Storied Land in the discussion of Indigenous Nation-building." *International Journal of Critical Indigenous Studies* 1 (1): 23–34, 32 (2008).

23. Neale, Timothy, and Stephen Turner, "Other people's country: law, water, entitlement," 5 (4) *Settler Colonial Studies* 277, 387 (2015).

24. Viotti, Vicki. "DLNR loses another deputy," *The Honolulu Advertiser* (February 12, 2005).

25. Neale and Turner, at 278.

26. Smith, A., *Conquest: Sexual Violence and American Indian Genocide.* Boston, South End Press, 50 (2003).

27. See Gover, K., "An Indian Trust for the Twenty-First Century." *Natural Resources Journal* 46(2): 317–374, 318 (2006). This has been true of federal Indian trusts that served as "intrusive means of denying Tribes control of their lands." Unlike the trust doctrine in Indian law, however, a trust applied to public lands more aptly describes a public interest in stewardship of natural resources. Tsosie, R. A., "The Conflict between the 'Public Trust' and the 'Indian Trust' Doctrines: Federal Public Land Policy and Native Nations." Neale 39: 271–311, 271 (2003) quoting Wilkinson, Charles F., "The Public Trust Doctrine in Public Land Law," *U. Cal. Davis L. Rev.* 14 (1980).

28. Tuck, E., et al., "Land education: Indigenous, post-colonial, and decolonizing perspectives on place and environmental education research." *Environmental Education Research* 20 (1): 1–23, 10 (2014).

29. Settler citizenship accomplishes a territorialization of land and body that pushes against an Indigenous recognition of a bond between community and land. Goeman, at 31 (2008).

30. Shorter, D. D. (2007). "Hunting for History in Potam Pueblo: A Yoeme (Yaqui) Indian Deer Dancing Epistemology." *Folklore* 1118 (3): 282–306.

31. Yúdice, G. *The Expediency of Culture*, 4. Durham, NC: Duke University Press (2004).

32. Goldstein, A., "Finance and Foreclosure in the Colonial Present." *Radical History Review* 118 (Winter): 42–63, 44 (2014).

33. Yúdice, G. *The Expediency of Culture*, 25; see also Arvin, M. (2009), "Sovereignty will not be funded: indigenous citizenship in Hawai'i's non-profit industrial complex." *Ethnic Studies*. San Diego, University of San Diego. Master's: 135.

34. Tuck, Eve, and K. Wayne Yang, "Decolonization Is Not a Metaphor," *Decolonization: Indigeneity, Education & Society*, 1, no. 1 (2012): 35.
35. Fanon, Frantz. *Black Skin, White Masks*, 66 n. 9 (Pluto Press, 1967).
36. Jean Dennison (Osage) offers the concept of "colonial entanglement . . . to mark the shifts created through the ongoing settler-colonial process, with a particular focus on the agency that is possible within this space." Dennison, J. (2013). "Stitching Osage Governance Into the Future." *American Indian Culture and Research Journal* 37 (2): 115–128, 116. Instruments of entanglement may be a "means by which colonized people can pick up the pieces of the current moment and create their own original patterns for the future." Ibid., p. 117.
37. The public trust may be said to enact a settler colonial politics of deferral. "Confirming postcolonial theorization of benevolent care, however, there is ongoing reluctance to accept Indigenous autonomy in service delivery. Indeed, the "impulse to improve and help Indigenous peoples is remarkably immune to critique, and there is an endless deferral of the time at which Indigenous peoples can be deemed 'ready to manage themselves.'" Coombes, B., et al., "Indigenous geographies II: The aspirational spaces in postcolonial poliics—reconciliation, belonging, and social provision." *Progress in Human Geography* 37(5): 691–700, 695 (2012). Hawai'i's public trust is not quite a charity device. And while it has a similar deferral effect, this is not necessarily a bad thing. Keeping the settler state on the hook to protect, manage, and allocate liability for lands and natural resources may be part of a canny tactic of instrumentalizing the settler state for decolonizing purposes.
38. For a similar emphasis in language-making in regard to Asian settler colonial histories in Hawai'i, see Isaki, B. (2012). Re-Archiving Asian Settlers in a Time of Hawaiian Decolonization; or, Two Walks Along Kamehameha Highway. *Transnational Crossroads: Reimagining Asian America, Latino America, and the American Pacific*. C. Fojas and J. Rudy Guevarra. Lincoln, University of Nebraska Press: 269–290.
39. Kawash, S. (1998). "The Homeless Body." *Public Culture* 10 (2): 319–339, 325.
40. Neale, T. (2013). "Staircases, pyramids and poisons: the immunitary paradigm in the works of Noel Pearson and Peter Sutton." *Continuum: Journal of Media and Cultural Studies* 27(2): 177–192, 183.
41. Coulthard, G. S. (2007). "Subjects of Empire: Indigenous Peoples and the 'Politics of Recognition' in Canada." *Contemporary Political Theory* 6: 437–460.
42. See e.g., DLNR's "community-based" process at Ka'ena. See Press Release, Dep't Land & Nat. Res., State of Hawai'i, DLNR Seeks Public Input on Designation of Roads at Ka'ena Point State Park Reserve (Oct. 31, 2011). Available at http://hawaii .gov/dlnr/chair/pio/nr/2011/NR10-305.pdf. This paper suggests that DLNR-structured processes here invoke community to make them easier to control. See supra Part I.C.

INDEX

248   Index

About the Authors

Born and raised on Oʻahu, JONATHAN LIKEKE SCHEUER helps organizations manage environmental conflict, seeking sustainable prosperity for the people and resources involved. He has played an integral role in the resolution of complex water disputes in Nā Wai ʻEhā (Maui) and the Waimea River (Kauaʻi). He has closed over 28,000 acres in fee simple conservation real estate acquisitions (of Mūʻolea Point [Maui], Wao Kele O Puna [Hawaiʻi], and Waimea Valley [Oʻahu]). He has advised fiduciary boards in policy development, including the Real Estate Vision Mission and Strategy of the Office of Hawaiian Affairs and the Water Policy Plan of the Department of Hawaiian Home Lands. As a facilitator, he has guided meetings for Hawaiʻi and the US Affiliated Pacific Islands on climate change matters, including the third and fourth National Climate Assessments. As a volunteer, he serves as the Chair of the State Land Use Commission and the Past Chair of the Hawaiian Islands Land Trust. He is also a Lecturer in Law at the William S. Richardson School of Law.

Scheuer has worked with the Office of Hawaiian Affairs, the Nature Conservancy, the Hawaiʻi State Legislature, Kamehameha Schools, the Hawaiʻi Department of Land and Natural Resources, the Hawaiʻi Conservation Alliance, the National Park Service, and the Waipā Foundation. Previous volunteer work has been on the Board of Mālama Mānoa and as a Kona Moku representative and Vice Chair of the Oʻahu Island Burial Council. He holds three degrees in Environmental Studies: a BA from the University of California, Santa Cruz (UCSC), a master's from the Yale University School of Forestry and Environmental Studies, and a PhD from UCSC. He was awarded fellowships from the Switzer Foundation and the US EPA's Science to Achieve Results program. He is a 1987 graduate of ʻIolani School.

BIANCA K. ISAKI is a writer, solo legal practitioner, community activist, and a member of the Board of Directors of the North Beach-West Maui Benefit Fund. She received her PhD from the University of Hawaiʻi at Mānoa Department of Political Science for research on Asian settler colonialism and plantation labor organizing, completed a postdoctoral fellowship at the University of Illinois at

Urbana-Champaign, returned to Hawaiʻi to teach Women's Studies, and then graduated summa cum laude from the William S. Richardson School of Law with certifications in Native Hawaiian Law and Environmental Law. She is coeditor of the North Beach-West Maui Benefit Fund books *Tourism Impacts West Maui* (2016) and *Social Change in West Maui* (2019).